MEDITATION™ S

D0206321

I CAN'T. GOD CAN. I THINK I'LL LET HIM.

DAILY DEVOTIONS FOR GIRLS

Jane Cairo, Sheri Curry,
Anne Christian Buchanan,
and
Debra Klingsporn

A JANET THOMA BOOK

THOMAS NELSON PUBLISHERS
Nashville

Published in Nashville, Tennessee, by Thomas Nelson, Inc.

Library of Congress Cataloging-in-Publication Data

See back of book

Printed in the United States of America
5 — 96 95 94

Life is a journey. It can be fun and exciting—a great adventure. It can also be treacherous and exhausting—a monumental pain. Either way, you can only experience it one step at a time.

That's also true of the journey called recovery. After a lot of mistakes, a lot of unhealthy behavior (your own and others'), you've started on the road toward healing and wholeness. You are putting one foot in front of another, watching out for potholes, gradually making progress. Sometimes you get tired. Sometimes you trip and fall. Still, step by step, you are leaving behind the destructive habits that caused you so much trouble and moving forward toward a sane and healthy future. It's not always easy—but boy, is it worth it!

As you travel, we hope you have some company—supportive family or friends, a recovery group, prayer partners, perhaps a counselor or therapist. (Recovery really is a hard road to travel alone.) And we would like to walk with you, too. We wrote this daily devotional as a kind of traveling companion to encourage you and help you along the way—to give a pat on the back, a shoulder to cry on, a steadying hand when you stumble, and occasionally, perhaps, a gentle nudge in the right direction.

You might not be able to relate to all the devotionals at first. If you have a problem with overeating, you might not think a meditation for someone with anorexia has anything to do with you. You might have an addiction to alcohol but never touch drugs. You might have a sex addiction, or you might never even have a date. But people on the recovery journey usually find out quickly that regardless of where they come from, the journey is basically the same. We hope you will look past the particulars in each devotional to find a word spoken directly to you.

And who are "we," anyway? We, the authors of this book, also come from different walks of life and widely varying experience. Two of us are professional therapists who work with teens in recovery. Two of us are just fellow travelers who happen to be writers. All of us have been teenaged girls not that long ago. And no matter where we're coming from, we all hope the scriptures and the meditations in this book will help make your steps a little firmer and a little lighter on the recovery road. (To help you feel the impact of the scripture, when the verses use "men" and "him" to refer to all humans, we've changed them to "people," "women," and "her.")

Most of all, we hope you're traveling this road hand in hand with God, your Higher Power, and with His road map, the Bible, tucked firmly under your arm. To be perfectly honest, if you aren't learning to depend on Him, you don't have much chance of a successful journey. But if you are on the road with Him, learning to follow His lead, He'll get you where you need to go. It really is true what His Book tells us:

In all your ways acknowledge Him,
And He shall direct your paths.
                                        Prov. 3:6

A NEW START

Oh, sing to the LORD a new song! . . .
Proclaim the good news of His salvation
from day to day. —PS. 96:1–2

A brand new year! A fresh start . . . a new beginning . . . turning over a new leaf. To people in recovery, those words have special resonance. Just the word *new* sounds so alive to someone whose "old" has been full of pain and struggle.

Before you now lie all kinds of possibilities, chances, risks, challenges, failures, blessings. Thank God for them—they can give you faith, hope, and joy. They may make you stretch, but they will also make you more flexible, more confident.

Try to welcome change in your life—don't fight it. Changing is part of growing. Growing is part of learning. And learning equips you to have a fuller, happier life. You are acquiring new information, forming new beliefs, formulating new opinions—becoming your own person and building your identity. You are seeing what fits you—what feels right and not what just feels good.

Allow this new year to be your best yet. You can make the necessary changes. You can step out on that limb and go beyond what you are used to doing. And as the year unfolds before you, be sure you take time to reflect. Each day, ask yourself whether you have your life in focus. Step up to the challenge—and take a little time to celebrate, too.

■ *Lord, thank you for the gift of a fresh start. My most important resolution is to live this year one day at a time, trusting in you.*

S.C.

GOD'S HOPE CHEST

This hope we have as an anchor of the soul,
both sure and steadfast. **—HEB. 6:19**

The cedar chest usually served as a bench at the foot of the little girl's bed. Today, however, she and a friend were playing house, and it was a dining room table. The little girl was serving "tea" in toy cups and saucers. After a while, her mother came in and suggested she show her friend what was inside the chest, which she called a "hope chest."

Inside the hope chest were real cups, saucers, and plates with a dainty floral pattern. A crocheted table-cloth and a silverware set in a mahogany box were carefully tucked in next to the china. The mother went on to explain that when her daughter got married, she would have these to use.

The mother was so certain her daughter was going to get married—that she had even collected household items her daughter would need.

Today's verse does not talk of wistful, uncertain hope. The hope it speaks of has that "hope chest" certainty—and much more. In reality, no one knows if a child will get married. But we do know God's promises are sure.

Recovery means growing up and "getting married" to healthy ways of coping. Our heavenly Parent has prepared His hope chest, the Bible, to help us mature. In it are the tools He knows we will need as we go through recovery and life.

■ *Heavenly Father, help me to open your hope chest,*
the Bible, and use the tools you've given me for a
successful recovery.

J.C.

A GOOD PLACE TO BE

My iniquities have overtaken me, so that
I am not able to look up;
They are more than the hairs of my head;
Therefore my heart fails me. . . .
O LORD, make haste to help me!
                                        —PS. 40:12–13

I never thought I'd be in a place like this," confessed Lindsay, her head hanging. "Things just got bad so fast—I couldn't cope anymore. I've really messed up my life; you wouldn't believe some of the things I've done! I guess I'm here because I'm desperate. I don't have anyplace else to go."

Lindsay had to hit bottom in her life before she would let her aunt put her into a treatment program. But she quickly learned from her counselor and her peers that desperate is not such a bad place to be in recovery. Coming to the end of your rope can help with one of the hardest parts of recovery—turning over the controls of your life to God and depending on Him instead of your own strength.

That's not to say you should wait until you're absolutely desperate before you get help with a problem. In fact, the sooner you get help, the more quickly the problem is usually resolved. But if it takes being desperate to get serious about recovery—desperate is not a bad place to be.

■   *God, I never thought I'd pray this, but make me desperate if that's what it takes to keep me going in recovery. Push me to the end of my rope if that's what it takes to make me grab hold of you.*

                                        A.C.B.

MASTERING THE MOUNTAIN

He gives power to the weak,
And to those who have no might He
increases strength.

—ISA. 40:29

When you begin recovery, you may feel like you're at the bottom of Mount Everest. The whole process looks huge and overpowering. Choices and challenges loom, and you wonder if you'll make it up the "hill."

But if you have ever climbed a mountain or watched someone else climb, you are aware that climbers don't just stride up the side of a peak. Instead, they proceed step by step. They take advantage of easy going to catch their breath and see how far they've come. They test each toehold to make sure it will hold their weight. They use ropes and other kinds of safety equipment to anchor themselves to the rocks in case they slip. They know better than to climb alone. Most of all, they enjoy the climb; they know that the process is just as important as the goal.

As you continue in recovery, take a hint from the mountain climbers. Keep your eyes on the trail, not the summit. Mark your progress a step at a time, testing for solid footing. Allow sponsors, counselors, friends, and family to catch you if you slip. And don't forget to enjoy the climb! Before long, what now seems almost impossible will seem like second nature.

■ *Recovery may be a tough climb, but it is one mountain worth scaling.*

S.C.

YOU ARE NOT ALONE

Bear one another's burdens, and so fulfill the law of Christ. —GAL. 6:2

I know I want to stay off booze," Melissa said doubtfully, "but I'm not sure I want to get involved with AA. Isn't that a bunch of old drunks who sit around in a smoke-filled room and swap war stories from their abusing days? That's definitely not me!"

That's not AA, either! One reason AA has survived over the years has been its ability to adapt. Today there are AA groups for teens, older people, nonsmokers, men, women, Spanish-speaking people—and groups that are specifically Christian. Sister organizations such as Narcotics Anonymous (NA) and Overeaters Anonymous (OA) address different recovery problems. If you have a recovery problem, there's probably a group for you.

The main reason for AA's success is found in today's verse. God knows we need each other; He made us that way. We are not to lean on others for things we can do ourselves, but we all need help when the load gets extra heavy. In a support group, you can meet friends your own age who are also in recovery. You can find ideas and proven plans of action for keeping straight. Best of all, you can be reminded that you are not alone in your problems—that someone is there to help you bear your burdens.

■ *A support group can keep me going when recovery seems too hard.*

J.C.

EVEN JESUS WEPT

*He will be very gracious to you at the
    sound of your cry;
When He hears it, He will answer you.*
—ISA. 30:19

I hate to cry. Crying makes my mascara run down my face. My nose turns red, my cheeks get splotchy, and my head hurts. I end up feeling like Rudolph the Red-Nosed Reindeer with a head cold. Boys hate it—they never know what to do with a girl who's crying. Something about crying feels embarrassing, uncool.

But crying is mentioned more than forty-five times in Psalms and thirty-five times in Isaiah. Eighty times in only two books of the Bible, someone cried out to the Lord. Even Jesus wept (see John 11:35). Tears are a sign of release, surrender, letting go. Tears can bring healing. Maybe what I don't like about my tears is making myself vulnerable. I want to hide behind my pretense of self-sufficiency. But self-sufficiency is a myth, just as thinking I can control people, places, and things around me is a myth. In letting the tears come, I acknowledge my hurt. I acknowledge that things aren't great, that I'm not self-sufficient. The good news is that Christ doesn't leave me there. Eventually the tears stop, I blow my nose, and then I move on, turning over the cause of the tears to the Power greater than me.

■   *Jesus, even you wept. When the tears come, let me lean into the pain, trusting you with the healing to come.*

D.K.

It's Really That Bad!

Have mercy on me, O LORD,
for I am in trouble;
My eye wastes away with grief,
Yes, my soul and my body! . . .
I am like a broken vessel.
—PS. 31:9, 12

Self-reflection is a painful, difficult process. It means looking at ourselves in a way we have never experienced. When we really get serious about making some changes, we have to be honest about ourselves, our behavior, and how we got to the point we did.

Minimization is a process that most likely has been an active part of your life. Pretending that something does not matter as much as it really does, invalidating your feelings or perhaps the feelings of others, refusing to look at reality—all these are a part of minimizing the ways your life is being affected by your attitudes or behavior. Minimization is a form of denial. It holds us back from being honest. When we feel that we simply cannot deal with what is going on, we minimize the situation. What we tell ourselves is at odds with what we feel inside.

If healing is going to replace hurt, we have to look at reality. Even though it may be difficult, we must face the pain and see it for what it is.

■ *Don't minimize the pain in your life. Take a good look at it and allow yourself to be honest with what you are feeling.*

S.C.

I'M WONDERFUL!

I will praise You, for I am fearfully
and wonderfully made;
Marvelous are Your works,
And that my soul knows very well.
—PS. 139:14

Jan looked into the mirror over one of her shoulders and began singing a song from *West Side Story:* "I'm so pretty, oh, so pretty. . . . Look at that pretty face in the mirror there! Such a pretty face, such a pretty hair, such a pretty me!"

Unfortunately, Jan did not really believe this about herself. She was only playing at feeling beautiful.

Can you honestly thank God for yourself? Do you really think you are "wonderfully made"?

Out of the billions of people past, present and future, there has never been and never will be another you. No one has the same fingerprints as you. No one has the same handwriting or the same set of teeth. Even twins are different in these respects. Our bodies are evidences of God's amazing creativity.

If God took such pains and time to make just one original of us and then broke the mold, why do we spend so much time trying to contort ourselves to fit into someone else's mold? We can never be as good at being them as they can!

Recovery means working at really being able to thank God for who He made you to be. It means that deep down in your soul, you know it "very well."

■ *Knowing I'm "wonderful" helps me keep going in recovery.*

J.C.

QUIETING THE CRAZY EMOTIONS

> *Since you were precious in My sight,*
> *You have been honored,*
> *And I have loved you.*
>
> —ISA. 43:4

I was standing by my locker and saw him walking toward me, but I didn't want him to *think* I noticed. So I got busy with my books, trying to look totally cool. And then I heard his voice behind me: "You want to go to the game Friday night?"

Do I want to go!? The one guy I would have paid money to go out with—and he asked *me* if I wanted to go out?

Now I'm anything but cool and relaxed. I hate this! Why does this have to be such a big deal? I've tried on four outfits and hate all of them. I can't believe my face broke out today of all days! I hate the voices within that scream, "I'm too fat. My hair is too thin. My jeans are too tight." I want to scream, "Shut up!" Some days I hate my clothes. I hate my hair. I hate my life!

So many crazy emotions tangled up inside. But I know I've got a way to quiet those inner voices and untangle the jumble of feelings. If Jesus were sitting here right now, He would tell me, "Your hair looks great, your jeans fit fine, and you are one terrific girl—so lighten up, will you?"

■ *God, I know your love for me is stronger than my insecurities and conflicting emotions. I'm a precious child of God, custom designed just the way I am. Remind me of that when I'm throwing my jeans on the floor.*

D.K.

THE END OF OURSELVES

As the heavens are higher than the earth,
So are My ways higher than your ways,
And My thoughts than your thoughts.
—ISA. 55:9

I once had a teenager say to me, "If this is all there is, then I have had enough." She had come to the end of herself and found there was not a whole lot there. In and of ourselves, we quickly reach the point of hopelessness. We really do need more!

The second step of the Twelve Steps of AA states, "[We] came to believe that a Power greater than ourselves could restore us to sanity." God in his greatness and love will often bring us to the end of ourselves so that He can show us His strength and power. What a relief to know that we are not all there is!

If you are on the recovery road, you probably know what it is like to feel insane. When your life is out of control—that is insanity. And God can restore you to sanity, but only if you admit you need Him and hand over the reins of your life. As long as you are the one running the show, you will never know His power nor experience His restoration.

Please allow God to restore you to sanity. You can experience a newness you have never known. God knows what is best for you far more than you do. He does not think the same way you do nor handle things the way you would. Trust Him today.

■ *Lord, I give up! Please take control of my life and restore me to sanity.*

S.C.

THE FIRST DECISION

But the man who has settled the matter in his own mind, who is under no compulsion but has control over his own will, and who has made up his mind not to marry the virgin— this man also does the right thing.

—1 COR. 7:37 NIV

What does this verse have to do with recovery? A lot. This verse is specifically talking about choosing a lifetime of sexual abstinence, but it can apply to abstinence of any kind. Abstinence means taking control of one's body. It's a decision of the will—and it's the first thing you have to settle in recovery.

Serious recovery means we have thought through the consequences of our dysfunctional behavior and decided we don't like what it adds up to: the blackouts, the throwing up, the school tardies and cuts, the bad trips, the stealing of money, the lies, the broken relationships. Serious recovery also means being willing to give up what you liked about your "problem": the highs, the temporary release from problems, the excuse to do things you always wanted to do but didn't want to be responsible for, the easy acceptance by other abusers. The math of successful recovery adds these two considerations together and concludes: the pain of staying in my addiction is greater than the pain of leaving it.

This decision of the will is not an easy one to make— but we don't have to make it without help. Philippians 2:13 tells us so: "For it is *God* who works in you both to *will* and to do for His good pleasure."

■ *My will, energized by God, is a tool for successful recovery.*

J.C.

Awaken the Dawn

Awake, my soul!
Awake, harp and lyre!
I will awaken the dawn.
—PS. 57:8 NIV

In a way, the whole process of recovery is like waking up after a long night of partying. I'm opening my eyes to the reality of what my life is . . . and what it can be. I'm becoming conscious of what I need and what I feel instead of hiding from those needs and feelings behind a sleepy haze of booze or pills or sugar (or whatever).

And the waking isn't easy. The light hurts my eyes—surely it's too early! Besides, who wants to awaken the dawn? Just let me sleep a little longer. . . .

Nope. It's time to open the old eyelids. Feet to the floor, then push off. (Groan.) One step and then another. I may need a Diet Coke™ or a bite to eat—or a splash of cold water in my face. But gradually the fog clears. And even though things aren't perfect—yesterday's dishes are scattered around the living room, and the air smells musty—the sun is still shining in. And somewhere, somehow, a bird is singing.

■ *Awake, my body, soul, and spirit! Lord, teach me to believe you (and your friends) when you tell me that waking up really is worth the agony.*

A.C.B.

LET HIM FILL THE VOID

That Christ may dwell in your hearts through faith; that you [be] rooted and grounded in love.
—EPH. 3:17

Brittany's parents never showed her that they cared. Except for passing in the hallway, she rarely even saw them. They either were not home, or they were busy. Brittany had a lot of pain inside her. It hurt to know that her parents did not care enough even to inquire as to what was going on in her life. That's probably why she turned to drugs and alcohol at age fourteen; they were a way to numb the pain. When she was high, life did not seem to be such a burden.

When we do not get our emotional needs met, we usually look to something else to help fill that void. So many times what we choose (whether it be a person, an activity, or a substance) is detrimental. The pain we inflict upon ourselves only adds to the hurt we already have locked inside. Drugs and alcohol (or whatever) may give momentary relief, but they don't fix the pain—and the addiction will have to be grappled with before the real hurt can be addressed. Addictions only worsen the pain and the problems.

■   *Allow God to fill the void in your heart.*

S.C.

I CHOOSE TO GET BETTER

> *O LORD my God, I cried out to You,*
> *And You have healed me.*
> —PS. 30:2

When an animal is ill, it goes off alone, either to get better or to die," observes Robert Rosenblatt.* That can be true of people, too.

Jennifer spent much of her first days of hospital treatment in the quiet room. This is simply a bare room with a bed. It is isolated from the rest of the unit and is used if a patient is very angry, hysterical, suicidal, or just needs to be alone. Jennifer lay in a fetal position on the bed. Sometimes she just sobbed.

The hospital staff was concerned. Some were afraid that Jennifer was withdrawing too far. Others felt she needed this time alone. And both were potentially right. Which direction Jennifer took during that difficult time was her choice. She could use the time to feel more hopeless and fall into a deep, dark pit, or she could use the time to reflect and gather strength. Like the animal Robert Rosenblatt described, she could "get better or die." But unlike the animal, Jennifer could depend on God to help and heal her.

Fortunately, Jennifer used the time in the quiet room to think about her options. She made a decision to get better, and she asked God for help. In the coming days, God would honor her choice by healing her.

■ *Lord, I will trust You and choose to get better.*

J.C.

*Roger Rosenblatt, "Self Reliance in Hard Times." *Life*, February 1992, 25.

LET THE DARK OUT

God is light and in Him is no darkness at all.
—1 JOHN 1:5

Mommy, let the dark out." She was only three years old. Daylight was just breaking, but the blinds were pulled. She had awakened from a frightening dream, and her mother had come into her room to reassure her, dry her tears, and hug the fears away. Knowing the sunlight would erase all the dark shadows, she asked her mother to open the blinds and "let the dark out."

Don't we all have that little girl within us? Wanting someone to erase all the shadows, dry the tears, and hug the fears away? We've lived with the darkness of our isolation, the anguish of addiction, the fears of spinning out of control. Jesus comes to us in our darkness, opens the blinds of denial, and fills our life with the light of honesty, healing, forgiveness, and recovery. In the safety of our support group, we find those who can be the face of Christ to us in our fears. Gradually, we learn to turn our lives over to Him and let Him hug the fears away.

▪ *God, let the dark out and let Your light in. You know what's ahead of me today. May I walk in Your grace, knowing I'm held in the safety of Your arms.*

D.K.

A MATTER OF PERSPECTIVE

*Do all things without murmuring and
disputing.* —PHIL. 2:14

Winter is an interesting time of year. Nature seems to go into hibernation. The grass turns brown, the trees are stripped bare, the days are short, and the weather is unpredictable. A flurry of snow may blanket the ground. Ice can cover the roads and make them impassable. Sometimes the gray days seem to go on forever.

But the ice that makes travel impossible is the same ice that makes tree branches sparkle in the moonlight. And the snow that blocks in our car is the same snow that makes sledding a blast and forms the greatest snowballs. The days that give us only a few hours of light are the same days that give us longer nights for cozy fires, warm talks, and hot chocolate.

Perception is a major aspect of recovery. We can complain of too-short days, too much snow and ice, too little sunshine. Or we can be grateful that each season brings change and opportunities. After all, hot chocolate on a hot July day doesn't sound too appealing.

Every rose has its thorns. Whether you choose to admire the flower or gripe about the thorns is up to you. Your perception of change and healing will be factors in your recovery process. You can appreciate your growth or complain about its hard work. The choice is yours.

■ *Please help me, Lord, to keep a healthy perspective on life in general and my recovery in particular.*

S.C.

A LOVE STORY

You did not choose Me, but I chose you.
—JOHN 15:16

What's it like to be chosen? Here's a true story about a woman who found out.

It was November. She and some other volunteers were putting up a museum display. The museum had hired him to take pictures of the display (and he took some of her). He told her some jokes. She laughed, then left with her friends and forgot about him. But he didn't forget about her. To find her, he quizzed the museum staff. He called many wrong numbers. He carried her pictures in his car.

It was the following July. Driving by a caramel popcorn shop, he did a double take. It was her, in the window, waiting on customers. He went in and bought popcorn he really didn't want. She didn't recognize him. So he came in every day to buy popcorn he really didn't want. They talked and laughed. One day, he showed her the pictures of that November day. She was amazed that he had been looking for her all this time. Eventually they were married.

Here is another true story. Jesus chose us to be His even when we couldn't care less. He loved us so much He had to tell us, so He left heaven and came to earth. He gave up everything, including His own life, to be with us. That's amazing love. And that should give us the confidence and hope we need to build a good future.

■ *God picked me to love!*

J.C.

Free Indeed

*Therefore if the Son makes you free, you
shall be free indeed.* —JOHN 8:36

It was a hot August day in 1963. Rev. Martin Luther
King, Jr., stirred the hearts of Americans with a message of equality and brotherhood. "I have a dream," he
said, "that one day on the red hills of Georgia the sons
of former slaves and sons of former slave owners will be
able to sit down together at the table of
brotherhood. . . . that my four little children will one
day live in a nation where they will not be judged by the
color of their skin but by the content of their character."
And he concluded that moving address with lines from
an old spiritual: "Free at last, free at last; thank God
almighty; I'm free at last."

It's important to remember what that grand old song
is really about. It's a spiritual—a song about God. And
it's a reminder that, important as political freedom is,
the most important freedom is spiritual freedom—the
freedom that comes from surrendering our wills to
God's will. That kind of freedom is the whole point of
recovery process. As we learn to "turn our wills and our
lives over to the care of God as we [understand] Him,"
we gradually break free from the addictions and com-
pulsions that run our lives. Then we, too, can sing,
"Thank God almighty; I'm free at last."

■   *Lord, keep reminding me that all true freedom is
rooted in you.*

A.C.B.

PEACE IN MY CONFUSION

In You, O LORD, I put my trust;
Let me never be put to shame.
—PS. 71:1

Gina came to my office one afternoon with a look of bewilderment on her face. So much was happening in her life, and she was getting conflicting advice from all sides. She felt overwhelmed and scared, and she could feel herself sliding toward the edge. Gina did not want to fall back on alcohol and drugs to help her cope, but she was not sure she could remain strong.

Gina's parents had just announced their divorce after seventeen years of marriage. Although they occasionally fought, Gina had no idea their marriage was in trouble. She couldn't help wondering if she was partly responsible. She also wondered what would happen to her. Some kids in her class told her to live with her dad; some said she should live with her mom. Certain friends told her it was not that bad to have two separate homes; others complained that going back and forth was awful.

Confusion is tough to handle. Feeling as though there is no direction, no reasoning to life's perplexities leaves one feeling alone and bewildered. But even in the depths of the confusion, God is there; we can lean on Him for answers. The world can be bewildering, but we can choose to place faith in the One who guides and directs.

■ *Father, help me remember that you are aware of everything that happens in my life. Please bring peace to the confusion I feel.*

S.C.

DO YOU WANT TO BE FOUND?

For the Son of Man has come to seek and to save that which was lost. —LUKE 19:10

Beth felt lost and forgotten in her home. Her two sisters were constantly fighting with one another, and her mother was always busy breaking up the fights. One time her sisters accidentally pushed their mother down the stairs when she intervened. Beth was scared that one day her mother or sisters would get seriously hurt. But she told no one of these fears.

Her father spent most of his time at work or at a bar. Beth heard him shout to her mother, "Who can relax with all this fighting?" When Beth's mother complained about his being gone, Beth secretly worried about them getting a divorce.

One day, Beth decided she couldn't take it anymore. She decided not to go to school. She stayed in bed and barely ate. All of a sudden, everyone focused on her, but by then, she could hardly care. Her youth pastor came to visit, but she clammed up. Her parents wanted to take her to see a counselor, but she initially refused to go. When she did go, she barely said anything.

When there are a lot of problems in a family, the quiet child gets lost in the chaos. Jesus sent help to Beth via her youth pastor and the counselor. Now it was up to her whether or not she would be willing to be "found," and give up the lost child role.

■ *Jesus seeks us out and offers His help through others, but we have to accept being "found."*

J.C.

SORTING OUT ANGER

Who knows the power of Your anger?
—PS. 90:11

As soon as she got in the car, she blurted out, "I *hate* my father!" Then the tears started. She was so angry. It doesn't matter what had happened. The things that trigger the anger usually aren't the real issue, anyway. What matters is what to do with the anger.

For so long, I anesthetized my anger—numbed the intense feelings with my substance of choice. But the relief of substance abuse was always short-lived. And then everything I was feeling before was still there, waiting for me, like awakening from a restless, fitful sleep.

Of all the emotions, anger can be the most helpful. Surprised? Anger is full of powerful adrenaline. Anger propels action. Anger gives us the motivation to change. Anger isn't necessarily our enemy; it can be our friend, telling us when to get out of neutral. Sorting out angry feelings, letting go of my need for control, and being willing to make changes is part of the recovery process.

■ *Lord, give me the willingness to look at my anger and listen to what my feelings are telling me.*

D.K.

CHOOSING TO BE POSITIVE

*And whatever you do in word or deed, do all
in the name of the Lord Jesus, giving thanks
to God the Father through Him.*
—COL. 3:17

Some folks seem to float through life like black clouds.
They have an incredible knack of finding the absolute
worst in life. And their gloomy outlook is catching. After
spending any time with a person of this nature, one
feels depressed as well. No wonder people seem to scat-
ter when the "black cloud" walks into the room.

What causes a person to be so negative? In my opinion, it boils down to a choice. Hardships are going to
cross everyone's path, but we can choose our response
to them. We can choose to feel singled out and unjustly
treated, "picked on" or persecuted. And we may indeed be the only one undergoing a particular crisis. But
even then, our attitude will make a difference in how
that crisis affects us. I am not speaking about pretending everything is OK when it is not; I am referring to a
decision to look for the positive aspects of the hardship.

Attitudes make all the difference in the world. How
we cope with pressures, predicaments, and even life itself will greatly be determined by our attitude. Being
negative brings us down and those around us. But an
"attitude of gratitude" helps carry us through the tough
times as well as helping us enjoy the good times.

■   *Do your utmost to be a positive person. Be aware of
how your attitude affects your outlook on life.*

S.C.

WALKING WITH THE WISE

> [She] who walks with wise [people]
>   will be wise,
> But the companion of fools will be
>   destroyed.   —PROV. 13:20

You become like the people you hang out with. If you want to know about clothes, stick with someone who can make an outfit from pieces of clothing you'd never think to put together. Go out with a car freak, and you can learn a lot about cars.

In the same way, if you want to learn how to do more sophisticated drugs or get some drugs, hang around those who do them. If you want to relapse, go to parties where drinkers will be sure to have alcohol there. The Bible calls these people fools. And God warns us to stay away from them because, if we don't, we will lose our ability to "discern words of knowledge" (Prov. 14:7 NASB). After a while, we may buy the lie of "I never really was addicted" or "I can handle just one beer."

If you want to recover, pick friends who are serious about their recovery or who never were addicted. Pick those who seem balanced. These are the wise. Today's verse says if you hang out with them, you'll also be wise. Wisdom has a way of rubbing off.

Your control is in the picking of friends. Decide who you want to be and then hang with someone who models those qualities. After that, things are pretty automatic. You become like those you spend time with.

■   *My hope for a successful recovery includes picking wise friends and staying away from fools.*

J.C.

FACING THE FACES

"Do not be afraid of their faces,
For I am with you to deliver you,"
says the LORD. —JER. 1:8

It was tough to finally hit bottom and face the fact that you had a problem. It was tough to go for treatment. Group sessions and therapy weren't a piece of cake. But now you're on the road to recovery. And now you've got to go back to school and face the people who know what's been going on with you.

You can feel the whispers as you walk in the lunchroom. You can see the looks on faces all around— curiosity, judgment, fear? Your friends, wondering if you'll dump them now. Acquaintances, wondering how you'll act. Teachers, wondering if you've really changed. In a sense, it was easier when you could numb yourself with addictive behavior. Facing all the faces without a "crutch" can hurt.

But you've got what you need to handle this. You've got a support system. You've got enough recovery under your belt now to believe the effort is worth it. And you've got God, who has promised to deliver you (even from acute embarrassment!). All you have to do right now is get through lunch. So take a deep breath, take a tray . . . you're going to make it.

■ *Lord, thanks for the people who support me. Thanks for bringing me this far. And thank you for you! You have promised to deliver me; I need that promise more than ever now.*

A.C.B.

GET IN THE GAME!

I press toward the goal for the prize of the upward call of God in Christ Jesus.
—PHIL. 3:14

Many of us have a tendency to sit on the sidelines of life. We may complain about what is happening, but we would rather wait for others to fix our problems than participate in the solution ourselves.

Perhaps it is fear that keeps us from taking action. Maybe we are idle because we have no idea what to do. Whatever the reason, it's hard to make progress when we're sitting in the bleachers! We must learn to be active participants and not passive observers in the recovery process and life in general. We cannot expect others to rescue us. And although talking about our problems can be a help, words alone are not enough to change situations. Action is what gets the job done.

I have known many kids who believe that "life happens" to them. They go about their daily lives with very little direction, hope, or plans. And usually they aren't going anywhere. Granted, no plan is infallible. But if we really are serious about changing the course of our lives, we need to have something to strive for.

Watching a sport may be fun, but the game means so much more when you are a player. It is the same with participating in life. Don't stand back and watch it go by. Get in there and be a part of it!

■ *God, give me the desire to be an active part of my recovery and of my life.*

S.C

Focus on Jesus

*So don't be anxious about tomorrow. God
will take care of your tomorrow too. Live one
day at a time.* —MATT. 6:34 TLB

It's hard to think of being sober for the rest of your life.
If you're sixteen and the average life span for a woman
is about seventy-five years, then you have fifty-nine
years to go. That's 21,535 days; 516,840 hours; and
31,010,400 minutes! And that can be overwhelming if
you just sit and think about it!

Jesus knows that type of thinking adds stress and
worry to life and can even lead to relapse. That's why
He urges us to just take it one day at a time. And instead of focusing on staying sober, He tells us to focus
on Him—to seek His kingdom first, and everything else
will follow (Matt. 6:33). When we do that, we learn
about who Jesus is and how we can do things His way.
When we do that, He gives us the power and wisdom we
need to complete the task successfully.

■ *I can lower my stress about maintaining sobriety by
focusing on Jesus and taking my recovery one day at
a time.*

J.C.

NOTHING'S TOO HARD

Behold, I am the LORD, the God of all flesh.
Is there anything too hard for Me?
—JER. 32:27

I want to peek around the corner of tomorrow. I don't have to see it all—just a glimpse. I want to know it's all going to be OK. I want to know things will work out. Sometimes I feel I'm being pressured to make decisions: What job am I going to get this summer? What college am I going to? (I don't even know if I want to *go* to college.) Sometimes it just seems too hard, too complicated.

When the pressure begins to build, I need to remember that I don't have to live my whole life today. I don't have to solve it, fix it, plan it, or decide it. All I really have to do is live faithfully today. If I do that, God has promised to take care of tomorrow.

That doesn't mean things will be easy. It doesn't mean I'm through with pain. But it does mean God is in control—and nothing is too hard for Him. I've already made my most important decision; I've turned my life over to God. I don't need to know any more than that today. I'll "let go and let God" take care of tomorrow.

■ *God, when I feel the pressure to make decisions, help me remember that nothing is too hard for you. When I'm worried about tomorrow, bring me back to today and the gift of life I have in this moment.*

D.K.

I DON'T DESERVE THAT!

Be kind to one another, tenderhearted . . .
—EPH. 4:32

Erica grew up believing she was a bad girl. Her alcoholic father told her that nearly every day. He called her hurtful names while her mother sat helplessly by. He would accuse Erica of immoral acts she did not commit. If he could not find a belonging, he blamed her for stealing it. Even when she did something well, he would find fault.

After Erica left home, she became involved with other abusive men. She did not realize that she did not deserve to be treated poorly. If she was verbally or physically abused, she accepted it; abuse felt normal to her. In fact, when someone treated her with kindness or respect, she would question their motives or their sincerity.

For Erica, life was a series of mistreatments. Unconsciously, she may have even sought them out. But in recovery she learned that *no one ever* deserves to be abused. We all have a right as well as a need to be treated well by others. This does not mean having all our desires fulfilled. But it does mean we deserve to have our souls nurtured by kind words and acts. It means believing that we can mess up without being bad people. Every one of us is precious in the sight of God.

■   *Lord, please show me how valuable I am to you. Help me understand the importance of never accepting mistreatment.*

S.C.

BE A FRIEND FIRST

A [girl] who has friends must [herself]
be friendly. —PROV. 18:24

Stephanie's favorite activity was sitting in front of the TV with a bag of chips and a bowl of double-chocolate-chip cookies. Predictably, she was overweight. But weight was not her only problem. Stephanie was so afraid of rejection that she ended up rejecting others first.

From time to time, friends would call and invite Stephanie to go out with them. She'd usually decline. She was sure she never really fit in with them. She was afraid she'd stick out like a sore thumb. After a while, people stopped calling her. Then she felt more rejected and turned back to her cookies and chips. They were safe. They would never reject her.

What was happening here? Stephanie was helping to bring about the very rejection she feared. She needed to believe that people did want to be with her, especially since they had called her. This would be a step of faith for her, since she was convinced no one really wanted to be with her. She reasoned that they were just feeling sorry for her.

Even if this were true, it would not have remained the case had Stephanie shown herself to be a friend in return. She needed to change her self-image from "reject" to friend. Even if she did not feel like it, Stephanie could choose to be friendly. That choice would open new friendships to her. Then maybe she wouldn't need her friendship with food.

■ *God says that if I want friends, I need to be one first.*
J.C.

DOES IT HURT TO BE REAL?

*Do not say,
"Why were the former days better
than these?"
For you do not inquire wisely
concerning this.*
—ECCLES. 7:10

*T*he *Velveteen Rabbit* is a classic childhood story about a stuffed bunny who wants to be real. Late one night, when the toys are talking together in the nursery, the Velveteen Rabbit asks the wise old Skin Horse if it hurts to become real. The Skin Horse answers, "Sometimes . . . [but] when you are Real you don't mind."

Does it hurt to become real? You bet. Does it hurt to face our addiction, our character defects, and our failures and allow God to begin changing us from the inside out? You bet. Is it worth the pain? You bet.

We're never ready for recovery until the pain of staying where we are is worse than the pain of change. Many newcomers are surprised to find more painful feelings emerging after several months of abstinence or sobriety. What had previously been anesthetized through substance abuse gradually comes to the surface. That's the point where many want to give up, thinking, "I don't want to feel this way. This is worse than before." Those feelings are normal and, thankfully, usually short-lived. When we lean into the pain, look at the issues straight-on, and take recovery one day at a time, the changes take care of themselves.

■ *We have it on good authority: The Skin Horse says that once we're real, we can never be unreal again.*

D.K.

THERE'S NO COMPARISON

*It is He who has made us, and
not we ourselves.*
—PS. 100:3

I recently overheard a conversation between two teenagers. One had braces on her teeth; the other was experiencing a break out of acne. And both were complaining about their looks.

What happened next was predictable. They began comparing themselves to each other. One wished she had the other's black, curly hair. Of course, that one wished for her friend's straight blond hair. Since one was tall and one was short, this became an issue as well; each one wanted the other's height. Weight was also an inevitable topic; each claimed to be "fatter" than the other. (Both were of average weight for their height.)

On and on the comparisons went. Finally, I could not help myself. I went over and told them that they were both unique, one-of-a-kind girls—fine just the way they were. They looked surprised, both relieved.

Comparing ourselves to others is destructive; we inevitably end up feeling inferior. We are not created alike. God formed each of us to be different and special. So accept your differences—in fact, celebrate them. You do not have to be perfect. You just have to be who you are. After all, "it is He who has made us"!

■ *Father, help me to stop comparing myself to others. Teach me to accept myself just as I am.*

S.C.

BREAKING THE CURSE

Just as you were a curse among the nations,
O house of Judah and house of Israel,
So I will save you, and you shall be a
blessing.
—ZECH. 8:13

Were you a curse to your family: staying out all night; using your parents' home (without their knowledge) as party headquarters, trashing furniture and rugs; stealing your parents' money; driving drunk and crashing the family car; lying constantly; expressing anger through explosive tantrums or silent suicidal gestures?

Were you a curse to your friends: "borrowing" their money but never paying it back; promising to meet them somewhere, then never showing up because you were wasted; cheating on a boyfriend to take advantage of a drugs-for-sex offer?

Were you a curse to yourself: damaging your brain by drinking too much; starving or stuffing yourself; flunking out because partying the night before was more important than getting up to go to school?

Now God has saved you from all that, and you're on the path to recovery. In fact, God says He saved you so that you can be a *blessing* instead of a curse. The blessing will come as you figure out new ways to relate to family, friends, and yourself. God's hope chest, the Bible, will tell you how to do it.

■ *I can become a blessing instead of the curse I once*
was with God's help.

J.C.

MY BODY IS NOT MY ENEMY

I beseech you therefore, [sisters], by the
mercies of God, that you present your bodies
a living sacrifice, holy, acceptable to God.
—ROM. 12:1

D₀ you ever feel that your body is out to get you? It's easy to fall in the trap of thinking that way. After all, your body can be a pain. You have to worry about feeding it (or not feeding it) and exercising it and giving it enough rest. It's full of needs and appetites that get you into trouble. It's usually the wrong shape or size (according to popular opinion). And if you want to get philosophical, it's sort of a lost cause: one of these days, it's just going to die on you!

So should we just "concentrate on the spirit" and ignore the body? Contrary to popular opinion, that's not the biblical approach. According to the Bible, my body is not all of me, but it's an important, God-given part of me. It talks, it walks, it touches—and thus it helps me connect with others. If I abuse it, I usually end up depressed or addicted or just preoccupied with my own flesh. But if I give it to God—along with the rest of me—it becomes part of my transformation and my ongoing spiritual growth.

■ *Lord, my body is not all the me there is, but it is an*
important part of me—and a gift from you. Help me
to see my body in proper perspective and to treat it
with gratitude and respect.

A.C.B.

TAKE ANOTHER STEP

When you pass through the waters, I will
be with you;
And through the rivers, they shall not
overflow you.
When you walk through the fire, you shall
not be burned,
Nor shall the flame scorch you.

—ISA. 43:2

Trials can be overwhelming. It is not easy to look a struggle in the eye and remember that you will make it. Often it is tempting to quit or abandon your purpose. But when water rises or the heat is on, that's usually a sign that you're heading in the right direction!

Anything worth achieving is going to entail effort and, most likely, a few obstacles. Do not allow the obstacles to be stumbling blocks or stop signs. Instead, take another step. And just when you think that you cannot go on anymore, God will crack open a door or a window. Through that opening a ray of hope will stream.

When you must pass through the water or walk through the fire, keep your attitude in check. Keep your mind focused on your goal. Most of all, remember God's promises. Remember, the object is not to avoid the trial, but to accomplish what you started. With God's help, you can see it through to the end.

■ *Trials are God's way of bringing us through things*
we never would have chosen to show us things we
never would have known.

S.C.

A SPECIAL HELPER

Two are better than one . . .
For if they fall, one will lift up [her] companion.
But woe to [her] who is alone when [she] falls,
For [she] has no one to help [her] up.
—ECCLES. 4:9–10

A new relationship you might want to consider is a sponsor. This is someone who has been involved in a support recovery group or in recovery and has a considerable amount of straight time under her belt. This person agrees to be your guide and support to help you maintain your recovery. The person you ask to sponsor you should be a Christian, preferably someone older than you, and someone you would not get romantically entangled with.

A sponsor will know by experience what the pitfalls are and what some answers may be. She can offer hope when things seem hopeless, because she's been through it before. She will be someone you can call in a crisis—perhaps even in the middle of the night. Usually, however, you will meet together once a week.

Sometimes it's hard to find a sponsor. If this is the case, you may consider "adopting" an older "spiritual sister" from your home church or from an organization such as Campus Crusade. She may never have had substance-abuse experience, but she can help you understand your Higher Power, God. Weekly, one-on-one Bible studies and just having someone you can be honest with can speed your recovery.

■ *My hope in recovery grows when I have a "special friend" to guide and support me.*

J.C.

ANGELS IN THE SNOW

*Behold, I send an Angel before you to keep
you ir the way and to bring you into the
place which I have prepared.*

—EX. 23:20

I have a friend who says her life purpose is to make angels in the snow. I've asked her to explain what she means. She won't. She just smiles. Meanwhile, my other friends are deciding what they want to be when they grow up, dreaming dreams, or resisting the imposition of someone else's dreams.

I remember making angels in the snow when I was a kid. I'd find a deep snow bank, fall straight back, move my arms up and down to create the depression in the shape of wings, then try to get up without disturbing the form left in the snow. My cheeks and nose were red from the cold as I brushed the snow off my pants, only to have it fall into my boots. My toes were so cold they hurt. Those were afternoons of laughter.

I left invisible angels in the snow noticeable only to those who had eyes to see. Silent witnesses to savoring the experience, to childlike joy, to losing myself in the moment only to rise, energized, ready to do it again.

■ *Maybe finding God's purpose for my life isn't really a matter of seeking out the grand and noble. Perhaps God is calling me to make angels in the snow.*

D.K.

THE ALTERNATIVE TO DENIAL

Therefore I will not be negligent to remind you always of these things, though you know them, and are established in the present truth.
—2 PETER 1:12

In each of our lives, a psychological defense mechanism called denial is at work. We all have used it and most likely still use it from time to time. And that's not always bad, because denial is intended to protect us. In the face of trauma, blinding ourselves to the seriousness of a situation may enable us to get through it. But denial can also be an obstacle to growth—when it "protects" us from a painful reality we need to face.

If you are in recovery, chances are that you are well acquainted with this unhealthy kind of denial. Telling others or yourself that you're fine—when you're not—is denial. Telling yourself you can handle your life is denial. Believing you are stronger than the obsession is denial. And denial must stop before recovery can proceed. That's why step one of the Twelve Steps of AA states, "We admitted we were powerless over alcohol—that our lives had become unmanageable."

Facing reality without the protective shield of denial is tough—too tough, if we try to do it by ourselves. We can, however, turn ourselves along with our problems over to the One who is stronger. We do not need to pretend we are strong when we feel weak. We don't need to pretend everything is OK when it is not. In fact, we don't need to pretend at all.

■ *Facing up to what truly is going on is the critical first step to getting better.*

S.C.

THE BASIS FOR YOUR HOPE

*I have come that they may have life, and
that they may have it more abundantly.*
—JOHN 10:10

If someone could just prove to me there is a God, then maybe I'd believe." Kate was stuck. She knew she was powerless over her addiction, and this scared her. She saw the destructive chaos in her life. She knew by experience she had no power to change that.

But to admit to God's existence or to accept Jesus as her Savior would identify Kate with her mom and dad. She felt they had put their brains on hold in order to be saved. She was proud of her agnosticism. To her, it was the only sound intellectual position. In fact, it was part of her identity. But it was destroying her.

Does a Christian have to put her brain on hold? What are the evidences of God's existence? The systematic orderliness of nature requires a Creator, someone who planned that order. (One would not point to a car and say it just happened to arrange itself.) Other evidences are the human conscience, fulfilled prophecy, the historical reliability of the Bible, and the person of Jesus Christ. God loved us so much that He became human through Jesus. Jesus showed us just who God is (see John 1:14, 18). However, the most powerful evidence of God's existence is a changed life. God offered Kate that chance to prove Himself personally to her. He offered her His power for a new life and identity.

■ *Hope for a successful recovery lies in accepting
God's offer for salvation. Have you taken Him up on
this?*

J.C.

NOW IS THE TIME

Behold, now is the accepted time; behold,
now is the day of salvation.

—2 COR. 6:2

Shelby was obsessed by the problems of her past. Her parents' divorce, physical abuse by her stepfather, a sister's suicide—all played and replayed in her mind. She had gone beyond the point of honestly facing her past; now she was allowing the past to paralyze her.

Jana, on the other hand, was carried away with plans for the future. Her past life hadn't been great, but she just knew everything would work out once she got out of school, once she moved out of her parents' house, once she got a job. Jana studied hard, worked hard, made plans—but she wasn't doing much about the buried anger and grief that sometimes emerged to sabotage her dreams.

The reason recovery programs put such emphasis on living "one day at a time" is that *now* is the only part of our lives we have any control over. We can process the pain of the past, but we can't change what happened. We can plan for the future, but we can't guarantee our plans will work out. But each day, each moment, we can make a new decision to depend on God, to be honest with ourselves and others, to make responsible choices. To grow in recovery, "now is the accepted time."

■ *Lord, you give me insight about yesterday and hope for tomorrow. But now is the moment for me to trust you and move forward.*

A.C.B.

WORTHWHILE WORK

*The LORD repay your work, and a full
reward be given you by the LORD God.*
—RUTH 2:12

A lot of folks sit in my office and discuss their problems. They find themselves in predicaments and want help to untie the knots in their lives. Sometimes they ask me, either directly or by their lack of action, to untie their knots for them. When I go over my typical speech of "I'm willing to work with you but not do it for you," most shake their heads in agreement. When I warn them that therapy is tough work, that it can be draining, and that they will only reap the desired results if they are willing to put forth the necessary effort, most readily accept that fact.

However, the attrition rate in therapy is high. Why? Because the majority of people are not willing to stick with the effort it takes, or they want the therapist to do the work for them. A therapist who works harder than her patient is not really helping. The patient does not learn to manage her life herself and continues to believe she is not capable.

If you have just begun treatment, be prepared to work hard. Do the assignments. Feel the pain. Be on time for your appointments. Make your therapy a top priority in your life.

■ *Nothing worthwhile comes easily. But when I am
willing to work at it, the results are well worth the
time and effort.*

S.C.

LEARNING TO LISTEN

*See, I have inscribed you on the palms
of My hands.*
—ISA. 49:16

Imagine someone loving you so much he'd tattoo your name on his hand! This act would symbolize a lifetime commitment, since tattoos last that long. God has already done that. He is lovingly committed to you. Are you as committed to Him?

A committed relationship thrives on communication. We can talk to God by praying and listen to Him by reading His words in the Bible. But listening to God as a person who loves us and not just as the ultimate authority figure takes practice. Evelyn Christenson, in her book, *"Lord Change Me!"* outlines how we can develop our spiritual ears.* First, she recommends reading a Bible passage only until God has spoken. God's voice can feel like a gentle nudge or like a shout. But once you hear it, don't read on. If you do, you may miss the message. Second, ask God why He stopped you at that point. Maybe He wants you to change something. Or maybe He wants to give you a word of encouragement. Whatever it is, write down what you hear Him saying. You will then have a record of God's personal words to you, written on paper, but also, hopefully, inscribed on your heart.

■ *Hearing God's personal words to me helps fill the hole in my heart where I used to pour drugs, alcohol, or food.*

J.C.

*(Wheaton, Ill.: Victor, 1989), 22–23.

WHERE TO DRAW THE LINE

Do not remember the former things,
Nor consider the things of old.
Behold, I will do a new thing.
—ISA. 43:18–19

Once you've gone all the way, how do you backtrack to purity? The hormones start bubbling, the desires start burning, and the compromises seem so easy.

So how do you draw the line and wait till the time is right? The same way you live in recovery—one day at a time, turning over the longings, desires, struggles, and failures to the power of Christ within.

Admitting I'm powerless is not the same as admitting I'm helpless, though. Temptation wouldn't be temptation if it didn't involve something I want. So in recovery I know there are certain situations that are a "no go" for me. I know my decisions about what's right for me have to be made *before* I find myself in a compromising situation. And I know that anyone who pressures me to compromise my integrity is someone I can choose no longer to hang out with.

■ *Lord, knowing what's right and finding the strength within to do it are two different things. I know that on my resolve alone, I can't make it. But looking to you, trusting in your power, and walking in your grace, I am becoming a new person. Thanks for making all things new.*

D.K.

BIG "I," LITTLE "U"

*Let each of you look out not only for [her]
own interests, but also for the interests of
others.*
—PHIL. 2:4

Have you ever been around a person who is so consumed with herself that no one else seems to matter? It is as though she is the center of the universe and the world revolves around her. There is certainly a "big I" and a "little U" in her life.

In the recovery process, much focus is placed on self. This is to balance an unhealthy focusing of attention on others—blaming, feeling overly responsible, protecting. But it's easy to become so engrossed with "self" that we begin trampling on others' feelings or needs. "Self" is important, but it is not the only thing that matters. People who become too wrapped up in themselves quickly find themselves feeling isolated and friendless.

The pendulum of "self" does not need to swing from one extreme to the other; it needs to gently rest in the middle. Being aware of our own needs, validating our feelings, respecting ourselves, establishing healthy boundaries, treating ourselves with dignity—all these are necessary and very important. But other people count as well. Respecting their needs is just as important as respecting our own.

I am responsible for my own treatment and recovery. I am not responsible for "fixing others." But each person is as significant as myself.

■ *Lord, help me today not to become wrapped up in myself.*

S.C.

WISE COUNSEL

Where there is no counsel, the people fall;
But in the multitude of counselors there
*   is safety.*   —PROV. 11:14

I know I need my support group. And I like the idea of
a sponsor. But therapy? Isn't that for crazy people?"
Not necessarily.

If you have been through a chemical dependency
program, having a therapist is not a new idea. If you
haven't, the idea of therapy might make you feel leery.
But if you feel stuck at any point, individual or family
therapy can help a lot.

As you have success in maintaining abstinence, other
issues may begin to surface. Pain from past physical
abuse, sexual abuse, or loss may become more
intrusive—pain that your unhealthy behavior was meant
to numb—might become more intrusive once you've
given up your "anesthetic." And the only way to get
better is to walk through the pain. But not alone. A
Christian therapist can walk alongside you and help
make you aware of Jesus' presence. (A support group
and a sponsor also come in handy at this point.) Therapy can help you understand the pain and its flashback
feelings. Finally, if the pain gets too intense and you feel
like hurting yourself or someone else, inpatient (hospital) therapy can keep you safe so you can continue the
work of healing.

■   *Today's verse doesn't mean you should have many*
    therapists—but a combination of supports promotes
    a successful recovery.

J.C.

"HAVE" OR "HAVE NOT"?

> *The LORD has appeared of old to me, saying:*
> *"Yes, I have loved you with an everlasting*
> *   love;*
> *Therefore with lovingkindness I have*
> *   drawn you."*
>   —JER. 31:3

Valentine's Day really tends to separate the "haves" from the "have nots"—at least for us female types.

If I have a caring boyfriend (or at least, someone who is interested), I'm a "have"—and the card or flowers to prove it. If I don't have anyone special (or if my guy just doesn't go for romance), I'm a "have not"—and it doesn't feel great. Amid all the hearts and flowers at school, at the mall, on TV—even at the grocery store—how can I help but feel at least a little left out? And that's a great temptation to fall back into old destructive habits.

If I'm feeling blue instead of pink on Valentine's Day, I need to rally my resources to stay on the recovery road. I can call my sponsor or a friend. I can spend extra time in prayer and pour my feelings out in my journal. Most important, I can remind myself that God's love, unlike *all* human love, is never a matter of "have" and "have not." He is always there for me. All I have to do is open my heart to Him.

■ *Lord, romance is great, but I can't let my happiness or my self-esteem depend on having a boyfriend or being in love. Teach me to look to you as the source of my fulfillment. (Then, if you happen to have a great guy up your sleeve for me—well, I wouldn't complain!)*

                                                      A.C.B.

DON'T WAIT FOR THE FEELING

*For it is God who works in you both to will
and to do for His good pleasure.*
—PHIL. 2:13

So many times in our lives we wait until we feel like doing something before we do it. But when we rely on feelings for motivation, we may not accomplish much. It is not that feelings aren't important. But feelings can be fickle. They seem to change with the wind. One day we might feel a certain way; the next day the feeling might have changed drastically.

Where recovery is concerned, there may be a conflict between the feelings and the will. It is important to will yourself to be committed to treatment, because you won't always feel like being committed. The *will* to preserve your sobriety needs to be stronger than the feeling of not caring. The will to eat properly and not purge needs to win out over the feelings of wanting to give in.

We have to act on what we know is right. If we wait to have the feelings before we pursue a goal, we may be waiting a long time. When we do act, however, our feelings have a tendency to follow. After the temptation to quit has passed, a sigh of relief can often be heard. A feeling of confidence and accomplishment is experienced instead of guilt.

Being committed to recovery is an act of the will. Feelings may have very little to do with it.

■   *Choose today to be committed to your recovery.*

S.C.

SAYING NO

. . . proving what is acceptable to the Lord.
—EPH. 5:10

Toni was a people pleaser. When she got her driver's license, her friends knew she'd take them where they needed to go—anytime. "No problem," was her motto.

Since Toni was abstinent, her drinking friends made her the designated driver. She ended up going to parties that she knew weren't good for her and that she didn't even want to attend. Sometimes she felt like her friends' chauffeur—except no one was paying her. Her friends were running her life (and car).

The first time Toni said no to a request, her friend went silent. Toni felt guilty; she was afraid she'd lose her friendship. But then she reasoned that if this girl really was her friend, she'd respect Toni's decision. After a few times, saying no was easier.

Instead of building her life around pleasing other people and avoiding their anger, Toni wanted to please God. Pleasing God may mean different things to different people. But to Toni at this time in her life, it meant no late-night chauffeuring on Saturdays. (This was so she could get enough sleep to hear what God had to say to her on Sunday mornings at church.) It meant making new friends who could support her recovery. It meant risking someone's anger when she said no to them so she could say yes to God.

■ *Recovery means focusing on pleasing God instead of pleasing people.*

J.C.

THE CREATIVITY WITHIN

*So God created man [and woman] in His
own image; in the image of God He created
him; male and female He created them.*
—GEN. 1:27

If I can accept that God is creative, and I can accept
that I was created in His image, then why do I have so
much trouble accepting that I am creative? If God is a
creative presence, and I'm created in that image, isn't
it logical to conclude that I, therefore, am a creative
person?

Our creativity, however it is expressed, is an inner
wellspring—easily damaged, easily squelched. Because
we may not be gifted in school, may not know how to
play a musical instrument, or may not know the first
thing about paints, we too readily dismiss having any
creative abilities. But look deeper. Take the blinders off,
and give God a chance to open your eyes. Where do
your dreams take you? When do you feel most fully
alive? Ask Him to show you what lies within. What you
find may surprise you, may delight you.

■ *God, I've had so many people tell me I'm nothing
special that it's hard to hear you telling me I'm
gifted, precious, a one and only. Could you speak a
little louder, God, just for today?*

D.K.

THE BECKONING FINGER

No temptation has overtaken you except such as is common to man; but God is faithful, who will not allow you to be tempted beyond what you are able, but with the temptation will also make the way of escape, that you may be able to bear it. —1 COR. 10:13

The word *temptation* conjures up a picture in my mind of a shadowy but appealing figure who summons me to quit what I have begun, slide back into old ways (if only for a moment), or lose sight of my goals. I hear a quiet whisper that says, "Come here and taste of this; I will give you pleasure." Accompanying the whisper is a beckoning finger.

A war ensues within me. Should I abandon my standards or goals? Or should I stand strong against the temptation? Perhaps it will be OK if I just don't get caught. Confusion overtakes me. Rationalizing comes easily. Sometimes other people make it worse—saying, "You only live once" or "Just enjoy yourself."

In the midst of the battle, however, I can usually feel a gentle nudge and a tender Voice reminding me to choose carefully and wisely. If I give in to the temptation, what will happen? What is the price in the end? And is it really worth it? If I only listen, I remember that God has chosen a better way—a higher road. If I let the beckoning finger lead me down a wrong path, I will be hurting myself and probably others.

■ *Saying no to temptation is tough—but the Lord really does give me enough strength to do it.*

S.C.

DRAWING THE LINE

[She] who commits sexual immorality sins against [her] own body. —1 COR. 6:18

The middle of a French kiss is not the time to decide your standards for sexual activity on a date. By then, who can think? Who wants to think?

Today's verse advises us to know how to handle our bodies with honor. When we have a guest of honor, we uphold her importance. We make sure others recognize her specialness, too. Your body is a guest of honor. Uphold its importance by not exposing it to venereal diseases or AIDS. And recognize its specialness by not using it as a sexual tease—not wearing clothes or using body language that hint at possible sexual intercourse.

If a French kiss arouses the desire for intercourse, then the line needs to be drawn before it gets to that kiss. For some, even a kiss on the lips may mean too much. Be clear where that line is for you (and take into consideration that the line usually comes earlier for males than females).

Use your early days of recovery to think this through. It's recommended that you wait six months to a year before dating. Once you do start dating again, honor your body by talking to your date early on about your values. Clearing the air about expectations can avoid later frustrations and unmanageable situations.

■ *I can avoid unmanageable behavior by (1) figuring out where my "line" is, (2) communicating it clearly, and (3) sticking to it.*

J.C.

CALL FOR BACKUP

He is their strength in the time of trouble.
And the LORD shall help them and
deliver them. —PS. 37:39–40

Do you ever watch TV cop shows? If you do, you know that it's standard police procedure to call for a backup before proceeding into a possibly dangerous situation. There they sit, the detective and her partner, outside the deserted warehouse. They've tailed the bad guys there, and they're ready to go in after them. But first they radio in their position and call for another car—just in case.

It's not just a "cop thing," of course. Calling for backup is always smart when you anticipate a challenge. If you're going to a party where you don't know people very well and you're afraid someone might be using, ask a friend to go with you. If you're heading into exam time and you know that pressure tempts you to binge, alert your support group. If you're at home and bored and tempted, call your sponsor or your prayer partner. And wherever you are, you can always call on God as well as your human backup.

■ *Calling for backup from other people and from God is a smart way to head into a recovery challenge.*

A.C.B.

HOW TO BE ANGRY

*Therefore, my beloved [sisters], let every
[woman] be swift to hear, slow to speak, slow
to wrath; for the wrath of [woman] does not
produce the righteousness of God.*
—JAMES 1:19–20

Anger shows itself differently in different people. Some become so enraged that they totally lose control. Others have difficulty even knowing they are angry. Some throw things. Some develop ulcers or become depressed. And all these are unhealthy expressions of a healthy emotion.

God gave us the capability of feeling angry, because there are times when anger is appropriate. It is how we handle the feeling of anger that makes the difference. Expressing our anger in a way that other people understand is very important. Keeping a tight rein on our words and actions is imperative. We are not to sin with our anger (Eph. 4:26). And we are not to let anger take root in our hearts. Anger that is stored up harms others as well as ourselves.

Feeling the anger and then *resolving it* are two significant actions. Don't shove it down, but don't let it go on indefinitely, either. Handle anger cautiously. Feel it, but try not to wallow in it.

Anger is not wrong, but it can be damaging. It can also be a tool used in healing. Think through your actions carefully; respond, but don't react.

■ *Use anger constructively in your life.*

S.C.

No More Rejection Thinking

*. . . looking diligently lest anyone fall short of
the grace of God; lest any root of bitterness
springing up cause trouble, and by this many
become defiled.*   **—HEB. 12:15**

An older couple adopted an orphaned baby girl. They
had waited a long time for a child, and they treasured
her. The mother spent a lot of time with the girl and was
very concerned about her well-being. They baked cookies. They made popcorn and watched videos. They
loved being together.

Then one day, in spite of the mother's carefulness,
the girl was sexually abused by a neighbor. She told no
one, not even her mother. Mistakenly, she assumed the
abuse was her fault. She felt so dirty and ashamed. And
her attitude toward her mother changed. Now, when the
mother told the girl to be careful, the girl thought she
was criticizing her. When the mother asked the girl to
come with her on an errand, the girl felt the mother was
"using" her for company. "Rejection thinking" made
the girl bitter, and she drank to numb the hurt.

One day, after a knock-down, drag-out fight, the girl
told her mother about the abuse. She learned that the
abuse was not her fault and that her mother's words to
be careful were said out of love, not criticism. A thaw
began in the girl's heart as she let go of the rejection
thinking. She still had a lot of work to do, but the healing process had begun.

■   *Lord, help me to weed out the roots of bitterness,
whose fruits of rejection thinking bring unmanageability to my life.*

                                              J.C.

GRAY DAYS AND WINTRY MOODS

Hear me when I call, O God of my righteousness!
You have relieved me when I was in distress;
Have mercy on me, and hear my prayer.
—PS. 4:1

Rainy days. Gray days. Yucky wintry days. I know the Serenity Prayer says, "accept the things I cannot change," and I know the weather is something I can't change. So why does it get me so down? Why does my mood match the grayness of the weather?

Isn't it interesting that the Serenity Prayer starts with "God, grant me . . ."? The Serenity Prayer is a plea for help, asking God to do for me what I can't do for myself. When I'm feeling down, that's probably a good place to start. How easily I forget that the Serenity Prayer is a *prayer*. Rather than falling too quickly into "shoulds" and "shouldn'ts," I first need to be honest about what I am feeling. Telling myself, "I shouldn't be feeling this way" is at least an unrealistic expectation and at best probably low-grade denial.

Gray days, sad times, and down moods serve a purpose. Even plants need a break from the harshness of bright sunlight. And we may take notice of nasty, rainy weather when we aren't taking notice of what's going on within. Maybe on my gray days I need to seek the quiet, pamper myself a little, and be nice to me.

■ *God, help me accept the things I cannot change and give me the willingness to look beyond the easy things to blame when I'm feeling down.*

D.K.

A PLACE OF SOLACE

In my distress I cried to the LORD,
And He heard me. —PS. 120:1

When I was a teenager, I used to have special places I would go when I needed to have some time alone. I lived on a farm, and my two favorite spots were the hayloft and the back pasture. I would climb up the ladder in the barn to get to the hayloft. Bales would be stacked all around. I would pick a bale of hay to sit on, pull my knees up to my chest, and just think about my problems. I did not have to worry about being interrupted. I might be up there an hour or two at a time. After I thought about things for awhile, life did not seem so bad.

The pasture was a place that felt open and free. I could talk to myself out loud and no one could hear me. Sometimes I would flop down in the grass and just stare up at the sky. Or if I needed to release some energy, I would run as fast as I could until I was tired. Again, after some time alone, life seemed manageable.

Even now, when I go back to my parents' home, I visit my favorite places. Being able to find a quiet spot to smooth out my troubles continues to be important. I frequently picture those places in my head when my life gets too hectic. My heart finds solace there.

■ *Do you have a quiet place—physical or mental— where you can go when you need some time alone?*

S.C.

LIVING THE TRUTH

[They] exchanged the truth of God for the lie.
—ROM. 1:25

Yeah, I think it's best if I quit the gang. I can get out any time. I was just "blessed into" the gang. I didn't become a full-fledged member."

Patsy was lying. She had no intention of quitting, but was saying what she thought her group members at the drug rehab center wanted to hear. Later, after group time, Patsy was caught in the lie when a peer confronted her. Patsy swore and told her there was no way she'd quit the gang.

Patsy was living two lives. In front of her parents and staff she was compliant and hard working. Privately, with her peers, she was scornful of authority figures and proud of her secret acting-out behaviors. Patsy had quit abusing substances, but her lifestyle was still that of an addict. She talked the talk but was not walking the walk. Consequently, people had trouble getting close to her—and she felt little support.

People who abuse substances often lead two lives—a public one and a secret one. This necessitates lying, which isolates them from deep and trusting relationships.

Eventually, Patsy did tell the truth about her real intentions. Telling the truth allowed her to explore her fears about quitting. Then, she did get some support, and she felt less alone.

■ *A lifestyle of sobriety means walking the walk of truth.*

J.C.

HOLY COINCIDENCE

*Grace to you and peace from God our Father
and the Lord Jesus Christ. I thank my God
upon every remembrance of you.*
—PHIL. 1:2–3

If anyone had predicted odds, they would never have
bet on us becoming friends. We were as different as two
people could be. She was flamboyant. I was a follow-
the-rules type. She knew stuff I thought only gray-
haired, bespectacled teachers knew—names of stars,
classical composers, artists whose works hung in muse-
ums. I did well to read my history assignments. But our
schedules threw us together and before I knew it, she
was my closest friend.

A writer named Janet Hagberg says that coincidences are God's way of remaining anonymous. You
could say our friendship was just a "coincidence," just
something that happened because we were in the same
classes. But I don't think so. She's been too good a
friend: believing in me when I didn't believe in myself,
confronting me when I was fooling myself, laughing
with me when I needed to lighten up.

God knows what we need and gives us what we
need—sometimes in the least likely people, at the most
unexpected times, and through none of our own efforts.
The theologians call it grace. I call it great.

■   *God, thanks for the "coincidences" that come my
way, filling my life with unexpected moments of joy.
May I be that kind of "coincidence" to others.*

D.K.

Smart Risking

There are many plans in a
[woman's] heart,
Nevertheless the LORD's counsel—that
will stand.   —PROV. 19:21

Life is a series of risks. Sometimes you come out on top and other times you end up in a heap at the bottom—but you can't really live without taking some risks. Driving a car, meeting new people, trying a new sport, signing a loan—all these things are risky.

Risk has its negative side. When we take a risk, we stand the chance of not meeting expectations or perhaps even humiliating ourselves. There is a positive side, too. With certain risks, we gain new knowledge, discover talents, and experience things we would have never known had we not made the attempt. Still, some risks are dangerous and unnecessary. Experimenting with drugs, driving while intoxicated, damaging our health through purging or starving—all this could have long-lasting detrimental effects, and they offer no possibility of long-term gain. They aren't worth the gamble.

As you face risks in your life, evaluate them as well as you can. If the potential outcome is worth the cost of the risk, you might want to try it. Be sure and seek good counsel prior to the decision, however. Above all, pray about your decision. Ask God to guide and direct you.

■   *Lord, grant me the wisdom to make wise choices*
    when I face risks in my life.

S.C.

WHOSE SLAVE ARE YOU?

*You were slaves of sin . . . and having been
set free from sin, you became slaves of
righteousness.*   —ROM. 6:17–18

Whose slave are you? No one's? You say you're your
own person and no one tells you what to do?

You're lying!

The Bible makes it clear that we're going to be slaves
of something—but we can choose either to be slaves of
sin or slaves of righteousness (Rom. 6:20). When you
are using, it's easy to tell whose slave you are. The unhealthy substance or behavior dictates your choices,
moods, and behaviors. And even when you are freed
from this dictator, other rulers are lurking. Dictator Codependency has a boyfriend for you to "solve" all your
problems of loneliness. Dictator Busyness tells you to
work hard at school and at a part-time job, to join the
yearbook committee, or to do anything necessary to
avoid thinking about your problems. The worst dictator,
however, is Self. She says, "I want to do what I want to
do when I want to do it." And all these substitute slave-
masters drive you toward disaster and unmanageability.

God is not a dictator. Instead He waits for you to
choose Him as King. And it's not a one-time decision.
He asks you every day to renew that choice. You are
free to dethrone Him anytime—but only a fool would.
When God has the controls, He gives you the power to
make healthy choices. And that's what freedom is all
about!

■ *Heavenly King, thank you for giving me a choice.
Help me to give it back to you every day.*

J.C.

IF THAT'S CRAZY—THAT'S ME!

*Then I turned myself to consider wisdom and
madness and folly.* —ECCLES. 2:12

Step two of the Twelve Steps of AA says, "[We] came to believe that a Power greater than ourselves could restore us to sanity." But I'm not really insane, am I? I don't roll my eyes and drool or think I'm Elvis. I may have some problems, but I'm not crazy. Or am I?

One of the most helpful definitions I've heard of being insane is "doing the same thing over and over and expecting the results to be different." Bingo! If that's crazy, that's me. How many times have I tried to deal with my loneliness or boredom by stuffing myself, knowing full well that binging in the past has just led to bloating and self-disgust? How can I expect things will be different this time? I'm like Wil E. Coyote thinking *this* time he's going to catch the Roadrunner—when every previous attempt has left him flattened on the road or crumpled on the canyon floor. Such thinking really is nuts!

One more thing about being crazy. I can't make myself uncrazy—by definition, insanity means being out of control. That's why I need the recovery process. That's why I need others to help me see my insane behavior. And that's why I need God to restore me.

■ *Lord, some of the time I can tell that my behavior is crazy; sometimes I can't see it. That's why I have to depend on you to make me uncrazy.*

A.C.B.

LEAN INTO THE WIND

Therefore take up the whole armor of God,
that you may be able to withstand in the evil
day, and having done all, to stand.
—EPH. 6:13

Being raised in the midwest, where tornadoes are frequent visitors, I learned about strong winds at an early age. Tornadoes leave a path of destruction. And even if a tornado is not present, winds occasionally gust at speeds of eighty miles an hour. Needless to say, it's hard to stand in the face of such a strong wind.

Strong winds will often blow in your life as well. Change can feel like a tornado that uproots you and wreaks havoc in your life. And pressing forward is not easy when you feel as if you are bucking a head wind.

There will be days when everything you do seems like a challenge. But don't let a strong wind of adversity set you back. Keep standing firm. Even if you have to lean into the "wind," keep pressing. However the wind buffets you, you can handle it especially if you have others standing beside you or backing you up.

Most houses in the midwest have basements or some sort of storm shelter. When strong winds blow, news reports advise people to seek shelter. In the same way, you need to prepare for adversities in your life. Know whom you can count on to be there when the strong winds blow. The storm will eventually cease, and if you have stood firm, you will be stronger and wiser for weathering the storm.

■ *Lord, help me to stand firm when the winds blow in*
my life.

S.C.

GOD'S SUPPORT SYSTEM

For where two or three are gathered together
in My name, I am there in the midst of them.
— MATT. 18:20

Jesus, please give Katy wisdom to know how to apologize to her mother." A young woman prayed for her friend. "And help Karen know what to do about her relationship with Robert," responded the other.

The two young people prayed together in short sentences. There were long pauses, but neither felt uncomfortable. They felt God's presence and encouragement from each other.

If you are God's child, you have a natural support system with His other children. The inheritance of praying together is part of that support. It's also a way of learning to build relationships with God and with others.

One way to find out more about this part of your spiritual inheritance is to ask God to send you a prayer partner. Then open your eyes to people whom you meet as possible partners. Ask. If someone says no, don't see her disinterest as a rejection. God is just narrowing the field down to His choice for you.

■ *A prayer partner meets some of my needs to relate to God and to people instead of substances or behaviors.*

J.C.

CHANGES SLOW IN COMING

*Therefore do not cast away your confidence,
which has great reward. For you have need
of endurance, so that after you have done the
will of God, you may receive the promise.*
—HEB. 10:35–36

In Minnesota, winters are long. As spring nears, the snow recedes ever so gradually, almost imperceptibly. The winter days sometimes feel as if the Ice Queen from the *Chronicles of Narnia* has unleashed her frozen spell and the world is captive to her icy, unyielding reign. Then, slowly, the jackets grabbed from the closet are lighter in weight, gloves are no longer necessary, hats are left indoors. The ground begins to be visible beneath the frozen snow pack. Still, for those longing for spring's warmth, the changes are painfully slow in coming.

Recovery can sometimes feel as if nothing is happening, as if my progress has been frozen. Recovery is so *daily.* Trying to measure my progress is like trying to watch the snow melt. But it isn't up to me to monitor or measure my recovery—this process is as gradual (and as wonderful) as spring emerging—and, like spring, the results aren't up to me. My job is to be willing, to let God be God, and to trust Him with the results.

■ *God, sometimes I get so impatient. Changes come so slowly. When my recovery feels like a Minnesota snow pack refusing to melt, let me feel the warmth of your Son.*

D.K.

THE WAY TO FREEDOM

And you shall know the truth, and the truth shall make you free. —JOHN 8:32

It's not that bad! You're just trying to make my life miserable, and I hate you!" screamed Susan as she headed out the front door. The house shook as she slammed the door shut, leaving both her parents tearful and a little terrified. They were used to Susan's outbursts, but they were concerned about her well-being. They had found a couple of bottles of vodka stashed away in the house. When they confronted her, she had an excuse, but it was obvious she was lying. Her eyes always shifted when she was not telling the truth.

These days, Susan consistently missed her curfew by an hour or two. On the nights when her parents waited up for her, she would walk right by them reeking of alcohol. They had talked with her about going into a treatment facility, but she was adamant about not getting help. After all, *they* were the problem; she did not have a problem.

No one likes to admit they are not in control of their lives. But denying the truth does not make the situation better; it worsens it. Denial is the refusal to believe—or even see—the truth. It is in truth, however, that freedom lies.

■ *God, grant me the courage to confront the lies in my life.*

S.C.

ADMITTING MY WEAKNESS

And He said to me, "My grace is sufficient
for you, for My strength is made perfect in
weakness." Therefore most gladly I will
rather boast in my infirmities, that the
power of Christ may rest upon me.
—2 COR. 12:9

Carrie sat in treatment group like a forbidding fortress, with taut arms steeled across her chest. No one was going to touch her life. In the past, she had let others get close, and they had hurt her—one had even raped her. It was safer to be self-sufficient.

Weeks later, in the same group, Carrie looked like a different person. She appeared animated and involved with others. She talked about how, after her rape, she had let others take advantage of her. The group empathized with her hurt and helped her see how she could remain open to others without falling into a victim role. This feedback gave Carrie new power and more choices. She changed from someone who did not need anyone to someone who could receive support as well as give it.

Just as it is important to admit needing others, it is important to admit we need God. When Carrie could admit her weaknesses before the group, she gained their power. When we tell God we can't do it on our own, we make room for His power to enter our lives.

■ *Lord, help me to see my weakness as a strength that brings me to dependence on you and on your unlimited power.*

J.C.

CHOOSE YOUR PAIN

Those who sow in tears
Shall reap in joy.
—PS. 126:5

Recovery is painful. That's just the truth. It hurts to face the truth about myself. It hurts to give up the things that numb my feelings—and to face life without them. It hurts to choose positive behavior when others laugh at or belittle me.

But here's another truth: Being trapped by my behavior is painful, too. The shame of depending on a substance just to get through a day hurts. Being out of control is painful. Seeing my health and my relationships go downhill is a pain that just doesn't go away.

So here's the difference: One kind of pain just gets worse; the other kind of pain eventually brings me joy. The pain of recovery is truly a form of "sowing in tears" so that I can "reap in joy." I choose to do the hard things of recovery in order to know the joy of freedom and growth. And it works—ask the people in your group who are further along than you are. The "tears" I invest in recovery really do result in joy.

So that's what it comes down to. In this life, I am going to have pain. Doesn't it make sense to choose a pain that gets me somewhere?

■   *Lord, I choose the pain of recovery. I trust you to keep your promise that I will end up with joy.*

A.C.B.

NOTHING IS HIDDEN

*Indeed, the darkness shall not hide
  from You,
But the night shines as the day;
The darkness and the light are both
  alike to You.* —PS. 139:12

To God, there is no darkness. His vision is just as clear in the nighttime as it is in the day. He has no trouble seeing our actions in the dark. We cannot hide from Him. But it is funny how we try to fool ourselves sometimes. I guess we believe that if we can conceal something from others, we can hide it from God. No chance.

I wonder what our actions would be like if we constantly had a bright spotlight on us so that anything we did could be seen by others. No doubt it would change our behavior.

Misty believed that her drinking did not count if no one found out about it. And she hid her secret well—it was almost like a game to her. Only when she was caught driving drunk did anyone realize she had a problem. Only then did she begin a Twelve-Step program to recover from her addiction.

The fact that darkness hides our harmful behavior better than the light does not mean we can avoid the consequences. Maybe we can keep it hidden from others for awhile, but we still know—and God knows. God's eyes pierce the darkness, and He is well aware of our actions. There is no way we can conceal anything from Him. Why try?

■ *God, remind me that you see everything I do and that nothing is hidden from your eyes.*

S.C.

STRAW IN THE WIND

They are like straw before the wind,
And like chaff that a storm carries away.
—JOB 21:18

If someone offered a drink to Meagan, she'd take it. If someone offered her pot, she'd take that too. If she didn't feel like going to school that day, she didn't. "If it feels good, do it," was Meagan's motto. But eventually, this motto made her life unmanageable. She was flunking school. She was addicted. She had no future. Wherever the wind of immediate gratification blew, that's where Meagan went.

Meagan's life was like the straw and chaff mentioned in this verse. Chaff is the hull of a seed; it's the stuff you can blow away in the birdseed tray. Straw is the leftover stalk of a grain. And neither of these substances have any stability. They have no roots, no life of their own. The only thing they are good for is to throw away. That's how Meagan felt about her life.

God wants us to grow. The roots that anchor us are God's values which guide our choices. When we have roots, we are like a tree that is firmly planted by a stream of water. When the drought of hard times comes, we will survive. We won't dry up like straw, but be green and bear fruit (Jer. 17:8).

If we base our decisions on what immediately feels good or is comfortable, we will end up like straw. If we base our decisions on Biblical principles, God promises us success.

■ *On what do I base my decisions? Am I more like straw in the wind or a firmly planted tree?*

J.C.

LONGING FOR A LITTLE SANITY

As the deer pants for streams of water,
so my soul pants for you, O God.
My soul thirsts for God, for the living God.
When can I go and meet with God?
—PS. 42:1–2 NIV

I can't believe I did it again! Doing too much, getting too little rest, staying too busy to take time for quiet. The game Friday night, hanging out at the mall all day Saturday, a party Saturday night, cramming for Monday's test on Sunday. Now I've got a short fuse—my family gets on my nerves, my friends are bugging me, and I don't particularly like my own company.

My friends love me, but it's not their job to take care of me. Only I can do that. Loving Christ means loving myself—responsibly. Making right choices means knowing when to say no, knowing when I've had enough and when it's time to have some down time. What I used to do when things went into "circuit overload" was self-destructive. Now I know God's there, ready to defuse my explosive emotions, ready to restore my sanity when things have been a little crazy—or maybe totally crazy.

■ *God, when I feel like a fuse ready to blow, short-circuit the explosion and show me alternatives. You are ever faithful, ever present, ever loving. Plugging into your Spirit is all I need to regain my sanity.*

D.K.

EMPTY BUT FULL

She is empty, desolate, and waste!
—NAH. 2:10

Claire was plagued by empty feelings. She did not know how to explain it to people, but she knew how she felt inside—as if her body were a shell with nothing but a heartbeat inside. She felt she did not fit in with anyone. Her friends were more like acquaintances, because no one really got to know her. The sad truth was that Claire did not know herself. She would ask, "Who am I?" and the answer would come back: "I don't know." This only made her feel more alone. No wonder she tried to fill up the emptiness with alcohol.

It hurts to feel empty. But what Claire learned in recovery was that her empty feelings were actually caused by being packed full—with buried anger, resentment, fear, and pain. In her efforts to keep those feelings down, she had come to the point that she couldn't feel anything at all. And in losing her feelings, she had lost all sense of who she was.

Very gradually, with the help of her therapist and her support group, Claire was able to empty out those dammed-up feelings and give them to God, making room inside for love, hope, joy, and peace.

■ *God can't fill me with good things until I make room in my life by emptying out the garbage I have packed inside.*

S.C.

ONE THING

*But one thing I do, forgetting those things
which are behind and reaching forward
to those things which are ahead.*
                            —PHIL. 3:13

At one time you were really good at one thing. You spent a lot of time thinking about it. You thought of different ways to improve how you did it. You exchanged ideas with others about it and practiced doing it with them. Your life was consumed by this "one thing." You lied for it. You went broke for it. You betrayed friends and family for it and lost time at school or at a job for it.

This "one thing" was drinking, drugging, eating, not eating. (Just fill in the blank.) But now God has turned you around. You are no longer focused on this "one thing." But you do know how to seek something so passionately that everything else feels lukewarm. So you can transfer that "one thing" single-mindedness to seeking God's plan for you. (Right now that plan includes your recovery.)

Think of ways to improve your chances at sobriety. Spend time with others who have this as their priority. Exchange your ideas. Build healthy relationships, job and school skills, a strong body. Base your decisions on how it will affect your recovery.

Unlike an addiction, recovery does not demand that you slowly kill yourself or give up having a life. All this lies behind you now. Exchange your passion for the old "one thing" for the new "one thing."

■ *Make recovery with God the "one thing" you do.*
                                              J.C.

A CRY FOR HELP

> *Deliver me out of the mire,*
> *And let me not sink;*
> *Let me be delivered from those*
> *   who hate me,*
> *And out of the deep waters.*
> —PS. 69:14

Jill was raised in a dysfunctional home. Although her family worked hard to maintain a "perfect family" image, painful problems festered behind closed doors. Jill was sexually abused by several members in her family. She kept it a secret; the shame she felt was much too great to tell anyone. She could not deal with the pain on her own, and she did not know how to find help. So Jill turned to alcohol to help her numb her pain. She also stopped eating; starving herself made her feel she had some control over her body.

Jill became thin for the first time in her life. She also began partying with her friends nearly every night. And everyone wondered what happened to the "good Jill"— the once-compliant child was now out of control. What they did not understand was Jill was crying out for someone to stop her. She knew she was on a "fast train" that was close to "derailing."

Dysfunctional homes are breeding grounds for dysfunctional coping skills. And no amount of starving, binging, overeating, or drinking will heal scars that run deep. Only the process of facing the pain and working through it will make healing possible.

■   *God, you know my hurt. Please help me deal with it constructively.*

S.C.

A NEW IDENTITY

*Yes, we had the sentence of death in
ourselves, that we should not trust in
ourselves but in God who raises the dead.*
—2 COR. 1:9

As the oldest of six children in her family, Margaret was the "responsible one." If a little knee needed bandaging, Margaret bandaged it. If a sister needed a ride to volleyball practice, Margaret took her.

But Margaret grew tired of no one meeting *her* needs (although she rarely admitted she had them). So she decided to make herself feel better with a little help from wine coolers—then, later from "Mr. Bud" and "Mr. J&B." Drinking made her hurt and anger feel distant and less painful. She could even deny there was a problem.

However, this "solution" gave Margaret another problem: alcoholism. It also began eroding her identity as the "responsible one." When she drank, Margaret didn't want to be bothered by her siblings. She forgot to pick up a sister from practice. She neglected her schoolwork. Her life was fast becoming unmanageable.

Margaret saw that her dependence on alcohol had the sentence of death in it. But she also needed to see that her "responsible one" identity was also creating chaos and death. Margaret's unmanageability came from trusting all in herself. God wanted her to grab onto the help He and others had to give to her.

■ *Father, you have made an identity just for me that does not have the sentence of death in it. Help me to accept it.*

J.C.

When to Keep My Mouth Shut

> *I will watch my ways*
> *and keep my tongue from sin;*
> *I will put a muzzle on my mouth.*
> —PS. 39:1 NIV

Before I even know I've opened my mouth, the words are spoken. Words that hurt. Words that sting. Words that are carefully honed weapons. Sometimes under the guise of "teasing"; more often openly sarcastic. And especially with those I love the most. Sometimes I wish I *could* put a muzzle on my mouth.

But as a Christian I'm not a puppet with strings to control my words and behavior. So when words come out that I wish had been left unsaid, I have to admit my wrong and make amends—even if making amends is embarrassing.

The psalmist says, "Create in me a clean heart, O God; and renew a right spirit within me" (Ps. 51:10 KJV). Words I regret never come from a "right spirit." They come from anger, fear, hurt, or resentment. So the best "muzzle" I can find is staying clean within, being honest with myself and God about what's going on inside—both good and bad.

■ *Emotions are neither good nor bad. Emotions are just real. What I say and do with my feelings is the issue. God, take the anger, fears, hurts, and resentments I feel and show me what to do with them.*

D.K.

WALK THE WALK

Even so you also outwardly appear righteous to men, but inside you are full of hypocrisy and lawlessness. —MATT. 23:28

Hypocrisy exists all around us. It is alive in churches, in governments, in schools, and—unfortunately, even in recovery groups. That's especially sad, because if there is one thing that blows trust out of the water, it is hypocrisy. When someone acts in a way that contradicts what they claim to believe, that person's credibility is destroyed.

People who begin the recovery process quickly pick up the buzz words that go with it: *denial, inventory, codependency,* and so on. The problem occurs when someone learns to "talk the talk" without "walking the walk." It is not enough to know the right words; we must be willing to live them. The same thing is true of religious commitment. It's not enough to talk about faith, hope, and love; these qualities must be part of us. People are always looking at our lives. Do we live what we claim? Are our actions in line with our words? If not, it is time to make our words and actions consistent with each other. Words come easy, but it is in our actions that we become genuine to others—and build the kind of trusting relationships that keep us going in recovery.

■ *God, help me to "walk the walk" in my life.*

S.C.

CELEBRATE!

*So you shall rejoice in every good thing
which the LORD your God has given to you.*
—DEUT. 26:11

Holidays can be tricky roadblocks on the road to recovery. Somehow, we have come to associate celebration with excess, sobriety with boredom.

St. Patrick's Day, for instance, has become not just a tribute to the Irish people, but a celebration of Irish whiskey and green beer. Look at the newspaper! All the bars are calling to you to come on down, and they don't care whether you're Irish or not.

So, how do you celebrate sanely and still have fun— today or on any other day? You might have to do some self-talk: Is it really celebration if the only purpose is to get bombed? It certainly helps to party with companions who don't equate being high with having a good time. It's important to keep current with your hurts (that way you are not as tempted to hide from your feelings) and to make a point of discovering some great sober pastimes (they really do exist).

Most of all, every day, make a point of thanking God—for life, for recovery, for the people who love and support you, for the beauty of creation and the fun of celebration (even sober). If you nurture a heart of thanksgiving, a spirit of celebration is bound to follow.

■ *Lord, you are the father of all rejoicing. Remind me
of that when I'm feeling left out of the celebration!*

A.C.B.

REBUILDING TRUST

Hope deferred makes the heart sick,
But when the desire comes, it is a
tree of life. —PROV. 13:12

Marita burst into tears. "Mom, see, you still really don't think I can make it. So why even try?" Marita, her parents, her teachers, and her therapist were in a meeting at her school. The topic of discussion was Marita's recovery and what support the school could offer. Marita had just been discharged from the drug treatment center. Her mother acknowledged the hard work she had done while in rehabilitation but was still feeling apprehensive about Marita's future progress.

Marita thought her mother's concerns meant she did not trust her at all. If this were true, then Marita felt it was hopeless to try. She felt heartsick. She needed the hope that she could gain her mother's trust back.

Once broken, trust takes time to rebuild—and it has to be earned. Marita's mother reassured her that she had earned a certain amount of trust by her hard work in rehab. And trust would continue to develop step by step as Marita followed through in her recovery program. As Marita took more responsibility for this, her mother would give her more privileges. Eventually, trust between them could be restored.

■   *I will hope for a better relationship with my parents as I work to earn their trust, step by step.*

J.C.

LIVING PAST THE LIES

"Behold, I am against those who prophesy false dreams," says the LORD, "and tell them, and cause My people to err by their lies and by their recklessness."
—JER. 23:32

Nobody likes to be lied to! You feel stupid. You feel angry. So here's something to make you really mad: Every day, you are being fed a pack of bold-faced lies!

Some of these whoppers are relatively harmless: "Cruncho Munchies are yummier than Muncho Crunchies." Some are potentially lethal: "Only sleek, sophisticated, athletic people smoke these cigarettes or drink this beer." And some are subtly devastating: "Every normal person has sex; if you don't, there's something wrong with you."

Some lies come from people who have been hoodwinked themselves. Some are a deliberate effort to sell you something or get something from you. Wherever they come from, they are tricky to sort out.

So, how do you live past the lies? By being alert to the fact that lies are all around you. By making a special effort to think critically about what you believe. By choosing your companions carefully. But most of all, by sticking close to the One who said, "I am the way, the *truth,* and the life" (John 14:6).

■ *Jesus, thanks for feeding me truth when so many others are feeding me lies. Thanks for picking me up again when I've fallen for a big one. And thanks for being with me as I try to sort out fact from fiction.*
A.C.B.

THE COURAGE TO CHANGE

For I, the LORD your God, will hold your
right hand,
Saying to you, "Fear not, I will help you."
—ISA. 41:13

Making changes in your life—even positive changes—can be frightening. It is human nature to want to go back to familiar ways—even destructive or unhealthy ones. Old patterns feel comfortable. We may not like them, but at least we know what to expect from them. Like gravity, old patterns may exert a steady downward pull.

Patterns are strong habits whose familiarity brings us comfort. And this comfort makes us willing to continue our crazy behavior—with all the pain it brings us—rather than finding a more effective way of coping. Once a pattern like drinking or binging and purging is established, it may feel like a safe, familiar way of coping. Not surprisingly, the thought of changing makes us anxious.

So how do we find the courage to face down our fear and change destructive patterns? We can start by reminding ourselves that it is normal for change to feel scary. We can weigh the pros and cons of changing as honestly as we can—it helps to write them down or talk them out with someone we trust. And then we need to take a step of faith, trusting God to help hold our hand as we move into the unfamiliar but fertile territory of growth.

■ *God, please take away the fear and anxiety that*
hold me down in my life. Give me the strength to
make the changes I need to make.

S.C.

DOING WHAT IT TAKES

*Let us lay aside every weight, . . . and let
us run with endurance the race that is set
before us.*
                              —HEB. 12:1

Can you imagine a guy shaving his legs? Could you
pay one enough money to do that? Imagine the comments: "Oh, look there's Rich. Doesn't he have nice,
silky legs? He must use Nair™." Believe it or not, some
guys voluntarily shave their legs. They do it to reach
a goal they feel is important—winning a bike race.
They're thinking aerodynamically, and they believe that
hair on the legs will slow them down. So they are willing
to make the sacrifice in order to win.

Our verse today tells us we need to have that same
attitude for a successful recovery. We must be willing to
lay aside any "weight" that slows us down. This does
not have to be a sin. For instance, having a boyfriend is
not a sin, but such a relationship can be a "weight,"
especially during the first six months to a year of recovery.

Recovery is a tough race to run. It calls for energy
and endurance. Doesn't it make sense to give ourselves
every advantage and do whatever we need to do to
reach the finish line?

■   *Heavenly Father, help me to be willing to give up
anything in my life that will make me slow down or
stumble in recovery.*

                                                    J.C.

THE PERFORMANCE TRAP

*And what does the LORD
   require of you
But to do justly,
To love mercy,
And to walk humbly
   with your God?*
—MIC. 6:8

The first week I walked into a Twelve-Step group, I thought, "OK, Twelve Steps, twelve weeks—no problem." I thought the Twelve Steps were no more than an assignment I could tackle, complete, and then get on with my life.

I'm a performer. Give me an assignment, and I'll do whatever it takes to deliver. But all my accomplishments—grades, awards, people pleasing—never convinced me of my own worth as a person. I ended up feeling empty, drained, emotionally exhausted. I tended to discount my abilities, thinking I had only been in the right place at the right time, that I somehow had faked, charmed, or manipulated my way through.

A person whose worth is based on winning other people's affirmation can never "perform" enough, never "prove" herself enough, never "do" enough. Living for the approval of others exacts a high price— my sanity, my strength, my character. It's a hard lesson to learn, but one worth learning: Only in giving up the need to "perform" can I find the real person within.

■ *"What other people think of me is none of my business." Those simple little Twelve-Step slogans. No wonder they've been around so long!*

D.K.

THE USERS

Bless those who curse you, and pray for those who spitefully use you. —LUKE 6:28

Some folks in our society are "users." Not drug users, but people who use others to get what they want and then cast them aside like old shoes. If you have ever been used, you know how horrible it feels. You feel like a fool. You scold yourself for being gullible. You feel drained and unhappy, robbed of your energy, and your self-respect deteriorates.

Many people in recovery know what being used is like. Addicts are often exploited by suppliers. Insecure girls from unhappy homes are easy targets for selfish guys. People who are dependent on relationships put up with all kinds of abuse rather than be alone. And here's another wrinkle: People who have been used often end up using others as well.

An important part of your recovery, therefore, may be recognizing that you have been used and getting the help you need to break free. This means resolving feelings of anger and humiliation as well as getting out of unhealthy relationships. Eventually, it means asking God's help in forgiving the person who used you. Until you can do that, the "user" will still have too much of a hold over you.

■ *God, please help me see the areas in my life in which I am being used (or using others). Guide me on the path to freedom.*

S.C.

A FEW GOOD FRIENDS

A [girl] of many friends comes to ruin.
—PROV. 18:24 NASB

Oh yeah, I've got about fifty close friends." Mary Ann was serious. "When I get tired of one bunch, I go to the next. I have partying friends, church friends, jock friends, and . . ." As we talked, Mary Ann's definition of *friend* became clearer. For her, a close friend was someone with whom she could gossip, talk about hair or makeup, or get high. None of these people knew the inside of Mary Ann. (Neither did she, for that matter.)

Going through an inpatient recovery program forced Mary Ann to know herself better. Talking to others about her hurts was a relief. Hearing about other people's pain helped her—and she helped them. It was a great feeling.

After discharge, Mary Ann ran into some of her old "friends." "It was boring talking to them. All they wanted to talk about was the latest rock video, the movie they just saw, or who's going out with who. That was OK for a while. But when I started talking about what I learned in treatment or my feelings, they got nervous and left."

Having many friends means you don't have time to get to know anyone really well. Then, when the hard times come, you have no ready-made support system. Mary Ann figured she could handle about two to three close friends. They could provide her with more support than fifty.

■　*Close friends are one of God's natural highs.*

J.C.

TIME FOR A BREAK

For lo, the winter is past,
The rain is over and gone.
The flowers appear on the earth;
The time of singing has come.
—SONG OF SOL. 2:11–12

You've heard it a million times: "You deserve a break today." That idea has probably been abused by people who think, "I deserve a break *all* the time." But it's still true. You do deserve a break today. In fact, you *need* a break today. You need time off from seriousness. You need a chance to leave your problems in God's lap for a little while and just enjoy the life He has given you.

Spring break time—whenever it hits during your school year—can fill an important need in your life. Resist the temptation to fill it up with "stuff I've got to do" or to make it such a blowout that you end up exhausted. Instead, take time out to relax. Take a long walk. Snooze in the sun. Play baseball. Call your sponsor—just to say "Thanks!" Dig in the dirt. Read a magazine.

And then, if you have a big paper to finish up or a huge test to study for or a room to muck out, get to work. If you're struggling with some area of your recovery, spend some extra time journaling and praying and talking to others in your group. But don't forget, even in the midst of all you have to do, you still deserve—and need—a break from time to time.

■ *Lord, teach me your rhythms of work and rest. Teach me that I don't have to go a million miles an hour all the time!*

A.C.B.

OLD BEFORE HER TIME

Even the youths shall faint and be weary,
And the young [women] shall utterly fall.
—ISA. 40:30

Samantha was ten years old the year her father left. That was also the year her mother started drinking and Sam started looking after her younger brother and sister. Now, at sixteen, Sam feels like the mom of the house. She gets the other kids ready for school, makes sure they eat properly, and tucks them in at night. She also disciplines them—someone has to do it. Sam rarely has time for fun—and she would feel uneasy about going out and leaving Bill and Buffy with their mom.

Samantha loves her family, but she already feels overworked and old. Sometimes she wants to scream, "It's not fair!" And it's not. Sam's a strong person, but her load is too heavy. And unless she finds some support, Sam may find herself going under. She, too, may turn to drugs or alcohol to ease the pain. She may get sick or depressed. Or she may turn into a control freak who gets her needs met by running everybody else's lives. Human beings were never meant to go it alone. And that's especially true when the load is heavier than normal.

■ *If you feel old beyond your years, you need help! Circumstances may have forced you to be "the strong one," but your health and happiness may depend on learning to lean—on a support group, on a counselor, on your pastor or youth director, and on God.*

S.C.

FILLING THE HOLE IN YOUR HEART

> *And the LORD, He is the one who goes before*
> *you. He will be with you, He will not leave*
> *you nor forsake you; do not fear nor be*
> *dismayed.* —DEUT. 31:8

Teenaged girls are the loneliest people," comments Josh McDowell on his radio program, *Why Wait*. He goes on to say that loneliness makes girls very vulnerable to becoming sexually involved.

"The sex was OK but the part I really liked was being held." Margy spoke softly, and her eyes looked wistfully beyond me as if she were remembering a private, tender moment. Margy had had several sexual encounters in her sixteen years. Her eyes looked back to me, and a sadness began to veil them. She just found out that during one of those sexual encounters she had caught a sexually transmitted disease.

Margy tried to take care of her loneliness by exchanging sex for hugs. However, this way carried an expensive price tag. In addition, she seemed to have added a sex addiction to her drug dependency.

In recovery, Margy learned other ways to take care of her loneliness. She worked at developing a better relationship with her father and her heavenly Father. She also learned ways to relate to her mother, whose problems were similar to Margy's but who wasn't in recovery. The hole in her heart called loneliness is still something she has to work on, but she is slowly finding other ways to get hugs.

■ *Sex will not take care of my loneliness, and it will make the hole in my heart bigger.*

J.C.

WHY PRAY?

Lord, teach us to pray.
—LUKE 11:1

Why pray if it feels like no one is listening?

Sitting down for a quiet time sometimes becomes a game of creative avoidance and aerobic distractions. Ooops, forgot my pen. Hmmm, think I'm thirsty. Uh-oh, almost time to go; better get my stuff together.

When I think I don't have time to pray, or when I don't *want* to pray—that's when I most *need* to pray. One writer calls it "creeping separateness"—that slow realization that I've put my relationship to God on "ignore." I can't hear the gentle guidance that comes from that quiet inner leading if I don't put myself in a position to listen. Instead of "Be still and know that I am God," perhaps it should be, "Sit still long enough to know that I am God."

■ *When I don't feel like praying, I need to start by telling God just that—and go on from there.*

D.K.

A NEW HEART

I will give you a new heart and put a new spirit within you; I will take the heart of stone out . . . and give you a heart of flesh. I will put My Spirit within you.
—EZEK. 36:26–27, 36

Hard times have a way of making hard hearts. A kind of callus builds up around the heart to protect it from hurt. Being let down creates a determination not to rely on anyone. Going it alone becomes a familiar and comfortable way of getting things done. Being used makes us determined to be "tough" and not let anyone do that to us again.

But a hard heart is also a lonely heart. A calloused heart may be protected against hurt, but it also loses its ability to feel joy. Developing a heart of stone may protect us from those who might use us, but it also barricades us from those who can help. It doesn't take long for a fortress to become a prison.

That's why it's good news that God is able to break through our flinty defenses. He is able to give hard-hearted persons a new, softer heart—a heart of flesh instead of a heart of stone. This softer heart can feel, not just tolerate. It can reach out, not just protect itself. It can be strong, not just tough. Best of all, it can grow. And it's far from defenseless, for God is still in charge of the whole process.

■ *Lord, I'm ready for you to do your special brand of "heart surgery" on me. I invite you to reach behind my stony defenses and teach my heart how to be strong yet tender.*

S.C.

NEW THINKING

Do not be conformed to this world, but be transformed by the renewing of your mind, that you may prove what is that good and acceptable and perfect will of God.

—ROM. 12:2

The world says:

"It's OK to have sex with someone as long as you love him."

"Safe sex means wearing a condom."

"If you love me you'll have sex with me."

"We are all gods."

"As long as I try to be good, God will accept me."

"If you want it, take it."

"I don't get angry; I get even."

"Drinking is OK as long as it's controlled."

"If it feels good, it's right."

"Bad things don't happen to good people."

If you believe any of those lies, then know your thinking has been partly shaped by the world. Not that the world in itself is all bad. After all, God made it! However, our thinking needs to be shaped by God's perspective. God has given us His thinking in the Bible. His perspective is our inheritance. It will "renew our minds" and show us how to think.

■ *Filtering life's events through God's perspective will help me have a successful recovery.*

J.C.

NOT A NO-SELF

For [she] who doubts is like a wave of the sea driven and tossed by the wind.

—JAMES 1:6

She's just a piece of fluff, a wimp. She ain't about a thing." That's what Carmen overheard two girls say about her. She was surprised and hurt. She had thought these two girls liked her. At least, she had tried to do everything to make them like her. She had never made a big thing about the clothes one of them had borrowed but never had returned. She had tried to agree with their opinions, even though sometimes she really didn't. At one point she even drank at their parties so they'd see her as one of them.

Carmen was a No-Self. She became like whomever she happened to be with, so no one knew who she was. *She* didn't know who she was. She wanted to please people, but in the end they took advantage of her. They lost respect for her, and she doubted herself.

Carmen's momentary pain due to her "friends'" comments caused her to think about her identity. At this point she was a people pleaser. Did she want to remain one all her life? All this identity did was get her into unmanageable behavior. So Carmen began studying her Bible to see who God said she was. It said she was God's child and so His heir. There were certain pieces of her inheritance she could have right now. Wisdom was one of them. All she had to do was ask her heavenly Father for it, and He'd give it to her.

■ *Heavenly Father, give me wisdom to develop the self you've planned me to be.*

J.C.

A HIGHER FORM OF FOOLISHNESS

If anyone among you seems to be wise in this age, let [her] become a fool that [she] may become wise. For the wisdom of this world is foolishness with God.

—1 COR. 3:18–19

Don't you hate feeling like a fool? Even on this day of good-natured pranks, it's more fun to be a "fooler" than a "foolee." So this verse and the mentality it represents is a little hard to comprehend. Why would anyone choose to be a fool?

I discovered part of the answer when I began working out. As I got into the routine of exercise, I was surprised to discover some basic facts about how the body works that seemed to fly in the face of common wisdom. Sustained exercise, for instance, actually made me *less* hungry. And on those days when I could barely drag myself home, moderate exercise actually gave me *more* energy. I learned these facts through actual experience—and yet they *still* feel foolish to the part of my mind that learned, "Exercise makes you tired and hungry."

That's one instance when I've learned firsthand that "choosing foolishness" really can be wise. I still have to take a leap of faith to believe it—but I do believe. And that leap of faith helps me understand the faith I need to follow God's life-giving way, which often seems foolish to a dying world.

■ *Lord, you are the Source of true wisdom. Help me to trust your way even when I can't see the sense in it.*

A.C.B.

REALLY RICH

Receive my instruction, and not silver,
And knowledge rather than choice gold.
—PROV. 8:10

Which would you rather have: instruction and knowledge or a thousand dollars? Most people would answer, "I'll take the cash!" But money is only temporary. Once spent, it leaves us with nothing. Perhaps that is why we are told by the Lord to choose His instruction and knowledge over silver and gold.

With the Lord's instruction, we receive guidance for living a life that really works. Common sense doesn't always cut it. Sometimes the wisest thing to do is the complete opposite of what seems natural. That's when we really benefit from God's instruction. Trusting His Word can save us a lot of grief and heartache and provide us with a lot of growth.

Knowledge opens up new doors and expands our horizons; it gives us something to build our lives on. But again, the Lord's knowledge is different from the world's knowledge. Human knowledge is limited. New theories replace old ones; what scientists believed ten years ago may no longer apply. But God's knowledge comes from the One who dreamed up the whole universe. It always proves trustworthy over the long haul.

■ *Lord, thank you for the gifts of instruction and knowledge from your Word. Help me always remember where true wealth lies.*

S.C.

WHAT ARE YOU HUNGRY FOR?

He has filled the hungry with good things.
—LUKE 1:53

"What are you hungry for?" That's a question my mother sometimes used to ask before she got started with dinner. And it's a question my life and my feelings ask of me every day. My answer, more likely than not, determines whether my life is frustrating or satisfying.

It's so easy to mistake one "hunger" for another. In fact, that's one reason I get in trouble. I am hungry for love so I turn to drugs. I am hungry for comfort, so I pig out on chocolate. I am hungry for control over my life, so I starve myself. The result? Surprise! I stay hungry. But I keep on trying again and again—insanely thinking that "this time" I'll be satisfied.

What I'm trying to do now, in recovery, is to reshape my response to those familiar empty feelings. When I feel "hungry," I need to recognize what I'm really hungry for. And then I need to put my hand out to the only One who really can fill me with good things.

■ *Lord, I don't know why I have such a hard time getting basic reality into my head, but thank you for being patient with me as I learn to depend on you for the things I need.*

A.C.B.

A SPARKLING PROMISE

> *You were sealed with the Holy Spirit of*
> *promise, who is the guarantee of our*
> *inheritance.*
> —EPH. 1:13–14

The restaurant was filled with the Easter pinks and blues of little girls' dresses. Restaurant employees costumed as bunny rabbits hopped from table to table giving out gifts to the children. One rabbit began hopping to a young couple's table. He clutched an orange stuffed carrot and a basket with a wrapped present in it.

The man exclaimed, "Oh look, honey, the bunny has a carrot for you." The bunny waved a furry white paw at the woman, who looked around, thinking the bunny was really waving to a nearby child. No, the bunny headed straight for her and handed her the present.

A crowd quickly gathered to see her open the box. Inside was a sparkling diamond engagement ring. (Instead of the carrot, the rabbit had given her a carat.) The woman accepted the ring. The crowd cheered.

What were they cheering for? In our society, when a woman accepts an engagement ring from a man, she accepts his marriage proposal. The ring symbolizes a relationship that promises future benefits.

When we accept Christ as our Savior, we become "engaged" to Him. The Holy Spirit is our "engagement ring" that "seals" us as belonging to God and promises us the benefits of (1) new identity, (2) new power, (3) new ways of thinking, and (4) new relationships.

■ *"Engagement" to Jesus promises hope for a good future.*

J.C.

SITTING ON THE FENCE

*When I was a child, I spoke as a child, I
understood as a child, I thought as a child;
but when I became a [woman,] I put away
childish things.* —1 COR. 13:11

Being a teen can drive you crazy sometimes. You're
treated like a child, but you're expected to take on adult
responsibilities. But is it possible you're making problems for yourself by acting irresponsibly while you nag
about adult privileges?

Think of a fence down the middle of a big yard. One
side of the fence is childhood. The kids playing there
can expect that someone else will take care of them—
making sure homework is done, feeding and clothing
them, getting them up on time. But there's a down side;
a lot of adults are standing around telling the children
what to do.

On the other side of the fence, there's a lot more
freedom. People drive. People stay out late. People
manage their own time. But people there are expected
to take care of themselves and act responsibly toward
others.

And there you are, sitting on the fence. Part of you
likes the childhood side; part of you longs for the adult
side. But you have to choose. You can't have the freedom of one side and the responsibility of the other. And
sitting on the fence too long will just give you a gigantic
pain in part of your anatomy.

■ *Pick the side of the fence you want to be on. Your
behavior, not your words, will indicate what you're
truly ready to handle.*

S.C.

THE WAY GOD SEES

For the LORD does not see as man sees; for man looks at the outward appearance, but the LORD looks at the heart.

—1 SAM. 16:7

It was a crime of fashion—but not like wearing 1970s bell-bottoms or having runs in your nylons. Two teen-aged girls murdered another girl because she refused to give up her leather coat to them.

Why would someone kill for a coat? The psychologist studying the crime attributed it to a lack of identity and self-esteem. To some teens, wearing certain clothes gives them a sense of prestige and importance. At the same time, a lack of self-esteem makes life seem cheap. If I feel I'm not worth much, neither are you—so killing becomes easier.

Even those of us who would never kill for a coat may be vulnerable to basing our self-worth on outside appearance—but God sees us differently. Today's verse refers to the prophet Samuel's search for a new king. He was looking for someone who looked regal, muscular, and tall. But God was looking for someone with only one quality—that he have a heart for Him. David was His choice. On the outside, David was young, small, and not very regal. But because of his insides, God took David from tending sheep to sitting on a throne.

■   *Our inside identity is more important to God than our outside appearance.*

J.C.

THAT WHICH IS HIDDEN

*If we confess our sins, He is faithful and just
to forgive us our sins and to cleanse us from
all unrighteousness.*   —1 JOHN 1:9

Before I came into recovery, I kept careful control of
how others saw me, saying and doing only what I
thought they wanted to hear. I tried to control my life
like a carefully rehearsed script with all the ugliness and
imperfection left out.

But that which I kept within, hidden, became an inner poison. As my pain increased, my control crum-
bled. I finally admitted I needed help. But the thought
of admitting "to God, to ourselves, and to another human being the exact nature of our wrongs," was the
source of more than a little anxiety. Admitting it all to
God wasn't so bad—He knew it all, anyway. But admitting my past to another person? Could I really tell another person all I'd done? The deceit, manipulation,
the failure? I didn't think I could do it. So I prayed,
asking for courage and willingness.

And then came the surprise: Only in allowing others
to see me as I really am did I come to know love, forgiveness, and healing. Only in letting go of control is
freedom found.

■   *Sometimes I have to jump in, trust the process, and
give it a try.*

D.K.

SELF-FULFILLING PROPHECY

*For God has not given us a spirit of fear, but
of power and of love and of a sound mind.*
—2 TIM. 1:7

Bethany slouched in her chair. Her support group wanted to know what was wrong. The more they pressed her, the quieter she got. When she did mumble something, it was barely above a whisper. Finally, she said that no one cared about her, so why should she talk? Irritation grew in the group as each realized what she had said. They had spent considerable time trying to draw her out, showing their concern. Now she was telling them they did not care about her.

Bethany had a habit of setting herself up for rejection—although she was totally unaware that she did this. Her fear of being rejected caused her to put up a wall around herself and refuse to let anyone help her. Eventually, what she feared came true. People got tired of trying to help and walked away. Others got angry because *they* felt rejected by her. Whenever this happened, Bethany blamed others. Her wall became even thicker in order to protect herself.

But God's Word promises Bethany that her fear of rejection doesn't come from Him. Instead, He has given her power, love, and a sound mind to overcome her fear. Bethany needs to risk opening up to her group. God can use them to help her develop better insight, to strengthen and love her. Eventually, she will be able to return the support.

■ *When I blame, I make myself into a victim.*

J.C.

A RAW DEAL!

But He was wounded for our transgressions,
He was bruised for our iniquities;
The chastisement for our peace was upon Him,
And by His stripes we are healed.

—ISA. 53:5

Life can be unfair. Somehow there always seems to be another person who has it easier—who makes friends faster, has wealthier parents, wears nicer clothes, and seems to have no problems. You may feel that person has the silver platter and you have the scraps that fell off the plate. And you may be right! Life may indeed have handed you a raw deal. Envy and perhaps even hatred may overtake you if you do not keep your perspective.

The sad truth, however, is life will not become fairer as you get older. There will always be those who will outshine you in some way. There will always be painful injustices. Learning to accept that fact now will save you a lot of heartache in the future.

When Christ went to the cross on our behalf, what was fair about that situation? When He was mocked, ridiculed, and beaten, was that fair? No! Nothing was right about that either; and yet He endured it. Christ was well acquainted with the unfairness of life, but He didn't fall into the envy trap. Instead, He depended on God to redeem the injustices and bring good out of evil.

■ *You can't expect life to be fair, but you can expect Christ to be with you.*

S.C.

TRACES OF GOD

He is not far from each one of us; for in Him
we live and move and have our being.
—ACTS 17:27–28

Remember Easter egg hunts? First, you scan the backyard for telltale signs of color. "Yes! There's one!" you tell yourself under your breath. A squeal of discovery comes from across the yard. Somebody found an egg behind a bush! Now, more bush eggs are easy to find. There's a pattern; every other bush hides a nest of eggs. Exhausted, you stop, thinking there are no more eggs. But is that true? You throw a questioning glance at your father (alias B. Rabbit). He answers by a glance up a tree. There on a forked branch snuggles the last egg. Chaos ensues! Everyone runs to be the one to get the last egg.

Finding traces of God is something like that Easter egg hunt. Have you ever experienced any out-of-the-ordinary happenings that met a need? A sweater you really liked but couldn't afford just "happened" to be on sale at the right price. Have you ever gotten exactly the same advice from different people who don't even know each other—then heard the same thing on Christian radio? Maybe God was trying to tell you something.

How about answered prayer? You are stuck on a test question. You ask God for help. Then, "miraculously," you remember the answer. Coincidence? Or God?

■ *God, open my eyes to see the evidences of your existence and care in my daily life.*

J.C.

LIVING INTO EASTER

The Spirit of the Lord GOD is upon Me,
Because the LORD has anointed Me . . .
He has sent Me to heal the brokenhearted,
To proclaim liberty to the captives,
And the opening of the prison to those
*   who are bound.*   —ISA. 61:1

She was a Christian. She was a good student. No one would have guessed her secret—and no one knew. Not her parents. Not her boyfriend. Not even her best friend. Then one day, along with the tears, her secret came tumbling out. She'd had an abortion. The secret had grown too painful to be borne alone; she finally had to tell someone.

Funny how we "rate" sins. We put them on a sliding scale of those we consider acceptable, those we consider worse, and those we consider unforgivable. And too often, the ones we can't believe God really forgives are the ones we hold within as our most shameful secret. We know Christ said He came to set the captives free, but we continue to live as captives within the prison of our mistakes, regrets, and hidden shame.

Christ didn't set conditions on forgiveness. He didn't say one sin can be forgiven while another can't. He died and rose again for all sins. Living as a captive to our shame means never living past Good Friday. Living in the freedom of forgiveness is living in Easter.

■   *Our most shameful secrets are no secrets to God. He knows us, he knows them, and he says, "My daughter, you are forgiven. Now, forgive yourself. Embrace the promise of Easter."*

D.K.

ROOTED IN LOVE

I bow my knees to the Father of our Lord Jesus Christ, . . . that you, being rooted and grounded in love, . . . may be filled with all the fullness of God. —EPH. 3:14, 17, 19

God didn't put me here on earth or lead me into recovery just so I could muck around in the dirt—uncovering painful secrets, weeding out destructive habits, putting up fences to protect my boundaries, organizing my cleaned-up life into neat rows. That kind of earthy work is vital—but it's not an end in itself.

The real purpose of digging in the dirt is to grow something! I'm here to "get rooted and grounded in love," then to sprout into the life God had in mind for me from the beginning. A life that's wide and full and wonderful and fun, not lonely and distorted. A life that's free and purposeful, not cramped by "shoulds" and "should nots." A life that's bright with love and fellowship, not dark and withered with dependency and abuse.

That's something to keep in the back of my mind even when the work at hand involves digging and weeding and fencing and organizing. Sure, I want a nice, clean garden. But eventually, if I hang in there, I'll see some flowers, too.

■ *Lord, keep me aware of your eternal purposes even as I live one day at a time. Root and ground me in your love so that I can grow and bloom in the fullness of your life.*

A.C.B.

FACING MYSELF

I have chosen the way of truth.
—PS. 119:30

Jennifer looked like a turtle. Her support group of peers had gently confronted her, pointing out that she was quick to see where others needed to change but slow in working on her own issues. And typically, Jennifer had withdrawn in silence. She had pulled her arm out of her long-sleeved shirt and hugged herself within the shell of the shirt. Occasionally she would even pull the neck of the shirt over her face, completing the turtle look.

The group gave Jennifer distance, temporarily. And slowly she came out of her shell. She shared her problem of being her own worst enemy. Being highly critical and demeaning, it was hard for her to look at herself— this made it hard for her to hear any outside confrontation. She'd amplify any negative comments and ignore the positive. No wonder she found it much easier to focus on others.

That day, however, Jennifer did a courageous thing. She looked at herself, sharing her struggles and shortcomings. In return, the group reflected back to her a more accurate picture of who Jennifer was and who she could become. Jennifer was a step further in knowing the positive truth about herself.

■ *Heavenly Father, give me the courage to look at the truth about myself. Maybe I'll be pleasantly surprised.*

J.C.

A NEW YOU

*Put on the new self, created to be like God in
true righteousness and holiness.*
—EPH. 4:24 NIV

It's a whole new you," trumpets the ad for the cosmetics line (or the clothing boutique, or the tanning salon). "Win a free makeover," tempts the magazine feature. "Your friends won't even recognize you," promises the hair stylist.

It's such a tempting idea. Just lie back, close my eyes, and be transformed.

But it doesn't really work that way. I can buy a new shade of mascara, or splurge on a new outfit, or even go from blonde to brunette to redhead. And the new look may lift my spirits temporarily. But underneath, everything's just the same. Same problems. Same failings. Same me.

And yet, in recovery, I *am* getting a makeover. (My friend Claire Cloninger calls it "the ultimate makeover.") And it goes a lot deeper than how I look or what I wear. With my cooperation, God is actually making me over from the inside out. It takes a lot longer than a day at the mall or a weekend at a health spa—but the results are a lot more long-lasting. In fact, they're eternal.

■ *Lord, I can't wait to meet the "new me" you have in mind. Please keep showing me what I need to do to participate in my own makeover.*

A.C.B.

Not God's Ways

*There is a way which seems
right to a [person],
But its end is the way of
death.* —PROV. 14:12

Knowing right from wrong is not as simple as it is sometimes made to sound. A person can have 20/20 vision but still be nearsighted where life is concerned. Only the Lord has all the facts and sees the whole picture. And that should be a strong motivation for us to consult Him. Yet most of us muddle through our lives with little awareness that the Lord's ways are different from our own. We base our choices on our own observations or common sense—often with tragic consequences.

Laurie began partying her junior year of high school. By the time she graduated, she was drunk at some party almost every weekend. Laurie saw nothing wrong with this way of life. All her friends were partiers, and nothing bad ever seemed to happen. Then one night, two weeks after graduation, Laurie's friend Gwen was driving home, drunk as usual. Evidently she passed out at the wheel. Her car slammed into a guardrail and spun into the oncoming traffic. A car crashed into Gwen's car and killed her instantly. That crash changed Laurie's thinking and propelled her into a recovery program. "I guess I'm not as smart as I thought I was," she says.

■ *Lord, I know that some ways seem right to me but are not your ways. Teach me to be able to discern the difference.*

S.C.

GOD'S WORKMANSHIP

For we are His workmanship.
—EPH. 2:10

"You Klutz." "Stupid." "Can't you do anything right?"

Imagine a friend who constantly shoots you down with such comments. You'd either want to leave her presence or tell her to shut up—or both! However, Genie could never escape from that critical friend, because she was the one who was saying those things to herself.

Step eight of the Twelve Steps involves making a list of all persons we have harmed—and that includes ourselves. Our negative self-talk can do a lot of damage in our lives. There is a saying that people rise to the expectations placed on them. We will rise or fall to the level of our own expectations. If we tell ourselves we will never recover, chances are we won't. If we tell ourselves we are failures, we are setting ourselves up to fail. Running ourselves down gives us an identity that leads to relapse.

Genie had done damage to her identity and her self-esteem. She needed to acknowledge that and to make amends to herself. And she needed to see herself for what she is—God's workmanship.

■ *In making a list of all persons harmed, do not forget yourself. Try to see yourself the way God sees you.*

J.C.

GIVE YOURSELF CREDIT

*A bruised reed he will not break,
and a dimly burning wick he
will not quench.*
—ISA. 42:3 RSV

She came into our recovery group looking pretty somber. Usually she was the one who joked around and made the wisecracks that got all of us laughing. Not this time, though. She was unusually quiet . . . until time came for her to talk about how she was doing. "I just came off the worst binge I've had since I began in the program, and I almost didn't come to our meeting." Tears started rolling down her face. We all knew the anguish, the sense of failure, the panicky fear of "What if I've lost it?"

And then someone said quietly, "But you're here. You came. Give yourself credit for that." Her lips trembled, and she simply nodded her head.

Give yourself credit. "A bruised reed he will not break, and a dimly burning wick he will not quench." We have a gentle, loving Savior. He takes whatever embers are still burning and brings us back to a full flame. Progress, not perfection, is what recovery is all about. God is bigger than our slips and our failures. Give yourself credit. You've come a long way.

■ *God, when I expect perfection of myself, remind me that perfection is your department. I only have to be faithful, willing, and open to your leading in my life.*
D.K.

THE REJECTION CHAIN

He is despised and rejected by men,
A Man of sorrows and acquainted
with grief. —ISA. 53:3

Rejection is one of the toughest experiences a person can face; it seems to cut right to the core of our being, creating self-doubt, feelings of inferiority, even self-hatred. Healing from the wound of rejection takes time, patience, nurturing, and self-examination. Unfortunately, some people, instead of handling their hurt in a healthy way, choose to take it out on an unsuspecting, innocent "next person in line."

When Lois's boyfriend dumped her, she felt humiliated and discarded. She cried for days, then decided that no one was ever going to do that to her again. Her feelings turned from hurt to anger, and she decided that she was going to do to someone else what had been done to her. She began dating a boy in her class. Once she knew that he really liked her, she turned on him and broke off the relationship. The result? One more person left with the sting of rejection.

If you have been rejected, resolve to handle your hurt constructively. Allow yourself to "feel your feelings" and cry, then begin picking up the pieces. But do not pass your hurt to someone else and make him pay for your pain.

■ *Jesus, you of all people know what rejection feels like. Heal me from my pain, and help me keep from intentionally hurting someone else.*

S.C.

SURPRISE ME, LORD

God has chosen the weak things of the world
to put to shame the things which are mighty.
—1 COR. 1:27

God is full of surprises. If He were a captain in gym class and had to pick a team, He'd pick the slowest, most uncoordinated people out of the group. Then somehow, through His patience, love, and power, they'd end up beating everybody.

Just look at the Bible. Joseph was a punk kid of about seventeen when he arrived in Egypt—and a slave, no less. He ended up as Egypt's "vice president." David, as a teen with a slingshot, killed an experienced soldier who was nine-and-a-half feet tall and armed to the teeth. Mary, who came from a poor family and perhaps was only fifteen years old, became our Savior's mother.

The reason behind all this celestial madness has to do with God's glory. The more hopeless the case, the more impossible things are, the more God has a chance to show His glory. . . . and the less we can boast about our own abilities.

The only thing God requires from us in order to be a player in this ultimate game is to give our will over to Him. This is a big "only." But once we get past that, He can turn our hopeless into hope and our weak into strong. You may think your addiction problem is incurable or your family situation is impossible or the damage you've done to your life is unsalvageable. But God will do surprising things in your life if you let Him do His job—and you give Him the glory.

■ *Lord, take my life and surprise me.*

J.C.

A PLACE TO HIDE

For in the time of trouble
He shall hide me in His pavilion;
In the secret place of His tabernacle
He shall hide me;
He shall set me high upon a rock.
—PS. 27:5

Sometimes I do great in recovery. It's so exciting to grow, to learn how to handle the behaviors that used to defeat me, to have a life that's going somewhere.

And sometimes it's just too much. I'm tired of working things out with my family, tired of juggling things at school. I'm tired of facing my problems, facing up to my feelings. Sometimes I just want to hide for awhile—just like I used to hide by holing up in my room with a bag of potato chips, a pound of chocolate, my stereo, and my stash.

God must know I have times like that. That's why His word to me is, "It's OK to hide out. But you don't have to crawl in a hole of compulsive behavior. Instead, hide out at My place. Spend some time with Me, depending only on My love. When you're ready to come out, we'll go out together on the high rocks and enjoy the view."

■   *Lord, thank you that you understand my need for time out. Hide me in your pavilion until I'm ready to carry on.*

A.C.B.

SPRING CLEANING

He has put a new song in my mouth—
Praise to our God.   —PS. 40:3

Spring signals new life and new growth. Flowers blossom, the grass turns green, trees sprout new leaves, and the air has a fresh, clean smell. Other delights come at springtime, too: warm breezes, cool grass, and birds chirping.

Spring is also the time of year that old clothes, unused items, and remnants from the past get thrown out. I remember when my mother did her annual "spring cleaning." She would open up all the windows and let the cool air drift in. Then, she would work her way through the house—sweeping, mopping, dusting, sorting. Several bags of old items would appear near the back door, ready to be given or thrown away. I always got to "participate" in the cleaning, but I really didn't mind. Just knowing the new was going to replace the old felt good.

It may be time to do some "spring cleaning" in your life. You may want to visit the "rooms" in your heart and clean out the cobwebs, junk, and garbage that have accumulated. Let the fresh air of change come in. Those old feelings and grudges that have weighed you down are probably in need of being thrown out. Put new attitudes in their place. Spring—what a wonderful time for a whole new life.

■ *Make this springtime a memorable season in your life.*

S.C.

JUST CALL ME PRINCESS

Now the LORD had said to Abram:
"Get out of your country,
From your kindred
And from your father's house,
To a land that I will show you. . . .
I will bless you."

—GEN. 12:1–2

Abram and his wife, Sarai, were risk takers. At God's command, this middle-aged couple left a familiar, comfortable home and set out for an unknown land. Then, almost twenty-five years later, God gave these pioneers new names and an amazing promise. Abram became Abraham, which means "father of a multitude." Sarai became Sarah, which means "princess." And both these new names were related to God's promise—that the two of them would bear a child. At age eighty-nine, Sarah found this promise a little hard to believe; in fact, she laughed out loud when Abraham told her about it. But when their son was born a year later she named him Isaac, which means (what else?) "laughter."

God gives us a new identity, too, when we trust in Him. The only catch is that, like Abram and Sarai, we have to be willing to leave our old way of life behind. What is our new identity? When we accept Christ as Lord of our lives, then we become God's daughters. We can call Him Dad or even Daddy. God is King and He is our father. And that means that, like Sarai, our new name is "Princess."

■ *Heavenly Dad, help me take that risk and leave the old, comfortable, but dysfunctional way of life. Thanks that you give me your royal life in exchange.*

J.C.

TEMPER TANTRUMS

Do not hasten in your spirit to be angry,
For anger rests in the bosom of fools.
—ECCLES. 7:9

Unfortunately, I've never outgrown temper tantrums. Slamming down the telephone receiver. Throwing my brush across the room. Slamming doors shut. At times I'm the model of maturity. Then again, sometimes my behavior rivals that of a tired, hungry two-year-old.

When frustration gets the best of me, the best thing I can do is take a time-out. Taking care of myself means learning to recognize when the fuse is ready to short-circuit and pulling the plug before it does. Instead of feeling disgusted or embarrassed when I find myself in a fit of frustration, I get out of the situation (even if that means momentarily locking myself in the bathroom) and ask myself, "What is it I need right now?" Have I been going in fast forward, losing myself in my haste? Usually, the answer is yes. It's time to shift gears, slow down, and ask God to restore my inner calm.

Although I haven't completely outgrown temper tantrums, I'm finding that they happen less and less. I don't claim the credit—I know to whom the credit is due. And for the Spirit that lives within me, I'm grateful.

■   *Lord, forgive me when I lose it, and give me patience with myself. I am growing. I am changing. Thanks for reminding me of that when I feel a little foolish.*

D.K.

HARD-WON HUMILITY

Where were you when I laid the
foundations of the earth?
Tell Me, if you have
understanding.

—JOB 38:4

Mary left the hospital eating disorder unit equipped with a wealth of newfound knowledge. She could spout psychological terms at will and discuss her problem with intelligence and understanding. In fact, when she returned home, she realized that she knew more about her condition than her parents did. Mary felt a burst of pride. Forgetting that just a few weeks earlier she had known next to nothing about eating disorders, she now studded her speech with psychological jargon and did everything she could to insinuate that her parents were ignorant.

But God has a unique way of humbling proud and presumptuous people: He lets them see themselves as they really are! That's what He did to Job when Job challenged Him, and that's what He did with Mary. It took a minor relapse to show her that knowledge about recovery is not the same thing as a successful recovery.

If you are in a recovery program, resist the urge to show off your knowledge and understanding. Instead, work at applying what you are learning to your life. Be understanding and patient with others, lest you have to learn a lesson in humility the hard way.

■ *Father, I need a strong dose of humility along with my newfound insight. Teach me to boast of your grace, not my understanding.*

S.C.

Ask, seek, knock

Ask, and it will be given to you; seek, and you will find; knock, and it will be opened to you.
—MATT. 7:7

How badly do you want to recover? (Choose one.)

A. I want it if someone hands it to me (silver-platter cure).
B. I am willing to ask for it and then wait for God to zap me with healing (magic-wand cure).
C. I am willing to go to meetings and get better by just associating with the right people (osmosis cure).
D. I will do whatever it takes.

Today's verse promises that recovery will be ours as long as we are willing to "ask, seek, and knock" for it. That implies action—actually doing something instead of waiting for a cure to come to us. *Ask* means figuring out what we need (information? encouragement?) and then making requests instead of expecting others to read our minds. *Seek* implies getting out and looking for help—actually going to the meetings or meeting with a sponsor. And *knock,* the most assertive of the three words, means being persistent about recovery. We work the program. If we relapse, we begin again. We take whatever action is necessary to keep on the road to recovery.

■ *Recovery is an active process—and I'm expected to participate.*

J.C.

KEEP ME LAUGHING!

A merry heart does good, like medicine,
But a broken spirit dries the bones.
—PROV. 17:22

Today started out so grim. My alarm didn't go off, and then Mom and Dad had another fight—before breakfast, no less. The dog had chewed my yellow flats, and Jake called to say he couldn't take me to school this morning; I'd have to ride the bus. (*I hate* riding the bus!)

And then, while we were hanging around outside, Wanda showed me a cartoon she had taped in the front of her notebook. It was hysterical; I started cracking up. While we were all laughing, Jerry came up and started telling these great stories. I love talking to Jerry because he's always so funny.

And that got me thinking. One of the things I like best about my support group is that even though we talk about a lot of heavy stuff, we also laugh a lot—and laughing really helps. Looking at the funny side of my crazy behavior helps put it in perspective. It's so ridiculous; how can I let it have so much power over me? Laughter also takes off some of the pressure when things get really grim. Keeping hold of my sense of humor—and deliberately seeking out people I can laugh with—can do a lot to help me in recovery.

■ *Lord, keep me laughing—not because everything is always funny, but because laughter is one of your gifts to keep my life in perspective.*

A.C.B.

A FRIEND TO PAIN

When my father and my mother forsake me,
Then the LORD will take care of me.
— PS. 27:10

Jenny's home life is turbulent. Her mother, Emma, who is mentally ill, constantly shouts obscenities at Jenny. When Emma takes her medication regularly, the home front is quieter. But war rages when Emma refuses her medication, and Jenny is always the loser.

It seems to Jenny that every time she begins to feel positive about something in her life, it is jerked away from her. She has learned to expect very little. Sadly, feeling bad about herself has become a way of life. It is so difficult to convince her that she is a good kid, worthwhile and special when her mother keeps screaming that she is a pitiful daughter who should never have been born. Jenny is afraid to feel good. At least when she feels bad, she is not disappointed.

A person like Jenny who is raised in an abusive home becomes "close friends" with pain. In fact, she may unconsciously sabotage herself from feeling good because freedom from pain does not feel like freedom at all. It takes awhile to "feel good about feeling good."

■ *If you find it difficult to allow yourself to feel good or enjoy life, that's a sign you have more healing to do. As you continue in recovery, the one who was "acquainted with grief" (Isa. 53:3) can help you be reacquainted with joy.*

S.C.

HOW DO I DECIDE?

*This book of the law shall not depart from
your mouth, but you shall meditate on it day
and night, so that you may be careful to do
according to all that is written in it; for then
you . . . will have success.*
—JOSH. 1:8 NASB

She had just recently returned to the States from being
overseas for ten years. "I went to the grocery store and
felt paralyzed by the choices. Over there, you only have
one or two picks of something. Here, if you want to buy
soda pop, you have to pick not only the brand, but also
if it should be regular, sugar free, salt free, or decaf-
feinated. Panty hose are sheer, regular, sandalfoot, designer, or support. How do you decide what to buy?"

It's true. We do have many choices to make—in life
as well as in the stores. What helps you make your
choices? A user bases her choices on what feels good,
but a successful recovery needs something better. God's
Word is that something better.

In today's verse, God is telling Joshua how to claim
the Promised Land. He is on the verge of entering a
new, exciting phase of his life. To have success in it, God
tells him to soak his mind in God's Word, the Bible.
God's Word will become so much a part of him that he
will know what choices God would want him to make.

It makes sense. If you know God's mind, you will
know His choices for you. If you follow through with His
choices, you will have success as you enter a new life.

■   *A successful recovery involves knowing what God's
    choices are for me and then going after them.*

J.C.

HE CARES

Casting all your care upon Him, for He cares for you.
—1 PETER 5:7

What aspects of your life worry you, drive you crazy, weigh you down? School pressures? Money worries? Guys? Parents? Your future? Whatever the concern, you are cordially invited to dump them all in God's lap. "Don't worry," He tells you. "I have it all under control."

But if that's true, why is it so hard to let go of our cares? Usually because part of us still wants to be in charge of them. Letting go of control is no easy feat, but it is necessary if we want to keep the stresses and strains of life from overtaking us. Human beings were not made to hold up without help under a constant load of care. For people in recovery that should be obvious. When we tried to carry too heavy a load of pain, we ended up numbing our feelings with drugs, booze, sex, or some other dangerous anesthetic.

God does care for us. He has a deep, loving concern for our well-being. He wants us to live joyfully and abundantly, and He tells us how in His Word. He admonishes us to trust Him instead of worrying, to hand over all our concerns to Him and relax in His loving care.

■ *Lord, today I am making the decision to cast my cares on you. I'll probably have to make the same decision all over again tomorrow, but that's the way the process works. Thank you for caring!*

S.C.

ANY TIME, DAY OR NIGHT

As for me, I will call upon God . . .
Evening and morning and at noon
I will pray . . .
And He shall hear my voice.
—PS. 55:16–17

The books say have quiet time in the morning. I'm semi-brain-dead until noon. The books say pray in specifics. If I knew exactly what to pray for, I wouldn't be feeling so confused. The books say sit quietly to pray. When I sit quietly, my fingers start to tap, a tune pops into my head, and before I know it, I'm humming. Sometimes I feel I don't fit the spiritual mold.

But the fact is, there is no right way or wrong way to pray, no right time or wrong time to seek God, no formulas for praying for what we need and want. If prayer and a quiet heart come more easily at noon or night, I can seek Him then. If knowing what to pray for seems elusive, I can simply place the concern in His hands and let Him decide on the specifics. If sitting still brings music to my head, then I can sing and dance before the Lord—the psalmist certainly did. Out there on the hillsides, with only sheep for an audience, the psalmist sang, played his flute, and danced for joy.

■ *The One who created me is the One who placed the song in my heart, the tunes in my head, and the energy in my body. If God were only a morning person, He wouldn't have created night.*

D.K.

METAMORPHOSIS

*But we . . . are being transformed . . . from
glory to glory, just as by the Spirit of the
Lord.* —2 COR. 3:18

Recovery is a type of metamorphosis. Just as a caterpillar changes to a butterfly we can change drastically
as well.

A caterpillar is burdened down by a body that moves
slowly. She does not get to see a whole lot of her world
because she cannot travel fast. We, too, may move
slowly through our lives weighed down by regrets, bad
habits, and worries. We crawl along, overburdened with
our emotional baggage.

When a caterpillar forms a cocoon, she is ready for a
life-changing process. And when a person enters recovery, she begins a similar process of dramatic change.
Old patterns are stripped away and replaced by new
ones. Old beliefs are demolished; new beliefs are for-
mulated. It's not always fun! Just as a cocoon is not
pleasant to look at, a person in recovery may be unpleasant at times as well.

But when the process is complete, she can now fly
freely. A person who has gone through treatment experiences a similar makeover. Her physical appearance
may or may not change, but her soul and spirit are
transformed. She is not the same person she used to be.
She has been given a chance to live life fully and freely.

■ *O Lord, I pray for a transformation in my life. Help
me break free from the areas in my life that weigh
me down.*

S.C.

FORGIVING MYSELF

In this is love, not that we loved God, but that He loved us and sent His Son to be the propitiation for our sins.

—1 JOHN 4:10

It's a death for a death. Isn't that what the Bible says? An eye for an eye, a tooth for a tooth. That's why I tried to kill myself—because I killed my baby. I deserve to die." At seventeen, two years after her abortion, Lisa was wrestling with the delayed shock waves of guilt and hurt she had tried to numb through drinking.

Lisa had two people to whom she had to make amends, her baby and herself. Making amends to the baby was easier. Lisa gave a name—Kristen—to her unborn baby. Next, she wrote Kristen a long letter of apology and read it aloud to her. Lisa cried and grieved for her act and for her baby.

Coming to terms with her guilt was harder for Lisa. She was right; she *did* deserve to die. The Bible makes it clear that we *all* have broken God's laws; we *all* deserve to die. But Jesus gave His life so we could live. When Lisa accepted Christ as her Savior, He saved her from death. It would take time for Lisa's feelings to catch up with her knowledge that God had forgiven her. But every time the feelings of condemnation washed over her, Lisa reminded herself that Jesus took care of her guilt—and took another step toward forgiving herself.

■ *Jesus, help me not to believe my continuing guilt feelings. As my Savior, You have already paid the penalty for my sins.*

J.C.

A TIME OF TESTING

When he has tested me, I shall come
forth as gold. —JOB 23:10

Final exam time can be tough on recovery. Schedules are off. Pressure is on. You're either cramming like mad or aware that you should be cramming . . . and knowing that vacation is around the corner makes it hard to concentrate.

There's probably no way to avoid extra pressure at exam time, but there are ways to make things a little easier on yourself. First, remind yourself that recovery has to be your priority. (If you spin out of control, you'll blow the tests anyway.) So try not to miss your meeting, your therapy, or your quiet time. Keep in close touch with your sponsor or supportive friends.

And do study! It may seem like such a daunting task that you're tempted to blow it off, but the stress of avoiding an unpleasant task is greater than that of doing it. Studying with a friend may help, but watch out for study parties, especially if you have a problem with food; many study sessions are really cookie and gossip fests where little gets done. Pace yourself to avoid "all nighters"; fatigue can be a real recovery buster. Finally, do your best, then hand your anxieties over to God.

■ *Regardless of how I do on my exams, I'm still on the growing road. And making it through challenging times helps me "come forth as gold."*

A.C.B.

SINK, TREAD, OR SWIM

But thanks be to God, who gives us the
victory through our Lord Jesus Christ.
                                                —1 COR. 15:57

When you are in the midst of recovery, it can become easy to lose sight of why you are there. When continual change is painful, the temptation to go back to old patterns is hard to resist. Attending meetings, going to therapy, journaling one's thoughts, praying—all these can become old and mundane. Listening to everyone's stories, rehashing painful events, examining and reexamining areas in one's life may seem like drudgery.

When a child first learns to swim, she is put in a potentially scary place. If no one gets in the pool with her, she feels alone and afraid. But if a teacher or parent climbs in with her and shows her how to swim properly, her confidence grows. Eventually she is ready to get out in deep water. And once she is there, she has three options. She can keep swimming, tread water, or sink.

Recovery may feel like the deep end of the pool at times. You may become tired of trying. If that happens, ask for help. (Others are in the pool with you—and there *is* a Lifeguard!) Catch your second wind, refocus on your goal, and then . . . keep paddling. Don't give up now.

■   *Are you going to turn back, stay in the middle, or*
     pursue the reason you got in the recovery process in
     the first place?

                                                              S.C.

ESP NOT REQUIRED

You do not have because you do not ask.
—JAMES 4:2

If Brenda ever took out an ad for a boyfriend, it would have to read: "Boyfriend needed. Muscular, possess a car, smart, *must* have ESP."

Brenda thinks that anyone who cares about her should be able to read her mind, figure out what she needs, and meet that need without her having to say anything. If her friends and boyfriend could do that, she would feel loved. Unfortunately, she hasn't found anyone who can do that. She never will, because God is the only One who can see inside our hearts. There are times when He will move to meet a need we don't even admit to ourselves. But not even He will do that all the time, because He loves us too much to hold us back from growth. After all, the more He does for us, the less we learn to do for ourselves.

Brenda's responsibility is to figure out what she needs and then to tell her friends about it appropriately. Sometimes she doesn't know what she wants and expects others to figure it out. Sometimes she does know her mind but expects others to prove their love by guessing it. But no one can know what's inside us unless we choose to reveal ourselves.

■ *I have a choice to make when it comes to relationships. I can expect the impossible and never be satisfied. Or I can pick up my end of any relationship, start working, and develop fulfilling friendships.*

J.C.

LEAVING EXTREMES BEHIND

Blessed be the LORD,
Because He has heard [my cry]!
The LORD is my strength and my shield;
My heart trusted in Him, and I am helped;
Therefore my heart greatly rejoices,
And . . . I will praise Him.

—PS. 28:6-7

Some days I'm a success waiting to happen. Other days I'm ensnared in insecurities. Sometimes I want to conquer the world. Other times I'd like to crawl in a hole. Sometimes I wish I were already grown up. And then again, sometimes I wish I could just hug my teddy bear and suck my thumb.

Vacillating between extremes is part of the addictive process. Exaggerated feelings—whether of complete confidence or total inadequacy—are really very similar. Thinking I'm worthless and thinking I'm terrific have something in common: Neither perspective enables me to see myself for who I really am.

Accepting myself means accepting all of me—character strengths and character defects, successes and failures, abilities and limitations. Neither the crest of the waves nor the bottom of the pits is a place I want to be. Learning to live in my own skin, content with myself, at peace with my world, and confident in my God provides the balance and inner calm I prefer.

■ *God is ever faithful, ever present, no matter if I'm flying high or feeling low. I only have to go to Him as the psalmist did—with a trusting heart and an honest prayer.*

D.K.

ADMITTING WHEN WE'RE WRONG

I acknowledged my sin to You,
And my iniquity I have not hidden.
I said, "I will confess my
transgressions to the LORD,"
And You forgave the iniquity of my sin.
—PS. 32:5

Admitting we have made a mistake is difficult to do. Sometimes we intentionally choose to do something wrong. If a rule exists that we do not like, we might choose to break it. If a curfew is established that we do not agree with, we might not adhere to it. Many areas in life are potential sources of wrongdoing.

Of course, there are unintentional mistakes as well. A word may slip from our mouth that sounds more cutting than we ever intended. We may forget about a promise to meet someone. We may neglect to say "thanks" when a "thank you" is in order.

Whatever the case—intentional or unintentional—mistakes or "transgressions" occur. And when they do, it is important to admit we are wrong. Step five of the Twelve Steps of AA states, "[We] admitted to God, to ourselves, and to another human being, the exact nature of our wrongs." Refusing to admit our wrongdoing places us in a box, so to speak, making us narrow-minded, rigid, and difficult. But admitting we were wrong frees us to accept responsibility for our actions as well as "right the wrong" with the person we offended.

■ *Admit your mistakes. Others will respect you for it, and God will forgive you.*

S.C.

TRUST MAKES THE DIFFERENCE

Oh, taste and see that the LORD is good;
Blessed is the [person] who trusts in
Him!
—PS. 34:8

What's the difference between positive thinking and denial? Between looking on the bright side and pretending there isn't a dark side?

I've heard so much advice that seems contradictory: "Be absolutely honest" about yourself and your feelings and your experiences, even if they're painful . . . but "focus on the good." The funny thing is . . . they're both true! If I back off from absolute honesty with myself, my self-deception holds me back from recovery. But if I just wallow around in my bad feelings, I stop growing.

To me, the thing that makes the difference between denial and positive thinking is *trust.* The only reason I can be brutally honest with myself without getting too depressed to move is that I trust God's promise that He has a better life in mind for me and will help me get there. Depending on God's love and grace is what keeps positive thinking honest and realistic. When I trust Him, I can face myself both honestly and positively.

■ *Lord, I choose to trust you with my feelings and my experiences. Only you can keep me both honest and upbeat about my recovery.*

A.C.B.

A HEAVENLY MOTHER

*As one whom his mother
    comforts,
So I will comfort you.*
—ISA. 66:13

We don't usually think of God as a "heavenly mother." Yet today's verse describes this side of God.

Mothers are usually depicted as nurturing and tender. Who hasn't seen a mother cuddling a baby in her arms? The little girl with an "ouchie" asks her mommy to kiss it, and the pain then magically lessens or disappears. Somehow, just knowing someone cares and hurts with you alleviates the pain.

A relatively happy mother can give her children living pictures of what God's softer side looks like. If this is your mother, take the time to thank her today for her love. If for some reason your mother is unable to be that comfort, God promises you His tender comfort.

In either case, take the time to honor your mother with a card, a gift, or words of appreciation. The book of Ephesians says that honoring your parents brings a better life for you (6:3).

Remembering your mother on this day can be an expression of thanks or a bridge towards a better relationship with her. Either purpose will strengthen your recovery.

■ *On this Mother's Day, I can choose to move my recovery along by honoring my mother.*

J.C.

A PURPOSE FOR HARD TIMES

Blessed is a [woman] who perseveres under trial.
—JAMES 1:12 NASB

There is a process used by silversmiths that seems to apply to the trials in our lives. When a silversmith melts silver down, he gradually raises the temperature. As the metal heats, impurities rise to the top. The silversmith skims off this dross and raises the heat again. After several skimmings, the silver is purer. And the silversmith knows the process is complete when he can see the reflection of his face in the molten silver.

Like heat under molten silver, our trials tend to bring impurities in our lives to the surface. And God allows such trials and tribulations to come our way—not as punishment, but as a way of bringing us closer to Him so He can remove the areas in our lives that are unhealthy.

The book of James refers to hard times as a means of producing endurance, wholeness, and maturity. We find out a lot about ourselves (and others) when trials occur, because difficulties expose much truth about a person. Her character can be either strengthened or broken depending on how she responds to the difficult situation.

God wants to see His reflection in our lives. Allow Him to apply heat to your life. Even though it may hurt and you may want to squirm out of it, the trial can bring purity and completeness.

■ *Lord, please use the trials in my life to make me stronger and more mature.*

S.C.

BODY LANGUAGE

> [You] *have put on the new* [self] *who is*
> *renewed in knowledge according to the*
> *image of Him who created* [you].
> —COL. 3:10

Look at me, young lady, when I talk to you." The principal stopped Judy in the hall during class changes. Sunlight danced in through a window and lit up the dreary hall like a stage, reminding her that she had better do some good acting. The sunlight also stabbed at her eyes. Her pupils were dilated from taking a hit in the girls' washroom. Judy averted her eyes and slouched over her books, mumbling something about being late for class. But her body language told the principal she was hiding something—and Judy was suspended when he found out what.

Judy went straight, but her body language still said she had something to hide. The principal continued to stop her in the halls. Frustrated, she threatened to give him something to stop her for.

Recovery means not only abstaining from your drug of choice but changing other related behavior. Judy's body language said, "I'm still a druggie." Teens who come through our inpatient unit are taught the ASERT Technique. It involves: using *A*ppropriate talk as you *S*peak clearly, with *E*ye contact and up*R*ight *T*all posture. The ASERT Technique could have helped Judy avoid unnecessary conflict with her principal and helped him take her more seriously.

■ *Self-respect in recovery may involve changing your*
body language.

J.C.

LEARNING THE SIGNALS

Be still, and know that I am God.
—PS. 46:10

Uh-oh. I can feel things inside beginning to go out of control. Feeling a little hyper—like I just want to do something, anything, to stay busy. Antsy. Restless. Nothing satisfies. I find myself avoiding prayer, avoiding moments of quiet, avoiding journaling. But what I'm really doing is avoiding myself and God.

Now I can recognize these antsy, restless feelings as signals that something is going on inside—and I need to listen to those emotions. Otherwise, I've learned through painful experience that the hyper "busyness" too often leads me back into my crazy behaviors. When things are feeling out of control, I know that's the beginning of being out of touch with God and myself. I can't avoid my feelings and stay healthy. Recovery means listening to the quiet—even when the quiet brings painful feelings.

■ *OK, God, time to sit still long enough to give my life back to you. Calm the restlessness within me and give me courage to feel my feelings and face what's really going on within me.*

D.K.

NOT DOUBLE-MINDED

*[She] is a double-minded [person], unstable
in all [her] ways.*
                              —JAMES 1:8

Have you ever known a person who says one thing but
does another? Being around such a person is frustrating. She may give conflicting messages—saying one
thing but really meaning something else. She may
change her mind frequently, and it is up to whomever
she is with to discern what she really wants. If by
chance, the other person does not actually read the
message as she intended, then she becomes angry or
sulks.

The book of James tells us not to be "double-
minded." It's speaking specifically of our prayer life,
but it also applies to the way we speak and act. We are
also told, "Let your 'Yes' be 'Yes' and your 'No,' 'No'"
(James 5:12). In other words, we should stick with what
we say. If we say yes, we should follow through with it.
The same goes if we say no.

Nowadays, people's words do not hold a lot of value.
In the past, loans were given on a person's word that
she would repay it. Even if she had nothing else, her
word was valuable. Can you imagine that happening
today? It is time to start "meaning what we say and
saying what we mean." Try to put an end to double-
mindedness in your life. A person who wavers in the
value of her word has a hard time receiving God's blessings.

■   *Lord, teach me the importance of not being double-
    minded.*

                                                    S.C.

A "GOOD GIRL"

*And all our righteousnesses are like
filthy rags.* —ISA. 64:6

Kelly was what you'd call a "good girl." If she was going to be late for curfew, she'd call her parents. She worked hard in school and had a part-time job on top of that. Nevertheless, Kelly landed in a psychiatric hospital because her "good girl" image covered a drinking and rage problem. Kelly's drinking problem had been a secret to her parents. Her rage problem had been a secret even to Kelly. After all, yelling and screaming did not go with her "good girl" image. So Kelly never saw herself as mad. Her anger came out in uncontrollable crying jags and suicidal thoughts.

Being a "good girl," Kelly was used to getting her own way. Her parents trusted her. Sometimes she took advantage of this and manipulated them. In the hospital, however, Kelly felt like she had no control. She wanted to leave, but her parents refused; they were afraid she would attempt suicide. Finally her rage came to the surface. Kelly *knew* she was mad. When it did, Kelly saw that others—even her parents—could still accept her. She learned to channel her anger into assertiveness and became less manipulative. She also found less of a need to be a "good girl." She could just be Kelly.

■ *Sometimes what we think is righteous can kill us. We need to exchange our righteousness for God's.*

J.C.

SUSTAIN ME

Sustain me with cakes of raisins,
Refresh me with apples,
For I am lovesick.
—SONG OF SOL. 2:5

This has to be the earliest recorded comment on compulsive overeating in all of history—and it's the story of my life before recovery. It's also the mentality I fall back into so easily whenever I neglect the ongoing disciplines of depending on God, seeking support, and keeping short accounts with what bothers me.

And it's not just about being "lovesick." As a friend and I used to joke, "I don't just eat when I'm happy or eat when I'm sad; I eat whenever I have an emotion."

And it's not just about eating. For some, it's "Sustain me with a credit card and two new pairs of jeans, for I am lonely" or "Sustain me with just one snort, for I am feeling rejected" or "Sustain me with a binge and purge, for I am feeling out of control."

But none of it really works, of course, because crazy behaviors just don't have what it takes to keep me going. The only dependable response to having emotions is found in the same Book that records that early compulsive behavior. "Cast your burden on the LORD," writes the Psalmist, "and *He* shall sustain you" (Ps. 55:22).

■ *Sustain me, Lord, with your unending love . . .*
whenever I have an emotion.

A.C.B.

SEX IS SERIOUS

*For this is the will of God, your
sanctification: that you should abstain
from sexual immorality.* —1 THESS. 4:3

God's standards for morality seem to be a thing of the past. "This is the nineties" is the excuse that is given. It is as if His Word was only written for a specific time frame and he had no idea that "the nineties" would ever roll around! Think of the messages you hear all the time from the media, from friends, from society: "Sex is OK, just as long as it is 'safe'!" "You can't have a male-female relationship without sex." "Sex is just clean, healthy fun—as long as you handle it 'responsibly.'"

But wait a minute! What about trust or commitment or love? What about self-esteem and self-respect? Sex has a powerful emotional component—especially for women. There are feelings that cannot be separated from the physical aspect. Sex is great when used as God intended. But sex is also serious!

The body you have been given is to be used for the glory of God, not as an object of lust. Think seriously about sex and the consequences. You do not owe anyone your body. But you owe it to yourself and God to take care of it.

■ *Father, I know you only want the best for me. Give me the strength not to compromise myself when the world tells me it is OK to go against your standards.*

S.C.

MISSING THE MARK

*If we say that we have no sin, we deceive
ourselves, and the truth is not in us.*
—1 JOHN 1:8

God expects us to sin. Not that He wants us to. But He knows we are all going to mess up sometime. Sin means missing the mark—like missing the bull's-eye on a target. Some people miss the bull's-eye by a lot. These people may rob, rape, or kill. Some people almost make the bull's-eye. Their sins may be telling white lies or just not doing the good they could. And yet both groups have still missed the bull's-eye. Both groups are sinful in God's eyes.

When we sin, it's common to say, "Not me, I didn't do it." To this, God says, "Get real, stop fooling yourself." And then He provides a healthy way to deal with the sin and the natural guilt that goes with it. (Stack up enough guilt-bricks on our shoulders and relapse is likely to happen.)

The old way of getting rid of guilt feelings was to numb them out by food, drugs, or alcohol. But God has provided a new way: Admit to messing up. Agree with Him that it was wrong and make restitution where needed. If you exploded at someone, apologize. If you blew it big time, you may need outside help in figuring out a restitution. And then, believe God's promise of forgiveness and cleansing (see v. 9). If you can believe God, then you should no longer feel the guilt. And you *can* believe God, because He does not lie.

■ *Believing that God is telling the truth about forgiveness helps me resolve my guilt feelings.*

J.C.

ALL OUT OF NICE

He withdrew, . . . knelt down and prayed.
—LUKE 22:41 NIV

The little girl was about three years old, obviously tired, and pushed beyond her limits. The grocery store "express" line was long and moving none too fast. The mother's nerves were fried and her voice was impatient. I was standing behind them, watching what I thought was going to be a "class A" brat's fit. As the little girl began to cry and whine, her mother told her to "straighten up and be nice." The little girl's response amazed and amused me. She said, "Mommy, I'm all out of nice."

She was only three years old, but she knew her limits better than I sometimes know mine. She was more in touch with her needs than I often am with mine. She knew she'd had enough people, waiting, and errands, and it was time to go home.

A classic Twelve Step slogan is H.A.L.T.: Never get too *H*ungry, *A*ngry, *L*onely or *T*ired. Recovery means setting my boundaries, knowing my limits, and recognizing when I'm "all out of nice."

■ *Christ, even you withdrew and took time alone to rest, to pray, and to let your heavenly Father replenish your spirit. Give me the wisdom to know when to do likewise.*

D.K.

I NEED HELP

*Not that we are sufficient of ourselves to
think of anything as being from ourselves,
but our sufficiency is from God.*
—2 COR. 3:5

I can do it myself" is a battle cry for many people. "If
you want something done, do it yourself" is another
favorite saying. But somewhere in the midst of all that
independence, you usually find an empty core of loneliness, fear, and inadequacy.

You may be talented, capable, or knowledgeable, but
you are not self-sufficient. From all our culture's propa-
ganda regarding a woman's ability to "do it all" comes
the false belief that needing help is a sign of weakness.
That's a lie. Needing help is simply a sign of being human.

Somewhere along the line you have to come to terms
with your insufficiency. You do not have to be everything
to everyone. You certainly are not responsible for meeting everyone's needs. And you don't need to tackle your
problems all alone.

Only one Person holds the position of being totally
powerful, self-sufficient, and lacking in nothing. Let
God have His rightful place, and you take yours. Do not
be afraid to ask for help. In fact, please ask. Let your
needs be made known.

■ *Lord, I can't do it on my own. Thank you that I
don't have to!*

S.C.

STATE OF ALERT

I sought the LORD, and He heard me,
And delivered me from all my fears.
—PS. 34:4

Trisha had to walk down a dark alley in order to get home, and she was scared. Her palms, feet and underarms got sweaty. She held her breath when she heard a noise. Just a cat—but her breathing was still shallow and rapid. Dark shadows seemed menacing. She quickened her pace and was ready to run if necessary.

When we feel fear, our bodies react the way Trisha's did—with shallow breathing, tense muscles and cold sweat. When the threat passes, our bodies should go back to normal. But some of us are always in this heightened state because of our fears. These fears may be flashback feelings—old feelings that emerge in the present because they never got resolved. These can be related to past sexual or physical abuse or losses in our lives.

Such a constant state of fear is bad for us. It causes wear and tear on the body. And it locks our thinking so that we are unable to see situations realistically. When I'm anxious I have a harder time thinking about my choices. I just react.

God promises His presence and deliverance from *all* our fears. Our part is to seek Him out. This means spending time with Him and talking about our specific fears.

■ *Fears can block recovery, but God promises me his deliverance from them.*

J.C.

A GOOD DAY

This is the day which the LORD has made;
We will rejoice and be glad in it.
—PS. 118:24

What do you do with a really good day?

It does happen from time to time. My skin is clear. My hair does just right. I ace a math test. I make good recovery choices without a lot of sweat. And the sun's shining.

So, what do I do on a day like that?

The way I see it, I have three choices:

I can get cynical, thinking, "Well, this can't last; something's bound to go wrong soon."

I can get cocky, thinking, "Hey, I've got this thing licked; life's a piece of cake."

Or I can be grateful, thinking, "Thanks, Lord, for a day off from working so hard. Thanks for the sunshine. Thanks for helping me stay on track. And thank You especially about the skin! I'm going to just lean back and enjoy this great day, knowing You are with me on good days and bad."

■ *Lord, thank you for good days that keep me going. I embrace them with gratitude.*

A.C.B.

TEAR DOWN THE WALLS

*I will say of the LORD, "He is my
refuge and my fortress;
My God, in Him I will trust."*
—PS. 91:2

Europe boasts some incredible castles. They served not only as homes for nobility of past centuries, but as fortresses. The high, thick walls were built expressly to guard against would-be attackers. The walls were built of stone—a substance that is difficult, if not impossible, to penetrate. These walls gave invaluable protective service to the people who lived behind them. Unfortunately, once the drawbridge came up, the inhabitants were cut off from the surrounding countryside.

In our lives we often build walls, too. Maybe not visible ones—but walls just the same. If you have been hurt by people you loved or trusted, you probably have some walls. If you are afraid to let people see who you really are, you have walls. If you carry around a lot of anger, your walls are solid. And yes, your walls have served to protect you, but they also isolate you. Unless you hand someone a chisel and let them chip away at your walls, or unless you choose to dismantle the stones yourself, no one will ever be allowed inside. You may feel safer with thick walls, but chances are you will be lonely, too.

■ *God, please teach me how to let others in my life so I
will not be afraid or lonely. Help me to tear down
the unnecessary walls I have constructed.*

S.C.

SOMEONE ELSE'S INVENTORY

And why do you look at the speck in your [sister's] eye, but do not consider the plank in your own eye?
—MATT. 7:3

It's such a drag being with her. All she does is complain about others. I tried to tell her to look at herself for once." Marla looked steamed and paused long enough to take a deep breath.

"That's really good advice, Marla," I said.

Marla did not miss a beat. "After all, she only has control over herself and not over those people she's always complaining about."

I repeated, "*That* is really good advice, Marla."

She looked at me puzzled. I had finally gotten her attention. She knew I was up to something, but was not sure what it was.

Do you get the point? What was Marla doing herself that she was complaining about? Right! She was doing the very thing she couldn't stand in her friend. She was taking someone else's inventory.

It's always easier to see someone else's faults. That's why Jesus gave us this warning in a hyperbole—an exaggeration to make a point. Jesus says we all have planks stuck in our eyes we need to pull out—so why bother with the almost invisible speck in someone else's eye? If we take our planks out, then maybe we can see better and then be truly helpful to someone else.

■ *Focusing on another's small speck and neglecting my plank is codependent behavior. The hope of my recovery lies in knowing myself first.*

J.C.

DANGER ZONE

Save me, O God!
For the waters have come up to my neck.
I sink . . .
Where there is no standing;
I have come into deep waters.

—PS. 69:1–2

When things are going OK, I easily think, "I can handle this. I don't have to go to my meeting today," or "Just this once won't matter."

When that happens, let the red lights flash and sirens blast, because I'm walking into a danger zone—the zone of self-destruct. Minimizing the dangers of addictive behaviors—that one bite, that one hit, that one sip—is part of the insanity. Only rigorous honesty with myself and God can keep me abstinent, clean, and sober.

Slips always start small. We never tell ourselves, "Hey, I'm doing great, so I'm really going to blow it!" Instead, one small action leads to another, and another, and another. But we in recovery have ways to beat the cycle and break the pattern. The tools of the program can bring us out of the danger zone and back into the safety of straight thinking. When the red lights flash, we can make a call, go to a meeting, take time for some recovery reading, or pray.

■ *No matter where we are, Christ is present, even in the danger zones, ready to send in the rescue squad.*

D.K.

SHOWING MERCY

The LORD is merciful and gracious,
Slow to anger, and abounding in mercy.
—PS. 103:8

Mercy is a concept that is rather foreign these days. It isn't talked about on TV. You won't hear it in too many songs, and unfortunately it is not practiced by a great number of people.

Mercy means showing compassion when you have a right to pass judgment. It was a very real part of the lives of people in the Bible. King David begged for God's mercy on his life. He knew the Lord had every right to withhold His compassion and kindness from him, but God showed Himself merciful. The people of Israel experienced God's mercy so many times. And Jesus poured out His mercy upon the people. He knew they were hurting, and He was kind to them.

In an age when most of us look out for "number one," we lose sight of being merciful to others. Our society is "sue crazy"; people are willing to go to court over the most trivial issues. Where did the mercy go?

We need God's mercy on our lives. We are also asked to extend compassion to others. The next time you are faced with the opportunity to be compassionate, try it. Even if someone deserves your anger, be kind. See if it doesn't feel good.

■ *Father, I pray for your mercy on my life. Please teach me how to be merciful to others.*

S.C.

PLEASING GOD FIRST

We make it our aim, . . . to be well pleasing to Him.
　　　　　　　　　　　　　　　—2 COR. 5:9

Carla's identity was all wrapped up in pleasing people. That's how she initially started drinking; she wanted to fit in with her partying friends. Now she knew better than to hang out with them . . . but she was still a people pleaser.

Her new friends were into expensive clothes—designer jeans and bags, cashmere sweaters—so Carla wanted them, too. This led into some heated arguments at home because her family simply could not afford the price tags. Carla's identity as a people pleaser was still getting her into unmanageable behavior.

God says we should make our ambition to please Him. When we do that, our recovery can go beyond just abstaining from our destructive behavior. Abstinence by itself is like cutting the top off of a weed. The roots are still there, and the weed is likely to grow back, perhaps in another form. But God can address some root issues when we focus on pleasing Him. With this new focus on our identity as His children, we can find a security we never had. And then we don't need to depend on TV, shopping, activities—or pleasing others—to make us feel OK.

■　*Pleasing God instead of people leads to self-respect.*
　　　　　　　　　　　　　　　　　　　　J.C.

A SMIDGEN OF FAITH

*And the apostles said to the Lord, "Increase
our faith." So the Lord said, "If you have
faith as a mustard seed, you can say to this
mulberry tree, 'Be pulled up by the roots
and be planted in the sea,' and it would
obey you."*
                                    —LUKE 17:5–6

According to Jesus, I don't need very much faith to
get started on the road to healthy, positive, effective living. (For me, that means getting started on the road to
recovery.) I just need a little "smidgen," a tiny dab—
miniature as a mustard seed. But as anyone in recovery
will testify, even a mustard seed of faith can be hard to
come by.

So where do I find the "mustard seed" of faith I
need to get going and keep going? In the beginning, I
may have to rely on the experience of others. (That's
one reason I need a support group.) Even though recovery doesn't *feel* possible, seeing it work in the lives of
people who were as messed up as I am gives me a tiny
glimmer of belief that it might work for me. Further
along, my faith is strengthened by remembering times
when I saw the process work in my own life.

I've learned that whenever I summon the courage to
act on the little bit of faith I have, I am given some more.
And bit by bit, my little "smidgen" of faith grows up to
do big, seemingly impossible things.

■ *Lord, I give you my mustard seed of faith. Help me
to trust your promise that you can grow it into something big and worthwhile.*

                                                    A.C.B.

SATAN'S SALES PITCHES

. . . lest Satan should take advantage of us;
for we are not ignorant of his devices.
—2 COR. 2:11

Satan is like a used-car salesman trying to make a sale on a "lemon." The scam is to make a big deal of the advantages and to avoid mentioning or minimizing the defects. "This car is a classic" (translation: it's old and rusty). "It's so roomy, you can pack a dozen of your friends in it" (translation: it's a gas guzzler).

At one time, you bought the lies about alcohol, drugs, or eating: "It'll make you look cool, feel good." But you got a lemon. Satan forgot to mention the throwing up (which definitely does nothing to enhance one's image), the cravings (which feel awful), or the loss of health. If you don't want to buy another lemon from him, be aware of the sales pitch.

These sales pitches usually have to do with denying or avoiding the truth. *Blaming* says, "I had nothing to do with this problem, it's your fault." *Denial* says, "Problem? What problem?" *Minimizing* says, "What's the big deal? It's just a little problem." *Excusing* says, "Problem? I couldn't help it because . . ."

God gave us the lowdown on Satan's and our own human nature. It's found in our hope chest, the Bible.

■ *Let the buyer beware!*

J.C.

THE GOD OF SECOND CHANCES

*He who did not spare His own Son, but
delivered Him up for us all, how shall He
not with Him also freely give us all things?*
—ROM. 8:32

If your god isn't concerned with your welfare, then fire
him." I couldn't believe my ears. Surely I hadn't heard
right. Did she really say that? You can't "fire God," can
you?

Well, wait a minute. Think about it. I've learned attitudes and ways of thinking about myself that I'm having
to let go of—attitudes that were damaged, invalid, what
some therapists call "stinking thinking." I could just as
easily have learned "stinking thinking" about God.

The God of the Old and New Testaments is a God of
grace, redemption, and mercy, not a cosmic score-
keeper anxiously awaiting our failure to measure up.
The biblical tradition is one of second chances—God
reaching out to us time and again to renew, restore, redeem.

So what's my image of God? The One who is my
greatest advocate and strongest ally? Or a harsh judge
ready to condemn and criticize? Will the real God
please stand up?

■   *Maybe learning to love myself and others is learning
first that I am God's beloved. He is my advocate, my
strength, my safety.*

D.K.

TIME TO REMEMBER

*And these stones shall be for a memorial to
the children of Israel forever.*

—JOSH. 4:7

It's a long, black wall of stone. If you look carefully, you
see that the names of all the Americans who died in the
Vietnam War are carved into its side. Remembrances in
the form of roses are placed carefully on the ground by
the names of loved ones. Tears and a hand tenderly
tracing the name of the loved one are other scenes at
the wall. People are there at the Vietnam War memorial
to remember. To feel.

God knows remembering is important. Today's verse
refers to the time when God miraculously stopped the
flow of the Jordan River so the Israelites could walk
across it on dry land. The stones from the middle of the
river were to be a memorial. They would remind the
people about the miracle God did. The memorial would
be a memory jogger of when God showed His power
and ability to help.

This might be a good day to stop and think about
God's miracles in your life. Write them down. They
don't have to be big miracles. It could be the time
someone offered you a hit, but before you could take it,
God intervened with an interruption. It could be that
time you felt all alone and then a friend called.

Once you have a list, you may want to keep adding to
it. Bring it out to read when you feel discouraged. It will
remind you of God's presence and power to help. Your
"remembrance list" will give you hope.

■ *I can make my own personal memorial to God.*

J.C.

CALIBRATING YOUR CONSCIENCE

*This being so, I myself always strive to have
a conscience without offense toward God
and [others].*   —ACTS 24:16

Always let your conscience be your guide." That's
great advice, except for one problem: Your conscience
can't always be trusted.

The little inner voice that tells you what's right and
wrong is basically a product of your environment. It re-
flects what you've been taught and what you've ob-
served, not necessarily what is true. It is possible to
suffer pangs of conscience over truly harmless behavior
and to feel perfectly comfortable with evil. And even if
your conscience does reflect a healthy set of standards,
it is easily numbed or silenced. If you ignore it long
enough, you won't be able to hear it.

But if the conscience is an unreliable guide, how can
we know what is right? That's where the Bible comes in.
Its truths have been tested over the centuries; they
really work. God's Word is a dependable yet flexible
source of direction. And here's something interesting: if
you spend a lot of time in the Bible, making it part of
your daily quiet times, it will eventually begin to work
on you. It will "calibrate" your conscience—fine tuning
it so it really does become an effective guide.

■   *Lord, shape me through your Word so that my
conscience—and all of me—becomes a reflection of
your standards.*

A.C.B.

LEARNING TO LISTEN

Listen to your father who begot you,
And do not despise your mother
when she is old.

—PROV. 23:22

When I was in high school, my parents were not very smart. At least, that is what I believed at the time. But then an amazing thing happened. The older I became, the more intelligent my parents became!

Obviously, my mom and dad were just as bright during my high-school years. I just assumed that, being older, they could not possibly understand what it meant to be a teenager.

What I gradually learned was that my parents knew far more than I gave them credit for knowing. I could have saved myself some heartache if I would have listened to them more often.

Listening to others (especially parents!) is hard. I think we all have a stubborn streak that wants to do things our own way. That may not always be bad; we learn a lot of lessons from our own mistakes. But listening to others, especially those persons older than us, can still save us much time and grief. It makes sense that older people have probably been through similar experiences to ours. Maybe they cannot directly relate to a specific problem, but they can still offer a helpful perspective. Take the time to listen to older people— even parents. Often, they are wiser than we want to believe.

■ *Learn to listen to others. Even if you do not agree,*
consider what is being said to you.

S.C.

SCHOOL'S OUT!

And further, my [daughter], be admonished by these. Of making many books there is no end, and much study is wearisome to the flesh.
—ECCLES. 12:12

Vacation. I feel relief when I hear that word. It's a break from school or work. Finals, papers, sitting at the library can be wearing. The writer of Ecclesiastes knew what he was talking about. Earlier, he wrote that there is an appointed time for everything (Eccles. 3:1). A change of pace is good. It keeps us sane and balanced.

What memory pictures does the word *vacation* develop for you? It may be hanging out at the beach late at night getting wasted. It may be of ferocious dieting to fit into that bathing suit, only to binge and purge or just starve.

Prepare for this summer by knowing where your weaknesses are and making a game plan for how you will deal with them. For some, it may involve staying away from the beach. (In general, any place you used to abuse could trigger old cravings.) For those with eating disorders, deciding to forget the bathing suit and swimming this year may help recovery.

So figure out what you won't do. Then (this is also important) figure out what you *will* do. Ask God for direction in this. Get involved with your church youth group. Attend more support groups. Learn a new way of having fun. Build new, healthy memories of summer. Refresh your body and mind!

■ *I can use my summer vacation to bring balance to my body and to my recovery.*

J.C.

WE CAN'T PICK AND CHOOSE

Teach me Your way, O LORD,
And lead me in a smooth path.
—PS. 27:11

My five-year-old daughter loves to pick and choose. When she's given a cup of mixed fruit, she picks out the maraschino cherries and leaves the rest. She picks out the hot-pink gum balls and gives the others to her little sister. She has to have the towel with the hot-pink stripes—the one with yellow just won't do.

Most of us aren't all that different. We like to pick and choose, too. It would be nice to pick and choose among the Twelve Steps—take the ones we like and leave the rest for others. But picking and choosing in recovery is not an option. We have to do it all. If doing a fourth-step inventory isn't difficult, then you probably haven't really done one. And giving up control—we keep trying to negotiate on that one: "God, I can give up this . . . but not that—anything but that." Unfortunately (or fortunately) I can't negotiate with God.

■ *Recovery requires rigorous honesty and a willingness to go to any lengths. Nothing less. Nothing else will do.*

D.K.

WHEN LAUGHTER IS A CRUTCH

> *To everything there is*
> *a season, . . .*
> *A time to weep,*
> *And a time to laugh.*
> —ECCLES. 3:1, 4

Sally is the comedienne in her family—not that there is a lot to laugh about! Her father is an alcoholic, and when he drinks he can become violent. Everyone else in the family is grateful for Sally, because she is the only one who makes their home life seem livable. She has a talent for making a joke out of nearly everything.

But there's a problem with Sally's use of humor. It has helped her survive at home, but it is also harming her relationships. Her friends complain that she jokes about matters that are serious to them. When they need her to listen, she is cutting up. And although she is always quick with a witty comment, fear and pain are building up inside. If she ever really thought about her mixed-up life, she feels she would fall apart.

Unfortunately, Sally's coping mechanism (the device she is using to survive) has become a way to hide from her problems. People will probably continue to appreciate her humor. But unless Sally learns to be serious when she needs to be, she will have a hard time growing past her pain.

Humor is a gift, an excellent gift. But it needs to be in balance with our lives. Knowing how to be serious is as important as knowing how to laugh.

■ *Lord, help me to use humor in a positive way—as a gift, not a hiding place.*

S.C.

A TRUSTWORTHY LEADER

*Women must likewise be dignified, not
malicious gossips, but temperate.*
—1 TIM. 3:11 NASB

Heidi loved to gossip. When she could get the latest
on someone, she felt powerful, and that helped cover up
some of her feelings of worthlessness. She used bits of
gossip to manipulate others and to get close to them
without really having to share herself. Eventually, however, Heidi noticed that people were avoiding her—and
even gossiping about her. They said she was two-faced,
that she couldn't be trusted. And they were right. Fortunately, Heidi decided to change. She did not like being
on the outside.

Today's verse talks about qualifications for women in
power positions. Being a gossip disqualifies one for
leadership because it breaks trust. No one wants to follow someone who cannot be trusted.

"But I'm not a leader," you protest. Everyone is a
leader in some respect. Your younger brother, sister or
cousin may look up to you and follow your example.
Friends may follow your lead. You may be on the student council or help out in church. Everyone influences
others in some way. And each of us is responsible for
how we use that power.

■ *Gossiping is an unmanageable behavior that destroys my potential for leadership.*

J.C.

RESPONSIBLE FOR MYSELF

*The son shall not bear the guilt of the father,
nor the father bear the guilt of the son. The
righteousness of the righteous shall be upon
himself, and the wickedness of the wicked
shall be upon himself.* —EZEK. 18:20

My mom's so messed up—no wonder I'm having trouble staying off drugs and stuff," complained Tiffany. "But I'm going to keep trying, 'cause I don't want to end up like her."

Hannah had the opposite problem: "You just don't know what it's like to be the only screw-up in a family of perfect people! I mean, my sister always got great grades and was really popular, and everybody thinks my parents are so great—the pillars of society. They must wonder what happened to me."

Our family environments contribute a lot to our particular pain and the way we handle it. That's why we spend so much time in recovery sorting out family issues. But learning to face up to our *own* issues is an important part of growing up—and a key to recovery. We have to reach a point where we take responsibility for ourselves—resisting the temptation either to blame our families for what we are or to waste energy trying to "live up to" their standards.

■ *Lord, thanks for reminding me that, in the end, I am responsible for me. Guide me to be the person you want me to be—not just the person my family shapes me to be.*

A.C.B.

TRUE TIME

The truthful lip shall be established forever,
But a lying tongue is but for a moment.
                                   —PROV. 12:19

When I was thirteen, my dad told me a story that I still remember today. I have told it many times to the kids I see in my office.

We had gone for a walk one day, and my dad said quietly to me, "If my watch tells me the right time every time I look at it, I will always believe it. But if for some reason it stops telling true time, I will always have to check it against another timepiece." We walked on a ways further and he finished his thought: "I will always believe you until I find out that you have lied to me. Then I will need to check your story out with someone else."

It was a short, simple, but powerful tale. There were many times in my growing-up years when I would much rather have lied to my dad than to tell him the truth. Always in my ear, however, rang those few words of wisdom. It was important for my words to be the truth. I wanted my parents to believe me, not someone else. I wanted to be the "watch" that told "true time."

Now that I am older, I look back and smile at my dad's good judgment in telling me a story. He could have said, "Don't ever lie to me, or you will get it." Instead, he chose a gentler way of getting his point across. It made a lasting impression.

■   *Are you a watch that tells true time?*

                                                        S.C.

PIT THINKING

Finally, [sisters], whatever . . . things are noble, whatever things are just, whatever things are pure, whatever things are lovely, whatever things are of good report, . . . meditate on these things. —PHIL. 4:8

I'm at the bottom of a deep, dark pit and I can't get out . . . may I sharpen my pencil?" As part of her treatment in our hospital adolescent unit, Kathy had to tack that "pit" prestatement to her every request or comment. That requirement annoyed her, to say the least, but it had an important purpose.

Underneath her alcohol addiction, Kathy also had an addiction to "hopeless-helpless" thinking. This thinking was part of her identity; she was reluctant and even afraid to give it up. It had led her to self-mutilation with a razor blade and to suicidal thinking. But Kathy could not see the connection—until she was forced to focus on it every time she spoke.

Gradually, Kathy began to see the pit of negativism in which she was trapped and to accept help in climbing out. When the time came for her discharge, she expressed fears about having a "thinking relapse." This time, instead of a prestatement, Kathy was encouraged to keep her thinking upbeat by meditating on Scripture and focusing on God's way of thinking.

■ *God, take me out of "pit thinking" into "straight thinking."*

J.C.

SOMEONE ELSE'S INSANITY

And the peace of God, which surpasses all understanding, will guard your hearts and minds through Christ Jesus.

—PHIL. 4:7

One morning I wake up, and my dad is in a great mood, joking about the breakfast cereal, asking me about something at school. The next morning he's a monster in a human disguise, ready to jump on me at the least provocation. One day I don't pick up my room and he doesn't even notice. The next day he explodes because I forgot to hang up my jacket. Life in our household can sometimes feel like walking on eggshells.

The temptation is to blame the other person, thinking, "If only he (or she) would . . ." That's the easy out—thinking the problem is with others. My life would be OK if only they didn't act so weird. But I can't change anyone but myself. When my dad gets weird, I can picture myself inside a protective bubble and remind myself, "This is not about me. I am not the cause nor the solution."

■ *God, I easily fall into blaming or "if onlys." By the power of your Spirit within me, I pray for the clarity to see where someone else stops and I start—and the wisdom to look with forgiveness and compassion on the other person.*

D.K.

GIVING UP CONTROL

*Do you not know that your body is the temple
of the Holy Spirit who is in you, whom you
have from God, and you are not your own?
For you were bought at a price; therefore
glorify God in your body.*
— 1 COR. 6:19–20

I can handle it," Kay told herself as she clutched her
knees to her chest. "I can handle it; things aren't that
bad."

It had been a horrible day. Mr. Flint would not accept
the fact that she didn't have time to get her homework
done. Amber had yelled at her. Donnie had decided he
wanted to be "just friends." And Kay felt that familiar
panicky feeling inside. She was really thinking of something else when she ate the first two cookies. Then came
more cookies . . . and a handful of tortilla chips . . . and
two cinnamon rolls. Before she knew it, the cookie
package and the chip bag were empty . . . along with a
carton of ice cream and a box of crackers. And Kay was
headed for the bathroom, full of anger and shame and
furious at herself for losing control again.

In recovery, control is a paradox. Trying to gain control of our lives in an unhealthy way—such as through
binging and purging—means losing control. And giving
up control of our lives by following the recovery road is
the only way to keep ourselves under control.

■ *Lord, being out of control is scary. But recovery can
be scary, too, because it means letting go of something that helped me cope. Give me the courage to
put control of my life where it belongs—in your
hands.*

S.C.

COOPERATING IN MY OWN RECOVERY

Work out your own salvation.
—PHIL. 2:12

Jeanine was one righteous girl. Any time the church doors opened, she was there, and her faith was an inspiration to many.

Then one day there were heavy rains in the town where Jeanine lived. The water rose, and her basement flooded. It kept raining. The waters reached the first-floor level. Jeanine looked out to see her neighbors making their escape in a lifeboat. "Get in!" they called. But she politely refused. "My hope is in God," she said.

The waters rose still higher. The Coast Guard sent a rescue boat to save Jeanine. She firmly refused, telling them her hope was in God and that He'd deliver her. By now she was being referred to as "that crazy girl."

Eventually Jeanine was forced to stand on her roof. A helicopter came by. The pilot yelled at her to grab the rope ladder. Jeanine yelled back (though politely), "No, thank you! My hope is in God, and He will save me."

Finally the flood peaked, and Jeanine drowned. St. Peter was shocked to see her in heaven. "You're not supposed to be here for another fifty years!"

Jeanine angrily snapped (not very politely this time), "I put my hope in God, but He let me down!"

St. Peter looked puzzled. "You mean the lifeboat, rescue boat, and helicopter we sent never got to you?"

■ *For a successful recovery, hope in God must be accompanied by my own efforts. I need to be involved in my own growth!*

J.C.

Keeping My Footing

He will not let your foot slip.
—PS. 121:3 NIV

One minute I was wading in the river on the big, flat rocks, waving at my friends on the shore, enjoying the rush of white water around my bare ankles. The next minute I was in the water, moving downstream, tumbling over and over. I couldn't get my footing. I couldn't catch my breath. It's a wonder I didn't drown.

Things get out of control so fast. One day I'm moving along in recovery, doing great; the next minute I'm back in the same old compulsive behavior, trying desperately to get my footing again. How does it happen?

When I think about it, the times when I tumble are the times when I get too confident in my ability to make it on my own—when I let go of God's hand to wave and say, "Look at me!" But the good news is that even when my foot slips, I can get back on firm footing by doing what I already know: asking for help, living one day at a time, and holding tight to the hand of the One who loves me best.

■ *Lord, I know that I can only stay in recovery step by step, one day at a time—and only with ongoing help and support. Help me remember that only when I hold tight to your hand can I keep from tumbling.*

A.C.B.

MAKE THE MOST OF TODAY

You do not know what will happen tomorrow. For what is your life? It is even a vapor that appears for a little time and then vanishes away.
—JAMES 4:14

The present seems to be a time frame that is tough to live in. We all have hopes for the future and regrets about the past, but the present seems to escape us. And there is nothing wrong with thinking about the future or the past except for when it clouds our vision for the present.

Too often we spend our time planning for the future but not living our lives on a day-to-day basis: "When I get to be older, I'll . . ." or "When I'm on my own, I'll . . ." Many alcoholics say, "When my life gets easier, I can stop drinking"—as though the future holds something magically different from what today has to offer.

Dwelling in the past can be detrimental as well. While it is true that we often have to go back to the past to understand the patterns in our families or to examine why we do what we do, camping out in the past is another story. It cripples our present. We cannot read today's chapter of the book if we continually reread yesterday's.

Sometimes it is difficult to stay in the present. Planning for the future is a necessity and gleaning information from the past helps us learn. But today is all we have been given. None of us are guaranteed tomorrow.

■ *Make as much of today as you can.*

S.C.

ASSOCIATED CRAVINGS

*Make straight paths for your feet, so that
what is lame may not be dislocated, but
rather be healed.* —HEB. 12:13

What places and activities do you associate with your old habits? Did you drink at parties, shoot up in the woods, binge at a certain friend's house? Whatever your associations, a successful recovery may mean avoiding the places and events that trigger them. There may not be anything wrong with those places and activities in themselves, but they can be a big problem for you because they stir up old cravings.

There is some evidence that such cravings may be biological as well as psychological. A recent public TV program featured a recovering cocaine addict who volunteered to participate in a research study on addictions. When shown a video of someone preparing and using cocaine, this addict reported feeling a rush—and researchers found changes in his brain chemistry identical to that of someone who was actually using. (After the experience, the addict asked to be detained. He knew that if he left, he would go out and buy cocaine.)

God knew about associated highs long before science could prove it—and He gives us practical direction that increases hope for recovery. In order to recover, we must be willing to change our lifestyle, to avoid not only our problem substances and behavior, but also the places and behaviors we associate with our past life.

■ *Why deliberately put rocks in your recovery path?*

J.C.

OUT OF THE DEEPEST DARK

Lord, I believe; help my unbelief!
—MARK 9:24

Ever noticed how much brighter the stars at night are when you get away from the city? A fascinating phenomenon: city lights dull the brilliance of stars. Get even thirty miles away from a major metropolitan area, and the sky seems almost luminescent, stars flickering like huge flecks of glitter someone threw up in the night sky.

Confusion, depression, discouragement can feel like a shroud of darkness—suffocating, endless, oppressive. We all have times when we think, "Things will never change; I'll always be this way." We feel as if darkness has descended and we'll never see the light. In those times of darkness, going to my support group can be one of the most helpful things I can do. Safe with those I know and trust, I can remember the darkness of times past and the faithfulness of God who has seen me through. He hasn't brought me this far to leave me where I am now.

One more thing. Darkness enshrouds, but bright light blinds. We don't need to see it all. Christ doesn't say He'll take the dark times away; He says He'll be the light shining through the darkness, giving us enough light to take one step at a time.

■ *We only need enough light for this moment.*

D.K.

End of take 11

THE COST OF REBELLION

Therefore whoever resists the authority resists the ordinance of God, and those who resist will bring judgment on themselves.
—ROM. 13:2

Heather wanted everything to go her way. Her parents were frustrated with her beyond belief. "She has always been a strong-willed child," her mother said. "Maybe we were wrong in the way that we disciplined her."

Although Heather lived at home, she did not respect her parents' rules. She came and went when she wanted. If her parents said she was not allowed to go somewhere, she would leave anyway. She had lost respect for authority and believed she could be self-governing. But Heather lost other possessions in the process: her parents' trust, her siblings' compassion, her friends' belief in her—not to mention her job, her driver's license, and her use of the car.

Heather did not realize that the price she was paying was much greater than the illusion of independence she felt she had obtained. Her rebellion had cost her more than she ever dreamed of.

Can you relate to Heather? Part of growing up is becoming our own person. It's OK if we do not always agree with our parents. (They probably did not always agree with their parents.) However, if we try to gain our independence by rebelling, we most likely won't gain much more than a pocket full of conflicts and a heart full of aches.

■ *Count the costs of your actions. You may be paying more than it is worth.*

S.C.

OWNING MY ANGER

*So when He had looked around at them with
anger, being grieved by the hardness of their
hearts, [Jesus] said to the man, "Stretch out
your hand." . . . And his hand was restored.*
—MARK 3:5

Isn't anger a sin?" Diane asked. She thought that
every time she felt anger, she had an "anger spirit" in
her—almost as if she needed to be exorcised of an anger demon. (Since she had never dabbled with the oc-
cult, this was not likely.) Because Diane persisted in
seeing anger as an "outside force," she failed to own up
to her anger. Instead, she tried to run from her anger by
ignoring and "stuffing" it. As a result, it grew inside of
her and spilled over in the form of sarcastic comments
and rude remarks. By then, the anger did feel as if it
had a life of its own.

Anger is not good or bad. It just is. Anger is energy
you can use in good or bad ways. Jesus used the energy
of His anger at the Pharisees to heal a man's hand. He
also used it to drive out the merchants who were turning
temple into a shopping mall (see Matt. 21:12–17; Mark
11:15–19).

Diane had used her anger energy to run away from
home. Stuffing her anger had slowly caused her to lose
control of her behavior, and her life had become unmanageable. When we give up control by refusing to
"own" our anger, we give Satan an opportunity to add
more chaos to our lives.

■ *I need to "own" my anger and then take care of it
on a daily basis—before it "takes care" of me.*

J.C.

MY PLACE IN THE MIDDLE

But the LORD said to me:
"Do not say, 'I am a youth,'
For you shall go to all to whom
I send you." —JER. 1:7

Sometimes I get tired of feeling stuck in the middle—not a child, not yet an adult. If I act silly and have fun, someone's bound to tell me to grow up. (They really say that when I do something stupid!) But if I want to do something like drive out of town for a concert, they say I'm not old enough. People are always asking me what I'm going to do with my life (as if I'm not doing anything yet). But then they tell me to enjoy myself because these are the best years I'll ever have—and that *really* worries me!

But this verse helps me realize that, no matter what others may think of me, God takes me seriously. He has a plan for me—one that doesn't have to wait until I'm old enough for a driver's license or a full-time job. As I continue to lean on Him in recovery, He is growing me up into the person I was meant to be. And best of all, He's doing it right now.

■ *Lord, thank you for taking me seriously. As I continue in recovery, keep growing me into being the person you want to speak for you.*

A.C.B.

FAITHFUL IN LITTLE THINGS

[She] who is faithful in what is least is
faithful also in much; and [she] who is unjust
in what is least is unjust also in much.
—LUKE 16:10

It's just not fair! I'm not using any more. Why can't they trust me?" Molly's angry outburst sounded familiar. I had heard it many times from teenagers who have abused their parents' trust. Molly had been an expert at slipping out her bedroom window to join her friends. She had skipped school so many days she was eventually suspended and had also been caught driving without a license. On several occasions, Molly had even managed to sneak into the house, drunk, without her parents noticing.

Of course, they did eventually notice—and admitted her to a hospital for treatment. And once she was released, Molly expected her parents to automatically return all her privileges to her. She was furious when they wouldn't trust her. She learned, however, that it takes time to rebuild something that has been torn down. She had to prove her trustworthiness in little things—not skipping out on chores, doing her homework, letting her parents know where she was, and following through on her Twelve-Step work. Sometimes she chafed at these mundane tasks, but she worked hard at being faithful. Gradually, she earned back the trust she had forfeited.

■ *Broken trust is repaired by faithfulness in little*
  things.

S.C.

OUR HEAVENLY DADDY

> *You did not receive the spirit of bondage
> again to fear, but you received the Spirit
> of adoption by whom we cry out, "Abba,
> Father."*
> —ROM. 8:15

The warm family car slows down, the motor quieting.
Headlights blink off. My mother's voice from the front
passenger seat: "Honey, wake up, we're home." It's
snowy and cold outside. I pretend I'm still sleeping. My
father's voice: "Don't wake her up; I'll carry her."

My father takes me in strong arms and wraps me in a
car blanket. We crunch through the snow quickly because my father can walk faster and is more sure-footed
than I am. I relax because I know I'm safe. I'm in my
daddy's arms.

Not everyone has a childhood memory of such security. Some don't even know who their father is. Some
fathers may be physically present but lost in the nether-
world of alcohol, buried behind a newspaper, "zoned
out" in front of the TV, or angry and abusive.

Whatever the childhood memory, all of us have the
chance to be adopted into a secure, loving family whose
Father is God. He is a Power greater than ourselves, but
He is not abusive or neglectful. We do not have to fear
that He will hurt us or forget us. His goal for us is a
return to sanity—the sanity of knowing someone loves
us and will take care of us. For you see, He not only is
"Father"; He is also "Daddy." That's what the word
Abba means.

■ *Heavenly Father, help me to trust you as my Abba,
my Daddy.*

J.C.

THE CALL OF THE MALL

Oh, how great is Your goodness, . . .
Which You have prepared for those
who trust in You. —PS. 31:19

I saw it on the rack in the front of the store. It had "me" written all over it, and I had to have it. It was almost as if a sign, visible only to me, was flashing and saying, "Buy me! Buy me!" So I did. Then I got home, pulled it out of the bag, and thought, "What did I think was so hot about *that?* I hate it. I can't believe I bought it."

Funny how buying something I don't really need can be as compulsive an action as any other addictive behavior. I have a whole closet full of clothes that fit (well, at least *most* of them fit). Buying something new does temporarily distract me from disappointment, worries, sadness, or loneliness, but the distraction is short-lived. Then back comes the nagging reality I was trying to avoid.

The only failsafe I have is the power of Jesus Christ— ever faithful, ever present, ever loving. I can't eat, drink, drug, or spend myself into happiness. But I can *grow* into happiness—by nurturing myself in prayer, by seeking His healing presence, and by listening to His gentle guidance.

■ *Lord, when I feel the "call of the mall," call me back to sanity, call me back to you. And when I'm taunted by the temptation to spend money I don't have, let me remember I have everything I need— maybe not everything I want, but everything I need.*

D.K.

THE RIGHT FRIENDS

Become followers of what is good.
—1 PETER 3:13

Sandie always believed herself to be a leader. After all, she was a cheerleader and a class officer. She was involved in a church youth group and many times was asked to be in charge of an event. Sandie was a leader in many ways. But she was also a follower. She had a tendency to go along with what her friends did just because she did not want to feel left out.

One time, for instance, Sandie and two friends went shopping. Her friends decided to shoplift a couple of swimsuits. Not wanting to appear self-righteous, Sandie slipped a swimsuit into her pocketbook, too. Just as they made their way through the aisles and out the door, a security guard stopped them. Sandie was caught red-handed. A flood of embarrassment rushed over her, then fear. What would her parents say? Would she be arrested? Immediately she regretted what she had done, but it was too late to undo it.

Peer pressure is difficult to withstand—that's why it is called "pressure." But peer pressure is not always negative. It can get us involved in positive things or cause us to reevaluate a negative choice or thought. Whether it is positive or negative depends a lot on the kinds of peers with which you surround yourself.

■ *Are your friends a good influence on you?*

S.C.

GOD'S WORD FOR A RELAPSE

God is our refuge and strength,
A very present help in trouble.
—PS. 46:1

Relapse is trouble—trouble we make for ourselves. But God still promises to be present to help us through it. We can sense His help when we read the Bible. His Word strengthens us and gives us directions on how to get back on track and prevent a relapse from snowballing:

(1) Commit to sobriety for the next twenty-four hours. In Matthew 6:34, Jesus advises us to take life one day at a time.

(2) Attend a support group within the next twenty-four hours and go as often as you need thereafter. Galatians 6:2 says to bear one another's burdens. Get some people to help you bear this burden. You need both support and accountability.

(3) Tell your sponsor, therapist, or a trusted adult what happened. Figure out with him or her what triggered the relapse so there's less chance of its happening again. Proverbs 26:11 says if we don't do this we are like a dog returning to its vomit.

(4) Read the Bible and a devotional (like this one) every day. Psalm 37:31 promises our steps won't slip if we make God's Word a priority.

(5) Rework the Twelve Steps, starting with step one. These steps are all based on Scripture.

■ *Pray for wisdom to know how to apply God's Word after a relapse.*

J.C.

YOU DON'T HAVE TO WANT TO

I press on, that I may lay hold of that for
which Christ Jesus has also laid hold of me.
                                    —PHIL. 3:12

"Just do it" advise the athletic shoe ads. They're talking about working out. (Well, actually, they're talking about buying shoes, but they make a good point about working out.) If you want to stay in shape, you have to exercise even when you don't feel like exercising. So sometimes it's better not even to think about it—you "just do it" because you know it works.

A friend of mine elaborated on that theme. She said, "You don't have to want to! All you have to do is cross your arms and do a sit-up." She didn't mean attitude isn't important. She meant that sometimes, when you don't have a lot of extra energy, it's a relief just to do what you have to do without worrying about whether you want to or not. Enthusiasm makes things easier, but it's not essential.

I find that advice helps in recovery, too, especially on days when everything seems hard. When I don't *feel like* journaling or going to my support group or staying straight, I tell myself, "You don't have to want to. You just have to do it." And that's usually enough to keep me going until I can come up with the "want to" again.

■ *Lord, thank you that recovery works—even when I*
don't want to. I trust you enough to "just do it" on
the days when my enthusiasm wanes.

                                              A.C.B.

SOMEONE YOU CAN TRUST

To You, O LORD, I lift up my soul.
O my God, I trust in You.
—PS. 25:1–2

Throughout our lives, people will fail us. Somehow, some way, we will be disappointed. If you haven't already experienced being let down, chances are you will before long.

Mandy's parents were always letting her down. They would tell her they would attend her volleyball game and not show, or promise to pick her up at a certain time and be forty-five minutes late, or say she could go to a special event and then forget they had ever talked about it. Mandy learned not to trust her parents' word, because it usually wasn't trustworthy. But unfortunately, she extended that lack of trust to everyone else. "If I just don't count on anybody, then nobody can disappoint me" became Mandy's motto.

It's true that there are people we can't trust. But it is also true that there is One who will never fail us. We can learn to trust God. He has proven Himself time and again. In the midst of some circumstances, it may seem that He has abandoned us, but time proves Him dependable.

Mandy is learning to rely on God, and she has found Him faithful. She is also learning that she can rely on some people as well. Their word is good, and they will keep their promises.

■ *God, please help me to have the faith to trust you and the wisdom to discern who is trustworthy and who isn't.*

S.C.

WHEN GOD SAYS NO

Certainly God has heard me;
He has attended to the voice
of my prayer.
　　　　　　　—PS. 66:19

The bus seemed to crawl in the rush-hour traffic. It was 5:15 P.M. The Catholic bookstore would close at 5:30. I wanted to get my Catholic mother-in-law a crucifix. Her birthday was coming soon, and I could not come this way again for a while. Not being Catholic, I didn't know of another store where I could buy the kind of cross she wanted. I prayed I could get that cross.

The clock read 5:25. Just in time! I saw the black skirt of a nun hurriedly disappear into the store . . . and lock it. I knocked on the door. *She has to hear me,* I thought. *I just saw her go in. Besides, it's not even 5:30.* I knocked harder. I yelled out, "It's really important for me to get something. I know exactly what I want. I won't take long." Silence. I fumed all the way home.

A couple of days later, my husband came home smiling. "Look what I got for Mom," he crowed. There in a black velvet box was the most beautiful crucifix. On its back was engraved "Blessed Pope John Paul II." My husband had actually met the Pope through his business affairs, and the Pope had given him the crucifix.

God's loud "no" to me in the form of a slammed door made sense now. A crucifix from the Pope certainly made a better birthday present than one from an ordinary store.

■　*God says no because he has something different and better in mind for you.*

　　　　　　　　　　　　　　　　　　　　　J.C.

WHO TO LISTEN TO

*I am the good shepherd. . . . My sheep hear
My voice, and I know them, and they
follow Me.*
—JOHN 10:14, 27

My mom tells me one thing. My friends tell me another. My sister tells me something else. Everyone is so quick to have an opinion about what I should do. Everyone so readily gives advice about things I ought to do, should do, or must do. Listening to conflicting voices leaves me churning inside.

But I really have only one voice to seek, one voice to heed—that's the voice within. Funny how the only voice I really need to hear—the one without the "oughts," "shoulds," and "musts"—is the quietest, the gentlest voice. That's the voice of God. His is the voice that says, "Listen to the stillness within." He doesn't give advice. He doesn't force or manipulate. He waits until I'm ready, then ever so gently leads me to answers already waiting within me.

■ *God, quiet the conflicting voices which sometimes come at me from all sides, so I can hear the only voice that matters—yours.*

D.K.

I AM WILLING

I can do all things through Christ who strengthens me. —PHIL. 4:13

Do you know anyone who uses "I can't" as an excuse? You may have done it yourself a time or two.

In a sense, of course, "I can't" is really true. On our own, without God and others, we can't make a go of our lives. Before we can make any progress in recovery, we have to learn to depend on Him. But I have to chuckle when I hear some people say "I can't." Nine times out of ten, they really mean "I won't": "I won't try anymore." "I won't give that up." "I won't stop acting this way." For them, "I can't" becomes a self-fulfilling prophecy.

A good friend of mine uses a phrase that I have incorporated into my vocabulary: "I have the willingness to . . ." That phrase eliminates the crippling sound of "I can't." God can use people who are willing to be available. A heart that has an "I'll try" sign usually has a successful owner.

In recovery, you need to pack away the words "I can't" and give them a rest. And as you change your vocabulary, open up your heart to the Lord and to change itself. You'll be amazed at what you can do.

■ *Lord, show me the difference between the "cannots" and the "will nots" in my life. Help me to have a willing heart.*

S.C.

TINTED GLASSES

> *I am the light of the world. [She] who follows*
> *Me shall not walk in darkness, but have the*
> *light of life.*
> —JOHN 8:12

Try an experiment. Wear your sunglasses in the house. Walk from room to room. Try to read, write, or watch TV. It's hard to do anything because you can't see very well, but it is easier to function in the rooms with brighter lights.

In one sense we all have sunglasses on—glasses that tint the way we see the world. Some people have rejection glasses. Everything that happens to them is filtered through lenses of rejection. If their mother has a frown, they automatically think they did something wrong. If they say "hi" to a friend and the friend doesn't answer, they think the friend is ignoring them on purpose. (That their friend may not have heard them doesn't occur to them.)

Some have failure glasses. They can only see what they did wrong. Sue made a birthday cake for her friend. It came out slightly lopsided, but she used extra frosting to level it out. It looked and tasted great, but she kept pointing out how lopsided it was. No one cared about it but her.

There are many other types of glasses: fear of abandonment, blaming others, control. But Jesus, who is our bright light, helps us to see our lives more accurately. The closer we get to the Light, the clearer our vision will be.

■ *Jesus, reveal to me what "glasses" I'm wearing.*

J.C.

SAFE FROM EL DESTRUCTO

Do not lay up for yourselves treasures on earth, where moth and rust destroy and where thieves break in and steal; but lay up for yourselves treasures in heaven.
—MATT. 6:19–20

Our puppy's name is Elliott, but we've started calling him El Destructo. That's because he'll chew anything he can get his mouth on—and I mean anything! He's gone through shoes, socks, books, plastic bottles. Last night I caught him mangling a paper clip. My small daughter has learned that none of her toys are safe on the floor. No matter how valuable or meaningful something is to us, Elliott sees it as a chew-toy.

Looking at life from Elliott's perspective helps me understand what Jesus meant about "laying up treasures on earth." If I look to earthly "treasures"—including substances, money, clothes, or even popularity—for my comfort or security or fun, I'm depending on something that is about as dependable as a puppy's chew-toy. Chances are, all I'll end up with are shredded shoes and mangled paper clips.

But if I stake my faith in spiritual reality—such as God's unfailing love and His ability to do for me what I cannot do for myself—I'm trusting in something both safe and dependable. I'm laying up treasure in heaven—building a life that is safe from any "El Destructo" that comes along.

■ *Jesus, thank you for showing me what is dependable and what isn't. Help me make the choice to depend on you.*

A.C.B.

MORE THAN MEETS THE EYE

Now faith is the substance of things hoped for,
the evidence of things not seen.
—HEB. 11:1

Faith is a paradoxical concept. How can something that is hoped for have substance? How can it be evidence when it is unseen? When we live in a world that says "I'll believe it when I see it," faith often gets squashed out.

What does it truly mean to have faith? Is faith just wishful thinking—or a positive attitude? Those are tough questions, but to live a life of faith is even more difficult.

Faith means choosing to recognize that there is more to life than the naked eye can see. It is like the backstage of a play. We may not see what goes on behind the scenes, but we know there is a flurry of activity—and eventually we see the results.

Faith involves a confidence in God's character—a confidence that He is still working even when we can't tell that anything is going on. Faith entails peace as well. When we trust in the One who is greater than us, we realize we are not all there is to this life. Just grasping that truth can relax a restless heart.

■ *Father, teach me what it means to have faith in you,*
in others, and in myself.

S.C.

LIKE A GENTLE RAIN

*And the LORD will . . . satisfy your desire
in scorched places, . . .
And you will be like a watered garden, . . .
whose water do not fail.*

—ISA. 58:11 NASB

Her feelings were like scorched leaves in a summer drought—shriveled and dried out. Of course, she did not know this. She thought she felt fine . . . until that day. They were meeting informally in someone's house. Their songs of praise were from the heart and directed heavenward. As if to reciprocate, the heavens poured out a gentle, warm rain of a spiritual presence.

She started crying tears of joy and could not stop. The tears seemed to soften a part of her heart that had grown hard through neglect and abuse. The frozen, barren ground of her life was being readied for future fullness.

At one time you numbed out your feelings so you could survive. Maybe the pain of sexual or physical abuse or never feeling quite good enough was too much. But now God has you in recovery. And part of His program involves unfreezing your ability to feel. He wants to connect with you on both a thinking and feeling level. God wants to be in relationship with you and satisfy your desire in the scorched places of your life. Having this living relationship with Him fills the emptiness left by your addictions. Keeping this relationship current will help keep you moving in recovery.

■ *God's love softens the hard ground of my heart so He can plant a new life for me.*

J.C.

BE SLOW TO JUDGE

For [God] knows the secrets of the heart.
—PS. 44:21

She always wears "polished apple" clothes. You know. Those neat little collars that button all the way up to the neck. Everything matches. Even when she dresses casually, she looks like something that walked off the pages of a magazine. She's also arrogant and obnoxious, and she always acts as if she's better than everybody else. I always feel just a little rumpled when she's around.

But I don't know what's inside her head or her heart. Just because she hasn't done some of the things I've done—that doesn't mean she's immune to pain. For all I know, she may be living in her own religious prison. Maybe her "do-good" behavior is really a way of trying to measure up to some invisible standard. Maybe her arrogance is really insecurity—like the way I act when I'm trying to impress someone. Maybe what irritates me about her is what irritates me about me. Maybe she and I aren't so different after all. Anyway, I might not like her, but I can still be Christ's person to her.

■   *Christ commanded us to love one another. He didn't say we had to* like *everyone—just treat each person with respect and compassion.*

D.K.

CLAIM YOUR FREEDOM

*If the Lord calls you, and you are a slave,
remember that Christ has set you free from
the awful power of sin; . . . remember that
you are now a slave of Christ.*
—1 COR. 7:22 TLB

When you have an addiction, you are a slave of it.
Slave Mistress Addiction has no respect for your body.
She will run your body into the ground until it dies. An
imbalance of electrolytes from binging and purging
courts a heart attack. Alcohol kills brain cells and damages the liver. Heroin needles can transmit AIDS, hepatitis, and other life-threatening infections. In spite of
these consequences, the slave will continue to obey the
mistress. Unless . . .

Jesus died to set us free from all of that. The only
catch in declaring our freedom is that we have to transfer ownership of ourselves from Mistress Addiction to
Jesus. This is what giving ourselves up to a Higher
Power is all about. Trying to be our own boss just leads
us back to Mistress Addiction. If you have tried to be
your own boss, you know how that goes.

Independence Day is a good day to declare your
freedom in Jesus. He gives you freedom from anything
that enslaves you: guilt, addictions, inferiority feelings,
past pain, whatever. Because you are His, He will do for
you "exceedingly abundantly above all that" you "ask
or think" (Eph. 3:20).

■ *Jesus, help me claim the freedom you offer me as my
inheritance.*

J.C.

EVERYTHING BUT

> *"Everything is permissible for me"—but not
> everything is beneficial. "Everything is
> permissible for me"—but I will not be
> mastered by anything.*
>
> —1 COR. 6:12 NIV

What a great verse for people in recovery! It reminds us that the problem with addictions is not really the external behavior, but the spiritual reality it reveals. The problem is not really alcohol or food or credit cards or people. The problem is me—my willingness to give up anything, even my freedom in Christ, to cover up my pain!

Everything is permissible for me. What a wild thought! Even a six-pack? Even an eating binge? Even a day at the mall with a purse full of credit cards?

Everything is permissible for me—but . . .

Because I have this tendency to hide from my feelings through drinking or binging or shopping, not everything is beneficial for me. Because, left to myself, I invariably surrender my freedom to substances or behaviors, I must depend on God to keep from being mastered by these things.

■ *Thank you, God, for keeping me going as I learn about what it means to be free in you.*

A.C.B.

Because narrow is the gate and difficult is
the way which leads to life, and there are
few who find it. —MATT. 7:14

Alicia wanted a way out of her problems. She tried manipulating others. She would make them feel guilty if they did not do what she wanted. She blamed others for her actions. If they had been more caring, then she would not have acted poorly. She became irresponsible with her schoolwork, chores, money, friends—just about everything. The more irresponsible she became, the more responsible (and frustrated) others had to become to compensate for her.

Deep inside, Alicia wanted to get better. She just did not want to do the hard work. She was attempting to reach a destination, but avoiding the direct route. Instead she constantly took detours and uncharted paths, looking for an easier way. Repeatedly she ran into obstacles.

Alicia had to learn that there are no easy roads to recovery. She was making it harder on herself by trying to avoid the path she needed to take.

In recovery, "the only way out is through." The road is narrow at times, but you must travel it. Go through the pain, not around it. Get to the healthier side.

■ *Choose today to take the narrow road. The destination is worth it.*

S.C.

PULLING TOGETHER

*Do not be unequally yoked together with
unbelievers.*
                                    —2 COR. 6:14

Imagine running a two-legged race with someone who is much shorter or taller than you. Or with someone whose timing is off. Or with someone who has a different idea of how to win than you do.

Let's take it further. Imagine that your leg is tied to a baby's. Or to a drunk's. Or to a dead person's.

God tells us not to tie our legs or get "yoked" with unbelievers. A yoke is a wooden frame that joins two animals (such as oxen) at the heads or necks so they can work together. The animals have to be the same—two oxen or two horses. Otherwise, the yoke rubs and chafes. Work proceeds slowly, if at all.

A yoke in human terms may be any long-term commitment in which two people have to work together, such as in a marriage. God wants us to only "yoke up" with spiritually alive people—other believers.

Let's take it further. If recovery is your work, you will want to avoid being yoked with people who hinder your progress. Being close friends with anyone who is actively using will definitely be an unequal yoke.

On the positive side, yoking with other believers can strengthen your understanding of God. And tying yourself to God can help you run a marathon.

■ *Pick your working partners with a view to moving
ahead.*

                                                    J.C.

RELEASING THOSE WE LOVE

> *[I] do not cease to give thanks for you, making mention of you in my prayers: that the God of our Lord Jesus Christ, . . . may give to you the spirit of wisdom and . . . knowledge . . . [that] the eyes of your understanding [may be] enlightened; that you may know what is the hope of His calling, . . . and what is the exceeding greatness of His power.* —EPH. 1:16–19

Someone I love is screwed up. Trying so desperately to fill the emptiness inside. Battling with depression. Her family is dysfunctional, but she doesn't see it. She doesn't *want* to see it. Maybe she's afraid that if she admits her family isn't perfect, she's admitting that she's not perfect. She can't see that she's not responsible for the craziness in others.

To do nothing, to stand aside and watch someone you love spiral into a deeper darkness, is tough. But knowing my life is in God's hands gives me the ability to release her to the same caring hands. I can't fix it, change it, or heal it for her. In recovery I've learned to detach myself from another's pain, to release those I love and turn them over daily in prayer to the healing power of Jesus Christ.

An anonymous writer wrote the words, "I love you. I bless you. I release you to your own indwelling presence of God." I can release those I love and entrust them to God's care.

■ *God, you know better than I the inner pain of those I love. Hold them close in your care and bring them into your everlasting arms.*

D.K.

YOUR HEART IS LISTENING

*Let the words of my mouth and the
    meditation of my heart
Be acceptable in Your sight,
O LORD, my strength and my redeemer.*
—PS. 19:14

What you tell yourself matters! If you are in the habit of belittling yourself, please stop. Your heart is listening to what you are saying. If you run yourself down, pretty soon you'll start believing your own criticisms, and your self-esteem will plummet.

Be aware that you react to your thoughts. If you tell yourself that you are stupid, weird, ugly, or awful, you will tend to live up to these derogatory beliefs. You may decide not to try hard on a test because you believe you cannot make a good grade, anyway. Or you may conclude you are not "good enough" to have close friends. Possibly you will withdraw from getting involved in activities because you believe no one would want to talk to you.

Everyone has faults—that is a reality. But you need to be in the practice of evaluating yourself constructively. If there is an area that needs improvement, work on it, but don't use it as a reason to cut yourself down. And be sure to evaluate your strengths honestly as well. Remind yourself of your good qualities. God has graciously bestowed unique characteristics to everyone. You do not need to have the same attributes as someone else. You have your own special set.

■ *Watch your self-talk. What you say to yourself influences how you feel and what you do.*

S.C.

THE ONLY SAFE SEX

For the turning away of the
simple will slay them,
And the complacency of fools will
destroy them. —PROV. 1:32

Have you heard the "safe sex" lie? The lie says a condom will protect you against venereal disease and AIDS. But there are already reports of people contracting AIDS even though they used a condom. Condoms can slip or leak. Yes, sex with a condom is safer than sex with no protection—but it is not really safe.

The only safe sex is between two people who never had any other sexual partners. When you have sex with one person, you also are having sex with everyone that person has had sex with. A male can be carrying a venereal disease and not have any noticeable symptoms. He can infect his female partner unknowingly. Venereal warts can lie dormant in females and later cause a tumor in the reproductive system. Many of these tumors are associated with cancer of the cervix and vagina.

The facts are scary. These days, being ignorant can kill you! It's also dangerous to be unconcerned or complacent about these facts.

God, however, promises that if we listen to him, we "shall live securely" and "at ease from the dread of evil" (Prov. 1:33 NASB). What does He say about sex? He says have one partner and keep the sex in marriage. Listening to Him is the only route to safe sex.

■ *My hope for safe sex lies in following God's truth about sexual behavior.*

J.C.

GROW UP!

Brothers, stop thinking like children. In regard to evil be infants, but in your thinking be adults. —1 COR. 14:20 NIV

"Grow up!" How many times have you heard it? And does it ever seem that the definition of "grow up" depends on what the other person wants? "Oh, grow up! (Everybody does it!)" "Grow up. (Don't get out of line.)" "Grow up. (We're depending on you to hold this family together.)" "Grow up. (Be boring.)"

This "grow up" scripture also has a specific slant, but a healthy one. In a sense, it summarizes the whole recovery process. "In regard to evil" (including our addictions and the pain that drives them) we need to be like little kids, totally dependent on our heavenly Parent to fill our needs and help us grow. At the same time, we need to develop the mental maturity to face ourselves honestly—to stop playing the childish mind games that keep us trapped.

It's not easy. Growing up never is. But it helps to remember that God, unlike some of the other people in our lives, has nothing but good in mind for us. And He doesn't just *tell us* to grow up. As we depend on Him one day at a time, He *grows us up*—into strong, sane (but never boring) maturity.

■ *God, today I turn to you, one more time, to get me through. I trust you to provide the childlike faith and the mental toughness I need to "grow up" in you.*

A.C.B.

A GOOD WORK

Being confident of this very thing, that He who has begun a good work in you will complete it until the day of Jesus Christ.
—PHIL. 1:6

Some days I feel like a total failure. It is as if I have the reverse of the Midas touch; everything *I* touch turns to mud! No matter what I say, it comes out wrong. No matter what I attempt, I mess it up. On those days, I cannot wait to get home so I can stop worrying about my next failure.

When I have one of "those days," it's easy to tell myself what an idiot I am. I begin to wonder why the Lord placed me here and to question whether He really knows what He is doing. How could He use such an incompetent person?

After I have my pity party for the day, I try to remind myself of some facts. First, it is *Christ* who has "begun a good work" in me. He is not asking me to be perfect, just available for His use. I also try and remember that it is a *good* work and not a shabby one—and that He will complete what He started.

What a relief! Christ is responsible for what He has begun, and He will see it through to the end—even if I fail!

■ *Thank you God for beginning—and completing—a good work in me.*

S.C.

KNOW WHO YOU ARE

The Spirit Himself bears witness with our spirit that we are children of God, and if children, then heirs—heirs with God and joint heirs with Christ. —ROM. 8:16–17

If a stranger came to my door and asked to borrow my car, I'd look at him like he was crazy and close the door in his face.

But if my daughter came up to me and asked, "Mom, may I borrow your car?" the chances are good that I'll say yes. She can also take my membership card to the local video store and rent some movies.

Without my car and card, my daughter's ability to go places and check out tapes would be limited. But she can do those things because she's my daughter.

Likewise, because God is our Father, we can do more things. On our own power, our recovery can be uncertain. But with God's power it's a sure thing.

That doesn't mean recovery won't be difficult or that we won't ever relapse. But it does mean we have a heavenly Parent who will help us if we ask. Know who you are, daughter of the Almighty God!

■ *When I know who I am, I'm more likely to act like it.*

J.C.

TURNING THE VOLUME DOWN

To everything there is a season, . . .
A time to keep silence.
And a time to speak.
—ECCLES. 3:1, 7

I live in the age of audiovisual assault—and I love it! No matter where I go, where I am, or what I'm doing, I've got electronic gadgetry to keep me company. Give me a great sound system and I'm happy. Whether I'm getting dressed, studying, sitting in the dentist's office, or shopping, filling the air with sound is the norm. Silence is uncomfortable; it feels like something is missing. And silence doesn't come easily. Silence comes only with a deliberate decision to seek an absence of external sounds.

Music can usher God in or drive Him out. Music can be an experience of beauty, passion, and fullness—or it can be head clutter. Only I know the difference. Only I know if I'm welcoming God in or tuning Him out. Either way, there comes a time for silence. If the silence is uncomfortable, then there's probably something in the silence I need to hear.

God doesn't drum His way into my life. He comes only at my invitation. He doesn't turn the volume of His voice up—He waits for me to turn the volume of my life down.

■ *God, learning to listen to the silence—to hear your voice—is a new thing for me. I'm not sure I know how to do it or even if I want to. Give me the willingness to give it a try.*

D.K.

THINKING AHEAD

You ran well. Who hindered you from
obeying the truth?
　　　　　　　　　　　　　　—GAL. 5:7

The apostle Paul often compared the business of living a successful life to that of running a race—and the comparison certainly applies to recovery as well. When a runner trains for a race, she has a lot of things to consider—the right food, the best shoe, the optimum training schedule. Most important, she needs to prepare mentally, anticipating possible obstacles. After all, it doesn't do much good to run well if you stumble and fall along the way.

Mental preparation is also vital to successful recovery. We need to think ahead and consider what could trip us up. For instance, there are usually people in our lives who will not applaud our recovery efforts and may even sabotage them. They may deliberately leave our problem substance where we can find it. They may try to coax or manipulate: "Oh, come on, don't be so self-righteous!" It just takes a little temptation, a little rationalization, and pow! we've blown it.

The good news, of course, is that stumbling doesn't mean we've blown the race. With God's help, we can get back in stride, keeping alert so that next time we can avoid the things that tripped us up.

■　*Lord, keep me aware of possible obstacles as I run*
　this challenging race in my life.

　　　　　　　　　　　　　　　　　　　S.C.

GOD'S STANDARD OF APPROVAL

*For by [faith], the men [and women] of old
gained approval.* —HEB. 11:2 NASB

She was a hooker. It was her last trick of the day. Her customer talked of some who were trying to take over the country. "They claim their God gave them *our* land. What a nerve!" Her heart skipped a beat when he mentioned the foreigners' God. Who was this God? Later, she found out from two foreigners who came to her house as spies. They said their God had promised this land to their forefather, Abraham, and now it was time to cash in on this inheritance. If she believed them, she could share in the reward.

She did. Her name was Rahab, and she lived in Jericho—you know, where "the walls came tumbling down." Her inheritance? She became the great-great-grandmother of King David of Israel (Ruth 4:21–22). And she was Jesus' great-great-et cetera-grandmother (Matt. 1). Rahab the prostitute did not get much approval in her hometown. But God gave her His approval—not for being a prostitute, but for having faith.

God's standard of approval is different from ours. If someone does well in school or athletics or looks attractive, we give them approval. But God is pleased when we act on what He says. Doing that means we believe Him. We believe He's not a liar and won't steer us wrong. Rahab had that kind of faith, because her identity was changed from prostitute to royal mother of kings.

■ *Faith is the way to get God's approval and claim my new identity.*

J.C.

ENOUGH

*And God is able to make all grace abound
toward you, that you, always having all
sufficiency in all things, have an abundance
for every good work.* —2 COR. 9:8

Sometimes I think the root cause of my compulsive behavior is the gut-deep fear that I'm not going to get what I need. That there's just not enough love or comfort or respect to go around, and I'm going to get the short end of the stick. Why do I begin thinking about a snack before I've even finished dinner? Why do I get jealous? Why do I get so miserable and fearful that I try to dull my feelings with my substance of choice? Partly because I'm terrified my needs won't be met.

I feel that way, of course, because I *have* gotten the short end of the stick in the past. I *have* been short-changed on love or comfort or respect—usually because the people I trusted to meet those needs were imperfect human beings struggling with their own problems.

And that's why I need the message of this verse. There *is* enough to go around. If I depend on God, He's going to see that I get the love and comfort and esteem I need—and more. I don't have to obsess about where my next "love hit" is coming from. In fact, I can even give some away!

■ *Lord, thank you for people who help fill my needs. But remind me, especially when I'm feeling desperate, that you are the real source of getting my needs met—and you are enough.*

A.C.B.

Riding the Waves

*Call upon Me in the day of trouble;
I will deliver you, and you shall
glorify Me.* —PS. 50:15

If you have ever been to the beach, you have seen waves. Large or small, they roll in continually—so swimming in the ocean is largely a matter of learning to deal with waves. If you are not paying attention, a wave may wash over you or even knock you down, and another wave may hit while you are trying to get up. If you do not know how to relax and go with the waves, swimming in the sea can be a frightening experience.

Sometimes trouble floods our lives like a wave. It hits when we least expect it, and another "wave" may wash in before we have recovered from the first one. Sometimes we may even feel we are drowning. And unless we learn to "ride the waves," we really are in danger of sinking.

Trouble in our lives is just as inevitable as waves in the ocean. And learning how to stay above trouble may be difficult. At times we bring troubles upon ourselves. Other times we have nothing to do with them; they seem to occur on their own. But regardless where troubles come from, you can learn to "swim" in them.

Let people teach you how to get through the troubled times in your life. Allow God to bring you above each wave. Eventually the waves will die down and the water will be smooth again.

■ *Trust God to help you ride the "waves" in your life.*
S.C.

Praying with a Partner

Confess your trespasses to one another, and pray for one another, that you may be healed.

—JAMES 5:16

Getting close to God through praying with someone helps meet my need for relationship with Him and with others. But praying with a partner can help me put away my denial, confess my faults, and deal with hidden sins. When the other person responds by praying for me and my problem, my burden is now shared: I don't feel so alone. God meets me in the form of my prayer partner and moves me toward healing.

Some ground rules can help this miraculous event be most effective. *Rule #1: Pray.* This may sound obvious, but too often, partners end up sharing requests more with each other and less with God. Spend at least half the time with your partner actually praying.

Rule #2: Make it safe to share. Make a pact not to tell anyone else what your partner said. This is called confidentiality. "Making it safe" can also mean not judging. Avoid any statements that sound like, "How could you do that?" or "That was really stupid."

Rule #3: Keep it simple. Having a partner of the opposite sex or someone who's using can make things too complicated. Prayer works best when the two of you can come before God honestly and without distraction.

■ *Miracles of healing in my recovery can come with a prayer partner.*

J.C.

A GIFT UNEARNED

You are My beloved . . . in You I am well pleased.
—LUKE 3:22

I saw her looking in a store display window. She was watching her reflection—completely absorbed in her pretend world. She couldn't have been more than five or six years old. She sang, posed, and performed for her own entertainment. Entirely unaware of my watching her, she was obviously delighted with herself.

I sat wondering, "When I see myself in a mirror, am I ever that pleased with myself? Do I enjoy my own company as much as that little girl does?" Not too often. I'm always thinking, "Is my mascara smeared? Does my hair look OK? Is my face breaking out?"

But God told Jesus at the moment of His baptism, *before He had done anything,* "You are My beloved." Before Jesus accomplished anything, before He healed anyone, before He became a "celebrity," God's love was assured, freely given as a gift. Just as Jesus was God's Son, so am I a child of God. If God can give me His complete acceptance, can I do any less for myself? Recovery is a daily process, a discovery of who I am and who—by the grace of God—I'm becoming.

■ *I take it one day at a time, trusting that I'm loved even when I have a hard time loving myself.*

D.K.

GETTING OFF THE ROLLER COASTER

*I will call upon the LORD, who is worthy
  to be praised;
So shall I be saved. . . .
In my distress I called upon the LORD, . . .
And my cry entered His ears.*

—2 SAM. 22:4, 7

It's Saturday afternoon at the amusement park, and you're next in line to ride the monster roller coaster. You slide into the seat. The bar clicks down. And now it's too late to get out; you're off. During the first big climb you feel that first surge of excitement, fear . . . or nausea. Regardless, you are on the ride for the duration. You are acutely aware that you are at the mercy of the roller coaster. It has all the power; all you can do is hang on. And normally all is well. You swoop down some hills, rattle around curves, loop the loop . . . and eventually arrive safely back where you started.

But what if the roller coaster didn't stop? What if you were stuck in a runaway car, hurtling faster and faster over the tracks? That's what living with compulsive behavior feels like. The behavior has all the power, you're just along for the ride. And you're certainly not having fun anymore.

But you don't have to stay on this white-knuckle ride. You can call for help. And as you depend on God and others in recovery, your roller coaster will gradually rattle to a stop and you can climb out—a little wobbly in the knees, but safe.

■ *God, help! Please help me end this roller-coaster ride and get my feet back on the ground.*

S.C.

HELP THAT REALLY HELPS

God has given each of you some special abilities; be sure to use them to help each other, passing on to others God's many kinds of blessings. —1 PET. 4:10 TLB

Cynthia was a helper with a capital *H*. If someone needed a listening ear, she extended it, sympathetically agreeing that the world was unfair and her friend was sadly misunderstood. If another friend was out late partying and didn't have time to do her math problems, Cynthia would share her answers. Cynthia's helping, in other words, was not always helpful.

The gift of helping is a special ability to aid others. God gives this ability to some of His children. It is part of our spiritual inheritance, one of many gifts that God gives. However, the gift of helping is often confused with enabling—which is what Cynthia did. Enabling doesn't really help anyone in the long run. In fact, it creates dependency instead of independence.

Some who have this gift may need to define what "help" is. Help should assist others to get back on their feet so they can take responsibility for their own lives. Feeding irresponsibility is not help.

■ *The gift of help should strengthen, not weaken, those we help.*

J.C.

IN MY HEART

Your word I have hidden in my heart,
That I might not sin against You.
—PS. 119:11

You get in the car. You switch on the radio, which is already tuned to your favorite station. First you hear the disk jockey talking, and then the first beats of a song.

Question: How many beats do you need to hear before you're singing along?

It depends, of course. But if you like the song, if your friends like it, and if it's been out awhile, you probably know the song in an instant—and you know all the words. That's especially true of the song you lip-synched or worked out to in aerobics class. The music you listen to all the time just seems to get in your bones. It's part of you.

Memory is a gift that lets us make whatever we hear or see or read a part of our lives. And as a rule, it's the stuff we spend a lot of time with that digs down inside of us. Doesn't it make sense, in recovery, to spend as much time as possible with material that brings us life and helps us in recovery—positive music, good recovery materials, and, most of all, God's Word?

■ *Lord, make your Word a part of me, so it will always be there when I need it.*

A.C.B.

NO ONE UNDERSTANDS ME

> *O LORD, You have searched me and*
> *known me.*
> *You know my sitting down and my*
> *rising up;*
> *You understand my thought afar off.*
> —PS. 139:1–2

No one understands me!" Suzanne cried. It was true. Suzanne's parents would shake their heads at her. They really could not relate to the issues she faced, her frustrations, or even her likes and dislikes.

It hurts to feel misunderstood. The tendency is to blame others for not listening, but here are some other possibilities:

(1) *We may not understand ourselves*—so how can we help others to understand us? But the disciplines of recovery are focused in part on increasing our self-understanding. Through the Twelve Steps, group meetings, prayer and journaling, and therapy, God can show us more about who we are and who we are meant to be.

(2) *We may not do a very good job of explaining ourselves to others.* We may not talk about our feelings or anything personal. Or we may just have a hard time communicating. If you feel misunderstood by people in your life, why not try some new ways for getting through—like making an appointment or writing a letter? Feeling understood is worth your best efforts at communicating.

■ *Even when no one else understands me, I know that you do, O God. Help me to know myself better and to communicate more clearly.*

S.C.

A WAY OF ESCAPE

*Deliver me in Your righteousness, and
    cause me to escape;
Incline Your ear to me, and save me.*
—PS. 71:2

Six months into her sobriety from alcohol, Belinda had done a good job of keeping herself out of compromising situations. One day, however, trouble loomed.

A girl in Belinda's church youth group invited her to a party. The girl's mother would be there. It sounded safe. But Belinda was surprised to find that beer was being served. The hostess's mother, who did not attend the church, felt that things would not get out of hand as long as she was there. Some youth group members were taking advantage of this "opportunity."

Belinda felt a familiar thirst—a craving she hadn't experienced in a long time. Panicked, she buddied up with a nondrinking friend who knew of her struggle and supported her abstinence. This friend eventually persuaded Belinda to leave the party with her and go home.

Belinda did not have the strength to leave the party on her own power. She did have the strength to ask her friend for help. This friend was God's door of escape for Belinda. If we ask God for a way out, He will provide one—but we have to cooperate. We need to ask for the door of escape, look for it, and take advantage of it.

■   *God wants me to recover and will provide a way to
    escape temptation. My part is to look for the door
    and walk through it.*

I.C

CREATED ON PURPOSE

*Then God saw everything that He had made,
and indeed it was very good.*

—GEN. 1:31

I have come to realize that the greatest trap of our life is not success, popularity or power, but self-rejection. It is the most dangerous human temptation," writes Henri Nouwen, a renowned theologian. Those are surprising words coming from one so accomplished, respected, and admired.

Knowing we are intimately loved and learning to accept that within the deepest part of us doesn't come easily—even for those who've grown up and achieved success. Yet we weren't created by accident. We were created by design, not by default. Ever thought of it this way? To criticize that which God has created is to think we are smarter than God. Even those things I don't like about myself, those personality traits I wish were different, are a part of who I am for a reason.

The creation story in the first chapter of Genesis records seven days of creation—and seven times says, "It was good." Obviously, the story is trying to make a point. Listen to it. Believe it. Trust it: When God creates something, it is good.

■ *Turning my life over to God is accepting that when God created me, He knew what He was doing.*

D.K.

A WHOLE, NOT A HALF

*You are complete in Him, who is the head
of all principality and power.*

—COL. 2:10

When someone mentions "addiction," we usually think of drugs, alcohol, or food. But it is possible to be addicted to people, too. Connie was addicted to men; she believed her life would be horrible unless she had a boyfriend. She didn't really care how she was treated, as long as she had someone to date. Connie depended on her boyfriends to meet all her emotional needs. But she could not keep a boyfriend long; her clinging and controlling behavior drove them away. Then she would begin the frenzied search to fill that void in her life with another guy—any guy.

Connie was looking to guys to fill a gap in her soul that no human was meant to fill. She thought she needed a boyfriend to make her feel secure and complete. But she would never find that security and completeness until she learned to depend on God to make her secure and complete in herself, without a boyfriend.

It took some time, and a lot of work, but Connie no longer needs a guy in order to be fulfilled. By God's grace, she is not a "half" waiting to be connected to another "half." She is a whole person. And by the way, she is involved in a great new relationship with a guy.

■ *O Lord, help me not to be dependent on others to make me feel complete or to give me self-esteem. Show me how to become a whole person.*

S.C.

WHAT TO DO WITH GUILT

*For godly sorrow produces repentance to
salvation, not to be regretted; but the sorrow
of the world produces death.*

—2 COR. 7:10

If you have been straight for a while, you have become more aware of your feelings. (This makes sense because substances anesthetize feelings.) Sometimes you may find yourself hypersensitive to feelings like guilt. For example, you may make a comment that offends someone. You spend the rest of the day feeling depressed and angry at yourself. Before starting recovery, you would have turned to your drug of choice to block out those guilty feelings. This is "the sorrow of the world" that leads to death. But now that you are no longer blocking your feelings, what do you do with them?

Feelings of guilt are from the Holy Spirit. Their purpose is not to punish, but to point out areas we need to correct. (When Jesus died on the cross for us and we accepted Him as our Savior, He took care of the punishment we deserve.) And today's verse tells us specifically what we are to do with our guilt feelings: repent. Repent is an old-fashioned word that just means admitting when we're wrong and then making amends.

Instead of silently yelling at yourself all day for being "insensitive," you can make a prompt, sincere apology to the one you hurt. Even if the apology is not accepted, you can know you did your part. Leave the results and any regrets in God's hands.

■ *Use guilt feelings to make amends, not to drown in regrets.*

J.C.

THE MYTH OF PERFECT

Every good gift and every perfect gift is from above, and comes down from the Father.
—JAMES 1:17

You've read the magazines. You, too, can have a sleek, toned body, fresh skin, a flattering wardrobe. You, too, can be popular and have great relationships with guys. You, too, can make good grades, go to a top college, and eventually build a great marriage and a stimulating career. ("To find out how you're doing, just take this quiz . . . .")

Sounds perfect, doesn't it? The trouble is—you can't do it! For one thing, even those people with sleek bodies, fresh skin, and lots of boyfriends have their share of inner pain. But more important, trying too hard to "get perfect" just leads to frustration—and perhaps a relapse. There's nothing like an unattainable goal to make you feel like a total failure!

But God doesn't expect us to be perfect—that's His department. He just expects us to depend on Him and let Him grow us into a better, more satisfying life. The results probably won't be magazine perfect. But they can be full, meaningful, satisfying—even fun.

■ *If I let him, God can move me past the myth of perfection and into the reality of growth.*

A.C.B.

REAL FRIENDS

I have hated the congregation of evildoers,
And will not sit with the wicked.
—PS. 26:5

Rebecca decided she was tired of her life's being out of control. She felt that she was never going to be normal again if she did not get some help, so she asked her parents to put her in a drug and alcohol rehabilitation program. Because Rebecca was ready for treatment, she progressed rapidly. In two months' time she was discharged from the hospital armed with new knowledge and a determination never to go back to her former way of life.

Much to her disappointment, not many of her friends were on her side. In fact, several of them made fun of her. She was ridiculed and mocked with sayings like "Oh, now you think you're too good for us" or "Did you get religion or what, Rebecca?" She decided she could not remain friends with people who wanted to see her fail. So she stayed away from them, and eventually they left her alone. Soon Rebecca found new friends who were supportive and helped her to maintain her sobriety. "It's nice to have some real friends," she told them.

■ *When you start changing you may have to endure put-downs from your peers. But is someone who would make fun of you for getting healthy the kind of person you want to be friends with?*

S.C.

THOSE WIGGLY LITTLE TOES

If you do not know, O fairest among women, . . .
Behold, you are fair, my love!
Behold, you are fair!

—SONG OF SOL. 1:8, 15

Ever watch babies play with their toes? "Oh my gosh, where did these wiggly things come from? Ooops, got away from me . . . aaah, got 'em again." Babies play a game of "grab and catch" with their toes as if they don't realize the silly little things are attached.

Sometimes we play "grab and catch" with God. We grab hold of a bit of His love, only to let ourselves become distracted by other concerns. Before we know it, we're right back in there trying to control our lives. Then we grab again with renewed fascination, only to let His love slip out of sight again.

But you know, babies grow. Not by trying harder, working smarter, or thinking, "Wow, I'd better practice this grab-and-catch thing." They just go right on embracing their world, living in the moment (that's all babies know how to do), and taking it as it comes. They aren't the least concerned with the master plan of their growth, maturity, or development.

When we're being too hard on ourselves, expecting too much, feeling disappointed with our "grab and catch" performance, maybe we need to watch a baby playing with its toes.

■ *I'll grow—just give it time. All God needs is a willing heart.*

D.K.

GOD IS NEVER SURPRISED

In Your book they all were written,
The days fashioned for me,
When as yet there were none of
*   them.*   —PS. 139:16

God had a purpose in mind when He gave you your hair and eye color, your height, your race, and your particular parents. He did not choose for you to become addicted. That was your choice. But He did see it coming. He also knew that later you would choose to recover. Knowing all this, He made plans for your life that took all of this into account.

It was not God's choice for Adam and Eve to sin. Their sin brought eternal death into the world. However, God was not caught off guard. He had a plan to counteract death—Jesus Christ. In fact, He made this plan even before Adam and Eve were created.

So whatever mistakes you've made, God already has you covered. God is never surprised. Certainly, there are natural consequences for mistakes we make. They may include lost time and broken relationships that need to be healed. But God can use even these as part of His plan.

God's overall plan for everyone is that we become more like Him. The more we are like Him, the stronger, the wiser, and the healthier we are. Working through our past mistakes instead of trying to forget them is our part in letting God do His work of rebuilding our lives.

■   *If we let Him, God uses our mistakes as part of His plan to make us more like Him.*

J.C.

INTO THIS GRACE

Therefore, having been justified by faith, . . .
we have access by faith into this grace in
which we stand. . . . God demonstrates His
own love toward us, in that while we were
still sinners, Christ died for us.

—ROM. 5:1–2, 8

Feeling the sun on my face. Reading a great romance or mystery. Getting to sleep late—no hassles, no guilt. Finding a great sale when I actually have money to spend. A good cry. A great kiss. Simple pleasures. Moments you can't plan or predict. Moments touched by grace.

Our understanding of grace is sometimes too narrow, sometimes too churchy. Perhaps our understanding needs to be updated.

Frederick Buechner says grace is something we don't deserve but are given anyway. Seen that way, *grace* isn't just a religious term, reserved for Sunday school and sermons. Grace is the mystery by which we are transformed from within. You can't explain it. You can't negotiate it. You can't earn it. Grace is what happens when we truly understand that we are loved—no strings attached, no expectations. That kind of grace empowers. That kind of grace changes people.

■ *Grace is the gift God offers us; we only have to accept it.*

D.K.

CLEAN AGAIN

Create in me a clean heart, O God,
And renew a steadfast spirit within me.
—PS. 51:10

Vicki felt dirty inside. She was so ashamed of her past, and she struggled with the shameful feelings daily, even though she wanted to let go of them. When she was very young, Vicki was sexually abused by her stepfather. She could always remember feeling different than the other girls her age. And she thought something must be terribly wrong with her for her stepfather to hurt her so badly.

When Vicki entered junior high school, she already felt "secondhand." So when boys approached her about having sex, she consented. She truly believed that if she were to receive love at all, she would have to give in. But Vicki continued to feel embarrassed, ashamed, and sinful. "It's too late," she thought. "I'll always feel dirty."

But it's not too late! The Bible speaks frequently of having a clean heart—and the Lord really can give us a heart that is spotless. Things in our past will often make us feel dirty and used, but God promises us that He will renew our hearts, cleansing and purifying them. We do not have to let the regrets of our past keep us feeling stained. We can ask God to remove the stains in our hearts.

■ *Father, make my heart clean. Let me feel you renewing my life and setting me free from yesterday.*

S.C

A REAL FRIEND

> *Open rebuke is better*
> *Than love carefully concealed.*
> *Faithful are the wounds of a friend.*
> —PROV. 27:5–6

The letter was waiting on the table when Pete dropped her off from school:

Dear Maggie,

It's hard for me to write this, but I think you're headed for trouble. I don't think going out with Pete is such a great idea. Pete is an OK guy. But since you met him, you've missed a lot of your support groups. I'm just worried for you. I hope you're not mad at me for writing this. Still friends?

Love, Carol

Sometimes it hurts to hear the truth. Maggie did get very angry when Carol pointed out this blind spot. In fact, she wouldn't talk to Carol for weeks. But Carol was willing to risk Maggie's anger if it meant helping her friend. And it did—but not before Maggie relapsed. When she did, she remembered Carol's letter. It helped her figure out where the problem started.

God says a real friend is willing to confront lovingly. This is better than keeping silent. If you have friends like this, consider yourself lucky. If you have the chance to be such a friend, take it.

■ *It's much easier to look like the good guy and not confront, but a true friend is willing to risk the friendship in order to help.*

J.C.

CHANGING ON THE INSIDE

Woe to you, scribes and Pharisees, hypocrites!
For you are like whitewashed tombs which
indeed appear beautiful outwardly, but
inside are full of dead men's bones and all
uncleanness.
                                        —MATT. 23:27

It's so obvious—and yet I'm always forgetting: Life is an inside job.

Negative, destructive behavior is evidence of something out of kilter deep inside of me. And healthy, positive change in my behavior can come only from healthy, positive change within.

So why do I keep thinking I can turn my life around by making a few superficial changes? I think I can go on a crash diet and eliminate my weight problem forever. I think I can shop at the discount mall and solve the problem of compulsive spending. I think I can just stick to beer and not have a substance abuse problem anymore!

To use Jesus' words, that's like sprucing up the outside of a tomb that is full of rotting corpses inside! Like decorating a house that's filthy and roach-infested and falling apart.

As I work the Twelve Steps, pray, journal, stay active in my support group, I'm not just fixing a few bad behaviors. I'm opening up my life to real change—change from the inside. I'm not just dusting a few knickknacks and hanging a poster. I'm letting God deep clean, repair, exterminate—replace what is broken and dysfunctional with what is useful and beautiful.

■ *Lord, I'm tired of wasting my time with surface remedies. I'm ready for you to change me on the inside.*
                                        A.C.B.

OUT OF THE HOPELESS PIT

He also brought me up out of a
horrible pit. —PS. 40:2

Hopelessness has a way of creeping over all of us at times. Its blackness can cover our hearts like a suffocating cloud—blurring our vision for the future and blotting out any dreams that we can be different from who we are right now. We may feel that we are in the bottom of a well whose walls are smooth and impossible to climb. Hopelessness is a very scary feeling.

What do you do when that kind of hopelessness overtakes you? Many kids, unfortunately, consider suicide. What a tragedy. Hopelessness makes you think that nothing can get better—but suicide *guarantees* it.

If hopelessness has made you think of killing yourself (or if a friend is feeling suicidal), holler for help! There really are "ladders" available to pull you out of the pit. Call a suicide hotline. Call a friend. Seek help from a trained professional; a little counseling really can make a difference. And tell yourself over and over again that God really does see your circumstances and He will help you.

Whatever you do, don't give up. Help is available, and hope is just around the corner.

■ *God, when I feel hopeless, please let me see that you*
hold hope in your hand.

S.C.

SUPER-GLUED TOGETHER

Therefore a man shall leave his father and mother and be joined to his wife, and they shall become one flesh. —GEN. 2:24

I felt like we were one person . . . and then when he told me he didn't love me anymore I felt ripped apart." Cheryl was describing her breakup from the first boy she ever had intercourse with. Her feelings were very biblical. Genesis describes this natural bonding of two separate people as that of becoming "one flesh."

Intercourse is one of the powerful, supernatural glues that God invented to help keep a marriage together. God intended marriage to last a lifetime, so this glue would have to be powerful enough to withstand illness, children, growing old, and possible poverty, disability, and senility.

No wonder Cheryl hurt so much. She was super-glued to someone and then pulled apart. The pain was almost unbearable. She had even thought of suicide. Instead, she relapsed.

Getting to know oneself again while straight is hard enough work. A relationship, especially a sexual relationship, complicates this. Sexuality involves more than intercourse. It involves your attitudes and behaviors toward the opposite sex. It involves your opinion of yourself as female. You need to take time to find out what God says about this.

■ *Sobriety also means finding out what God says about my sexuality.*

J.C.

LOVE IN ACTION

Beloved, let us love one another, for love is of God; and everyone who loves is born of God and knows God. [She] who does not love does not know God, for God is love.

—1 JOHN 4:7–8

Love is something when you give it away, you end up having more," goes the verse of a song children sing in the preschool at our church. I always thought it was just a silly little kids' song until I got serious about recovery. Recovery is love in action. Unless I give it away, I hit a stalemate.

Recovery isn't something I do for a while, then move on to other things because I've gotten better. Recovery is a way of life. And no matter what I've done, by God's grace my experience can benefit others who still suffer as I once did.

When I think about skipping my support-group meeting, I need to remember the desperation I felt when I first began going and the hope I had from listening to those who were further along in their recovery. They talked easily about God. They laughed. They were comfortable with themselves, humble about their successes, and tolerant of their failures. They were my lifeline when I wasn't sure life was worth living. The Big Book of AA reminds me, "You can help when no one else can."*

■ *The way to maintain my own recovery is to give it away, to put love into action.*

D.K.

Alcoholics Anonymous, 3rd ed. (New York: Alcoholics Anonymous World Services, 1976), 89.

I AM ACCEPTABLE

*To the praise of the glory of His grace, by
which He has made us accepted in the
Beloved.*
—EPH. 1:6

Susan's mother was a perfectionist. For as long as Susan could remember, she had worked to meet her mom's high expectations: "Don't get dirty." "Make sure your clothes match." "Act like a little lady."

Weight seemed to be a big issue in Susan's family. Her mother made fun of large people. So Susan grew up assuming that thin people were "good" and acceptable; overweight people were "bad" and undesirable. Since she craved her mother's approval, she was always very careful not to gain weight.

Susan enjoyed food, however. When she and her friends would go out for pizza, she would gorge herself. (She knew she could never eat pizza at home and not be ridiculed for it.) Because of her fear of gaining weight and her intense need to avoid her mother's disapproval, Susan would purge.

Susan's mother is still very critical of other people's weight. But Susan is learning that acceptance from others comes not from looking perfect, but from being herself. Occasionally she finds herself still striving for her mother's approval. Fortunately, she is finding out that even if she does not meet her mother's expectations, she is still a very valuable young woman— acceptable and desirable in her own right.

■ *Lord, I pray that you will show me just how valuable I am to you. Thank you for loving me just as I am.*

S.C.

FATHER OF THE FATHERLESS

A father of the fatherless, . . .
Is God in His holy habitation.
—PS. 68:5

The chair where her stepfather usually sat was empty. Angie felt abandoned. Even though she was sixteen years old, she felt like a four-year-old who was lost in a deep woods. Angie had lost her real father when she was four; after the divorce, she lived with her mother and rarely saw him. When her mother remarried, Angie had called her stepfather Dad. He had fulfilled some of her longing for a dad. But now her mother and stepfather were getting a divorce, and she was afraid that he, too, would disappear.

Many girls feel they have no father. Many "divorced" kids see their fathers once a month or twice a month—if they are lucky. And many others have fathers who are addicted to TV, alcohol, drugs, or work. So even if Dad is in the home, he's not.

God promises to be a "father of the fatherless," But we have to be willing to be His daughters. First, we need to claim our place in His family by accepting Christ as our Savior. Then we need to make time to spend with our Father. We go to His house, the church. Daily we read His love letters to us in the Bible. Even though we may not feel it, we act as if He's standing next to us every minute of the day. (He is! Psalm 139 says He's watching every move we make.) And eventually we don't have to act "as if"—we *know* He is there.

■ *As the Father's daughter, I can be as close to or as far away from Him as I choose.*

S.C.

GOD OF MY BOREDOM

But the rebellious dwell in a dry land.
—PS. 68:6

God, I'm so bored!" I've said that a million times—
and usually I'm not praying! In fact, that's often when
I'm in danger of relapse—when things seem so blah, so
ordinary, when I can't think of anything to do except
what I really don't want to do.

But maybe that's part of the problem. Maybe one
reason I get bored is that part of me is rebelling. I don't
want to do something I need to do, and so part of me
withdraws and says no to life. I end up shutting myself
off from the billions of possibilities that are all around
me.

Say, for instance, that I need to clean my bedroom,
but I don't want to, so I putter around doing everything
but. And I still feel restless and dissatisfied—bored. Or,
on a more spiritual level, I sense God is calling me to
commit more of my life to Him. I don't want to, so I put
my spiritual hands over my spiritual ears. Not surprisingly, life seems muffled and dull.

Jesus experienced slow times and busy times in His
life on earth. But as far as I can tell, He was never
bored. Maybe that's because He was saying yes to life
and yes to God instead of wasting His time worrying
about what He didn't want to do.

■ *Father, when I'm bored, open my eyes to the inner
negativity that may be causing the problem. Help
me to say yes to life and to you.*

A.C.B.

LEARNING TO LET GO

Show me Your ways, O LORD;
Teach me Your paths.
—PS. 25:4

Letting go of things we cannot control is so difficult. We often try desperately to control people and situations in our lives. Sometimes we end up driving people away because we are striving to make them do what we want or be who we want them to be. It is easy to end up manipulating, scheming, and conniving. We can easily offend and irritate others by being controlling. We damage relationships by our anger or refusal to accept others the way they are. Until we learn to "let go," we wear ourselves and others to a frazzle.

Sometimes letting go means evaluating hurtful relationships and backing off from the detrimental ones. Sometimes we surround ourselves with people who are harmful to themselves (abusing alcohol, drugs, food). Even if we try to stop them, our efforts usually do not work—and those people end up influencing *us!* Why do our efforts fail? Because it is not up to us to change others! We're responsible only for our own actions.

Letting go also means giving up on the idea that we can make someone think a certain way about us. People will believe what they want to believe. It is not our responsibility to choose their feelings or thoughts for them.

■ *Today, I will begin letting go of my efforts to control others. Instead, I will concentrate on my own behavior—and turn over control of that to God.*

S.C.

A SPIRIT OF GENTLENESS

*If a [peer] is overtaken in any trespass, you
who are spiritual restore such a one in a
spirit of gentleness, considering yourself lest
you also be tempted.* —GAL. 6:1

I wanted to pound her into the ground at first." Debra
bit her lower lip and hit the arm of the chair. "But then I
thought about my first recovery group meeting and how
off the wall I was. I told everyone I didn't need to be
there, but it was fine for them since they did. It's amazing someone didn't smack me."

Debra was applying an important principle in carrying the message of recovery to another. It would have
been easy for her to have gotten into a power struggle
with the new group member or taken the role of "expert." Instead, she remembered her early days of recovery and how strong her denial was. So she just
shared some specifics about how her life had been unmanageable. Debra took a risk and let a stranger know
about her past mistakes. She did not put herself above
the stranger, but alongside her. She chose to express the
spirit of restoration and gentleness.

The experience also helped her remember how fragile recovery can be. Debra talked about how denial is an
ongoing issue throughout recovery. In carrying the message of recovery to another, Debra had an opportunity
to instruct and encourage herself.

■ *Heavenly Father, help my confrontations be done in
a spirit of gentleness and restoration. Remind me
that as I confront others, I confront myself as well.*

J.C.

HEALING TAKES TIME

*For the thing I greatly feared has come
  upon me,
And what I dreaded has happened to me.*
—JOB 3:25

The unthinkable happened. What existed only as statistics in a police report became my living nightmare. I kept thinking, "This can't be happening." But it did. The smell, the roughness, fighting the tears and wondering, "When will he stop?"

One out of four women is sexually abused or raped. One out of four. I'm not alone. God didn't cause it. I didn't deserve it. And if it hasn't happened to me, it's happened to someone I know.

Jesus knows I'm not a statistic. He knows what it is to be physically harmed, victimized, and abused. And He didn't stop at Good Friday. He could have. He could have said, "Forget this, God, it isn't worth it. Let me out of the deal." But He didn't. The Man who saw it through to the resurrection is the same living Christ who will see me through. There is no image so ugly, no memory so painful, no abuse so grim that it can't be brought before His healing presence.

■ *With His strength and by His grace, I can face the pain, walk through the memories, and embrace the hope knowing that healing takes time, but healing will come.*

D.K.

FEELINGS WON'T KILL YOU!

Search me, O God, and know my heart;
Try me, and know my anxieties.
—PS. 139:23

If you have worked hard at not "feeling your feelings," having them surface can be very scary. And this happens a lot in recovery. As issues are uncovered, feelings emerge that you never knew were there. Anger, hurt, bewilderment, and sadness may come rising to the top like air bubbles. The process can be overwhelming at first. The intensity of some feelings may be frightening. Trying to label them can be confusing. The uncertainty about what you feel can produce anxiety.

If you have learned to stuff your feelings with food, purge because you did not like what you felt inside, starve yourself to become numb, or rely on alcohol or drugs to dull the pain, you probably are afraid of feelings. But it's a fact: *feelings cannot kill you!* They may feel uncomfortable and foreign, but they are not lethal. The behavior that results from the feelings is what needs to be kept in check.

As you learn to rely on God and the people who support you, allow yourself a little freedom to experience your emotions. Relax . . . breathe . . . and feel. There'll be some pain. But many wonderful feelings such as joy, contentment, peace, and relief await you, too. Feelings open up a whole new world and give you the chance to feel more alive inside.

■ *Father, help me to understand what I am feeling in my heart. Give me the courage to feel the emotions.*

S.C.

GOD MEANS IT FOR GOOD

But as for you, you meant evil against me;
but God meant it for good.

—GEN. 50:20

Joseph was a middle-aged man when he spoke the above words to his brothers, but he spoke out of a lifetime of pain.

When he was a teenager, his brothers had physically abused him and then sold him as a slave! He had ended up in Egypt, serving a high government official, Potiphar, and eventually was given responsibility for Potiphar's huge household. Then Mrs. Potiphar tried unsuccessfully to seduce him. Frustrated by his refusal, she yelled "Rape!" and Joseph was thrown into jail.

Here was a young adult forcibly separated from his family, sold into slavery, physically and emotionally abused, sexually harassed, and falsely accused. What would you do if it happened to you? Feel sorry for yourself? Use substances to numb out all those feelings of anger, fear, and abandonment? Get lost in a relationship?

Joseph didn't. He kept on track and eventually rose to be the second most powerful man in Egypt. What helped him keep on track? The knowledge that God was in control, even though he wasn't.

■   *Because God is in control, He can use the bad others*
    do to me for my good.

J.C.

Not a Victim

*We are more than conquerors through Him
who loved us.* —ROM. 8:37

Yesterday we read about Joseph, who suffered incredible abuse and yet managed to keep his life on track. It would have been very easy for him to derail himself with rebellious behavior. Instead, Joseph learned about giving up control to his Higher Power, God.

An important part of giving up control is surrendering our right to hold a grudge. Joseph had every right to hold a grudge. But if Joseph had done that, others would have sensed his anger and would have been less willing to trust him with power over others. He might have been stuck in jail the rest of his life. Instead, Joseph chose to let go of his grudges and practice forgiveness. He turned his hurts over to God rather than hanging on to them. As a result, he eventually rose to be "vice president" over all of Egypt. God was with Joseph, and so "whatever he did, the LORD made it prosper" (Gen. 39:23).

How can we make unfair circumstances work for us? Joseph's secret was that he saw God in control over all aspects of his life—even the ones that seemed unfair. He refused to see himself as a victim, because he trusted that God was at work for good—even in his painful circumstances.

■ *Lord, keep me from seeing myself as a victim. Help me to choose a winner's viewpoint.*

J.C.

TAKING PLEASURE IN DANDELIONS

I take pleasure in infirmities, in reproaches, in needs, in persecutions, in distresses, for Christ's sake. For when I am weak, then I am strong. —2 COR. 12:10

If I have a lawn, dandelions are a real problem. They're prickly and oozy and uncomfortable to dig up, and I can never get all the root. But if I'm a child, dandelions are wonderful. They're bright and cheerful. They're free for the picking. When the blossom is gone, they turn into delicate, puffy rounds, and I can make wishes on them.

The same plant, in other words, can be a curse or a blessing—depending on who's responsible for maintaining the lawn. If it's my job to keep it manicured and perfect, the dandelions can drive me crazy. When a perfect lawn is someone else's responsibility, I'm free to enjoy the dandelions.

I'm learning that my worst faults and my greatest strengths are usually part of the same "plant." The same passionate caring that makes me an effective crusader for good also makes me my own worst enemy. The same attention to detail that makes me a valuable worker can make me a hopeless worrywart. So instead of spending all my time trying to uproot my "bad" qualities, maybe I need to relax and trust the Gardener—who not only planted my "lawn" in the first place but is working to make it a place of beauty.

■ *Lord, help me to thank you for what I am even while I am trusting you to change me.*

A.C.B.

Rethinking Illogical Thoughts

The LORD knows the thoughts of man,
That they are futile. —PS. 94:11

Andrea became anorexic several years ago when her emotional pain became so intense she could not eat. At first her appetite seemed to drop off on its own. She felt a few hunger pangs every now and then, but after the first week or two, she really was not hungry. Losing weight was reinforced by everyone's comments on how great she looked. For the first time in her life she felt she had control over her body and her life.

A strange thing began happening to Andrea. Although her thoughts made sense to her, they did not make much sense to others. Andrea was convinced that if she ate anything—anything at all—she would become fat. The thought of putting food in her body terrified her.

Andrea eventually had to be hospitalized and fed through a tube. Even after weeks of group and individual therapy and education, she still had a difficult time retraining her thought patterns. Logically, Andrea realized her body would turn food into energy. Illogically, she believed all food would turn into fat.

Andrea still struggles with believing she can control her emotional pain with food (or the lack of it). Old ideas are difficult to change. But as Andrea is learning, difficult is not the same as impossible.

■ *God, help me to examine my illogical thoughts and*
understand how futile they are.

S.C.

THANKFUL THINKING

For all things are for your sakes, that grace, . . . may cause thanksgiving to abound.
—2 COR. 4:15

But I didn't deserve this consequence essay!" A male peer had broken the hospital adolescent unit rules by stepping into Robin's room to talk to her roommate. Robin had gone along with this. Now she, the roommate, and the boy all had to write essays.

Rules were a problem for Robin—but God was giving her plenty of opportunities to learn to follow them before she went back home. If she did not get a handle on this, life with her mother would always be conflicted— and fights with her mother often precipitated Robin's relapses. But Robin did not see this particular event as God's opportunity to give her practice in accepting limits. As long as she remained defensive instead of thankful, she was missing out on a chance to work on her recovery.

The habit of giving thanks for everything (1 Thess. 5:18) keeps us open to God. It helps us realize that He is using every circumstance for our sakes—to help us grow. Thankful thinking is based on the character of God, who is all powerful and loves us more than we can know. Because God is all powerful, because He loves us, we can have the confidence that whatever happens to us is part of His loving plan for us.

■ *Thanking God helps me use the circumstances of life to grow stronger.*

J.C.

ICE AGE EMOTIONS

*Likewise the Spirit also helps in our
weaknesses. For we do not know what we
should pray for as we ought, but the Spirit
Himself makes intercession for us.*
—ROM. 8:26

Walking into my house can sometimes feel like walking into the Ice Age—not knowing what I did, but feeling I must have done something. I'm greeted by that tight-lipped, grim, "I'm mad at you and you know why" expression only a parent can have. But I don't know why. I just know my relationships at home just hit the subzero temperatures, and who's to say when things will thaw?

But this Ice Age may not be about me. I don't have to take responsibility for my parents' issues. Maybe this is between them. And whether it's about me or between them, I've got healthy ways to handle the freeze. Without fear or shame, I can look at my behavior and actions, asking God to help me see clearly if I have any amends to make. I can call a friend or my sponsor and talk the situation through with someone whose emotions aren't freeze-dried. And then I can do what's right, turning it over to Christ and listening for His leading.

■ *Jesus, when I'm confused and unsure about what's really going on, be with me. Let me see with your eyes, praying before reacting.*

D.K.

POWER THROUGH THANKS

> *. . . and be thankful.*
> —COL. 3:15

Straight thinking means seeing things from God's point of view, and giving thanks in everything is a way to do that. But that kind of thankfulness takes some mental gymnastics for most of us.

For example, how can I give thanks for my addiction? We can get some hints from the apostle Paul who did not have an addiction, but he did have some kind of handicap. Whether it was physical or otherwise, no one knows for certain. However, he called it a weakness—and an addiction is a weakness. How did Paul see his weakness? He saw it as something to boast about (see 2 Cor. 12:9) because it forced him to rely on God's power. Paul's power could only take him so far. God's power could take him anywhere. When Paul quit depending on himself, he could then depend on God. Human power can be likened to a bicycle that can take us to the local park. God's power is like the Starship *Enterprise* that can take us "where no man has gone before."

It's not God's will that you give thanks for AIDS or the untimely death of a friend or having an abusive parent. But it is His will that you give thanks while going through such tragedies. That's not because He wants you to be a masochist, but because thanking Him reminds you that His power is always available to you.

■ *Giving thanks takes supernatural thinking.*

J.C.

How long, Lord?

Do not forget this one thing, that with the Lord one day is as a thousand years, and a thousand years as one day. The Lord is not slack concerning His promise.

—2 PETER 3:8–9

How long until we get there?" That's the constant chorus from little kids on a car trip. And it's a frustrating question because, with little kids, there's no way to answer! You can say, "Another hour and fifteen minutes," and they'll ask, "How long is that?" To a small child with no concept of time, fifteen minutes doesn't sound very different from an hour.

Sometimes in recovery I feel like a kid in a car, asking my heavenly Father, "How much further? How long until I'm better?" I get tired of taking the recovery journey one day at a time. I want to get where I'm going. And one day, God has promised, I really will get there. But telling me *when* has to be as pointless as telling a little kid exactly when the car will reach its destination. With my frame of reference, I couldn't understand the answer.

God doesn't measure time or growth by my standards, but God does keep His promises. Like a little kid in a car, I just have to trust His word that if I ride with Him, I'll end up in the right place. Once I decide to do that, then I can relax and enjoy the journey.

■ *Heavenly Father, I guess it's only natural to ask "How much longer?" Thank you that I can express my honest impatience to you—and that I can trust you to keep your promises in your own time.*

A.C.B.

NO PLACE TO RUN

> [She] who flees . . . shall not get away,
> And [she] who escapes . . . shall not
> be delivered.
> —AMOS 9:1

Michelle has an incredible talent for running away. She has never physically run away from home; she runs away in her mind. She learned to do this when she was little, growing up in an abusive home. She had a fantasyland where she would escape when she was scared—a place where people were nice to her and she felt loved and accepted.

Michelle doesn't live at home anymore, but she still escapes. She often tells me she wants to run away. My reply to her is that she can never run far enough away. You see, Michelle isn't running from the abuse anymore. She's running from her pain and her fear. For Michelle, reality has been cruel. Her pain is very deep, and there is no way to escape it. She has tried drinking, drugs, binging and purging—but the pain always returns.

Escaping from our past is impossible—but healing *is* possible. There will never be a place to go where you won't feel pain anymore. So stop running. Turn around and face the pain. With help from counselors, friends, family, and God, you can make it.

■ *Lord, I ask you to give me the courage to face those things I am running from and the strength to stand firm.*

S.C.

Worth Getting to Know

I have chosen you and have not
cast you away.
—ISA. 41:9

Tania yearned to see a warm glint of approval in her father's eyes. But no matter what she did, she could not please him. The one time he did attend her volleyball game, he told her she looked like a blimp. And he abused her verbally at other times, too. Tania coped by trying to stay out of her father's way as much as possible. However, she still carried him in her head. Even when he was not there, she would remember his comments and repeat them to herself: "stupid," "fat cow," "blimp." She didn't need him to be there to do the job of running her down.

Not surprisingly, Tania grew to expect rejection from other people. If she did start to get close to someone, she fell apart if the other person seemed to let her down. Instead of checking out what really happened, Tania told herself, "I knew it! You can't really depend on anyone."

Gradually Tania gained more weight and used that as an excuse to keep her from close relationships. She reasoned that no one would want a fat girl as a friend. Rejection thinking was keeping her overweight and isolated. She needed to learn to look at herself the way God did. God cherished her and had chosen her. If the God of the universe thought that way about her, who was Tania to disagree with Him?

■ *Assume you're worth getting to know. God thinks you are!*

J.C.

WHEN THINGS ARE GOING GREAT

Hear, O LORD, when I cry with my voice!
Have mercy also upon me, and answer me. . . .
Do not hide Your face from me; . . .
You have been my help;
Do not leave me nor forsake me,
O God of my salvation.
                                                              —PS. 27:7, 9

Overconfidence. Something as easy to deny as the craziness of my behavior before I found this program of recovery. When things are going great, my program sometimes gets a little sloppy. The signs of overconfidence are all too obvious: not taking a few moments of quiet to connect with God, skipping my support-group meeting, letting thoughts creep into my mind like, "I can handle it. Just this once won't hurt . . ."

"It is easy to let up on the spiritual program of action and rest on our laurels. We are headed for trouble if we do, for [our compulsive behavior] is a subtle foe. We are not cured. . . . What we really have is a daily reprieve," say the authors of the AA Big Book.*

The founders of AA knew what they were talking about. I can take a cue from those who know the pitfalls well. My recovery is a gift, a daily reprieve that results from living grounded in faith.

■   *When things are going well, that's the time to take a*
    deep breath and say a humble word of thanks to my
    Redeemer, letting my heart feel the depth of grati-
    tude for the peace, hope, and happiness of this mo-
    ment.

                                                              D.K.

*Alcoholics Anonymous, 3rd ed. (New York: Alcoholics Anony-
mous World Services, 1976), 85.

A SUCCESS STORY

*Finally, my [sisters], be strong in the Lord
and in the power of His might.*
—EPH. 6:10

Rae is a friend of mine whom I respect and admire. She had a very difficult, confusing childhood. Her minister father was distant and withdrawn; he gave his daughter little affection or support. Even when she was sexually abused by a family friend, he worried only about possible scandal. Rae never knew quite what to expect from her mother; she would run "hot and cold." Rae could never tell what mood her mother would be in, what made her happy, or what the rules of the house were from day to day.

As Rae grew older, life in her home became unbearable. She left home and lived with another family for a period of time. To help her escape from the turmoil she felt, she began using drugs. This only made her world turn upside down. What Rae eventually learned was that the pain she felt needed to be dealt with, not escaped from. Drugs only compounded her problems.

It has taken Rae several years to heal from her childhood trauma. She has hung in there through thick and thin. There were many times she would much rather have given up than to keep dredging through the muck and mire of her life, but she kept going. Rae is living proof that healing is possible.

■ *Lord, keep me going so that I, too, can be a "success story" one day.*

S.C.

WRONG!

Therefore let [her] who thinks [she] stands take heed lest [she] fall. —1 COR. 10:12

Whenever I blow it, I know I forgot about being powerless over my addiction—step one." Christine went on with her sharing. "I start thinking I'm doing better. I don't need anymore meetings; I can do it myself. Wrong!" As if to emphasize that last point she placed her finger to her temple as if to shoot that thought dead. "It's like this false sense of security because you forget just how out of control your life was."

Christine was describing relapse thinking. Relapse does not start with that first drink or hit; it starts in the mind. Relapse is always a serious concern. One is especially aware of it during those first few months of taking the baby steps of recovery. But after six months or so, it does not seem to be such a threat. Memories of hangovers and nausea and desperation are fading. In fact, they may be remembered with some fondness as "war stories." "Wrong!" as Christine would say.

When we are pretty sure of ourselves and our recovery and think we do not need support, the Bible says to be careful. As today's verse points out, relapse is a possibility at any time. This does not mean we should remember our mistakes in order to wallow in them. But we should use the memory to keep us dependent on God and on our support system.

■ *Recovery: Fragile—handle with care.*

J.C.

"MORNING AFTER" MERCIES

His compassions fail not.
They are new every morning.
—LAM. 3:22–23

The morning after." That's the familiar term for that horrible time when you come back down after a binge or a relapse and feel—here's another familiar term— "like death warmed over." Mixed in with the physical discomfort of a hangover or bloating or just plain old fatigue is that agonizing sense of guilt, shame, and hopelessness. "Oh no, not again. How can I be so stupid? Why do I keep doing this?"

That's why, along with the ice pack and the aspirin, we need a good dose of God's "morning after" remedy: "His compassions . . . are new every morning." That doesn't mean we have a blank check for failure. God loves us too much to want us to fail. The physical, psychological, and spiritual consequences of a string of relapses are real, and we will have to deal with them. Yet God makes it clear that He is always ready to allow us a fresh start, no matter how many times we screw up.

That's hard to believe. In fact, every time I slip, part of me wonders how much of my "forgiveness quota" I've used up. Yet God says that's not the way it works. His compassions are new *every* morning. He's always ready to forgive when I repent and return to Him.

■ *Father, it's hard to believe you could still love me after I've failed you so many times, but you do. Thank you! With your help, maybe this will be my last "morning after."*

A.C.B.

THE BLAME GAME

Let no one say when [she] is tempted, "I am tempted by God"; for God cannot be tempted by evil, nor does He Himself tempt anyone.
—JAMES 1:13

Kaila had the tendency to blame others for her problems. No matter what went wrong in her life, the first words out of her mouth were "It's your fault!" She accused others of making her feel a certain way, not understanding her, and not being sensitive enough to her needs. She blamed her behavior on others. She even blamed her parents when she had to take some courses in school she did not want to take. The year before, she had manipulated her schedule to be in classes with her friends. Now, in order to have enough credits to graduate, she was stuck with boring classes. "If you hadn't made me go to this stupid school in the first place, I wouldn't be in this predicament!" she yelled.

Like Kaila, we all have some things about our lives that we don't like—and it's tempting to point an accusing finger at others. We may even choose to blame God for our problems. But blaming only alienates us from God and other people and retards our growth. Blaming others may take the focus off us, but it does not cure our problems or help us become responsible people.

■ *Father, help me to accept responsibility for my actions and not keep playing the blame game.*

S.C.

HEALTHY EXPRESSIONS OF ANGER

*"Be angry, and do not sin": do not let the
sun go down on your wrath.*

—EPH. 4:26

When you get angry, are you an exploder or a stuffer?
An exploder vomits her anger over whomever happens
to be near. A stuffer may have a smile pasted on her
face yet be furious on the inside. Both ways of handling
anger are harmful. An exploder hurts those she loves
and gives them ulcers. A stuffer hurts herself and can
give herself an ulcer.

Does that mean anger is wrong? No. Today's verse
says, "Be angry." God gave us our feelings to make life
fuller. How boring life would be without feelings! However, in addition to "Be angry," the Bible also says "Do
not sin." The sin comes in *how* we express the anger.
Exploding and stuffing harm others and ourselves and
so are sinful. And these responses do little to resolve the
problem that caused the anger in the first place. That
means we are more likely to sleep on our anger, which
the rest of the verse cautions against.

Exploding, stuffing, and holding on to anger over-
night give Satan an opportunity to turn our anger into
unforgiveness and bitterness—which are definitely sins
(see v. 26). God gave us feelings, but wants us to express them in a healthy way.

■ *Anger is not sin, but the way I express it can be
sinful.*

J.C.

THE REAL NEW YEAR'S

Behold, I make all things new.
—REV. 21:5

The beginning of the school year will always be the real New Year's Day for me. New clothes, new supplies, new teachers and classes—it all feels like more of a beginning than that day in midwinter. So why not mark this other New Year the way most people do January 1—with a few reflections?

First of all, last year is over; I can put it behind me and begin again. Even if I'm still in the process of taking inventory and making amends, this "backward" work is really a means of removing obstacles that keep me from moving forward.

Second, a fresh year stretches before me, but I can only experience it a minute at a time. I derive motivation from my plans and goals, but my moment-by-moment decisions—to maintain my abstinence, to ask for help, to let God be God—are what determine the course of my life. I do best when I look to the future but live in the present.

Finally, I'm not facing this year alone. My support group is a lifeline. My therapist and my friends keep me going. And I really can depend on God to be actively at work for good in all my circumstances.

■   *Happy New Year, Lord. Teach me to depend on you all through the coming school year.*

A.C.B.

PICKING THE RIGHT FRIENDS

Do not be deceived: "Evil company corrupts good habits." —1 COR. 15:33

She is not a bad influence on me. We've been friends since the age of seven. I can handle it."

I had hit a sore spot with Sherri. We had been exploring what she needed to do in order to ensure her recovery. The atmosphere between us had been calm until the topic of friendships arose. Now the air crackled with tension.

Sherri had neglected to mention that this girlfriend had let her use her address to obtain mail-order amphetamines so Sherri's parents would not know of her habit. This friend had also agreed to hide Sherri's supply of drugs at her house while she was in rehab. Sherri felt she could simply tell this friend to get rid of the drugs and continue their friendship. Even though this friend was also a user, Sherri was certain she could keep herself clean around her.

Sherri was fooling herself. As today's verse warns, those we hang around with do influence us. We become like the people we spend time with. It's like a law of nature over which we have little control. Where we do have control is in the picking of our friends. If I want to stay straight, I'll hang around those who also want to do that.

■ *I decide who I want to be by the friends I choose.*

J.C.

POSITIVE CRITICISM

Rebuke is more effective for a wise [person]
Than a hundred blows on a fool.
—PROV. 17:10

There are two types of criticism—destructive and constructive. Destructive criticism tears down feelings of self-worth, demolishes hopes and dreams, and plants seeds of self-doubt. It makes people defensive, and rightfully so; they are being attacked. The natural response is to retaliate verbally or withdraw emotionally. A person may come to believe that she is as insignificant as she was made to feel. Or she may dwell on what was said and become bitter and hateful toward the speaker. Whatever happens, the outcome will not be positive.

Constructive criticism, on the other hand, promotes change, teaches new thoughts, and builds confidence. It gives the person who is criticized a chance to improve. Everyone can benefit from someone else's perspective. But the manner in which it is presented is vital. The key component to constructive criticism is to discuss a person's actions or performance without attacking the person.

We all need constructive criticism in our lives, but we can do without the other kind. If you need to criticize someone's actions, be gentle—and check your motives. If you are being criticized, try to be understanding and really listen. The criticism just might be the very thing you need to hear.

■   *Father, help me learn to give and receive criticism*
constructively.

S.C.

An Angry Man

Make no friendship with an angry man,
And with a furious man do not go.
                                    —PROV. 22:24

One of seven adolescents are in violent dating relationships, according to a director of a domestic violence shelter.* She went on to say that "girls are beaten in the name of teenage love."

If a guy overreacts and explodes on different occasions, that's a warning sign to stay away. To associate with him would expose yourself to verbal and possible physical abuse.

When he's not angry, he may be the kindest, most thoughtful person. When he does explode, he may apologize and really feel sorry. His inability to control his anger does not make him a bad person, but it does mean he has a problem. Do not make the mistake of thinking you will be the one to help him overcome that problem. Don't forget you have your own recovery to work on.

There is also the danger that you will learn his way of expressing anger. If you hang out with someone who has a habit of shouting or of being physically aggressive, it's easier to act that way yourself. If you are the one being yelled at or pushed, you will feel angry. Your anger may come in the same way back at him or others. Violence stirs up more violence. Successful recovery requires better ways of handling one's anger.

■ *Abusive relationships make recovery rocky.*

                                                        J.C.

*Lou Ortiz, "Law Omits 'Date Violence,' Panel Told," *Chicago Sun-Times*, 22 November 1991, 130.

LIVING FROM WITHIN OUT

For indeed, the kingdom of God is within you.
—LUKE 17:21

I'm not the same person I was. The school is the same. The places to hang out are the same. My old friends may be the same. But I'm not. I've changed within. I don't *have* to please everyone. I don't *have* to be cool. I don't *have* to perform. I just have to be me.

For so long I let myself be defined by things outside of me—what kind of grades I made, who I dated, who my friends were, what activities I participated in. Whether or not I felt good about myself was determined by external things, accomplishments, and relationships. I lived from the outside in, rather than being me from the inside out. The author of *Letters from the Scattered Brotherhood* writes, "Your only safety is to be within the center of your kingdom, living from within out, not from without in."* I now live within the kingdom of God, and Christ is my centerpoint. The externals no longer determine my moods, my self-esteem, my recovery.

■ *I can go through this day with an inner calm, knowing that who I am doesn't depend on how others react to me. I am loved by Christ the King.*

D.K.

*Quoted in Frederick Buechner, *Telling Secrets* (San Francisco: Harper & Row, 1991), 56.

SPIRITUAL SUSTENANCE

Cast your burden on the LORD,
And He shall sustain you.
—PS. 55:22

It did not matter to Melinda what anyone said about her weight. In her mind, she could never be thin enough. Even though she had lost fifty pounds and was down to skin and bones, in her mind she remained fat. The fear of being fat was so intense that she had not eaten in two months. Except for chewing gum, diet soda, and water, nothing had passed her lips.

When a friend or family member would make mention of how thin she was, Melinda became even more determined to lose weight. Her thoughts turned paranoid: "They just want me to gain weight so they won't feel bad because they are fat!" She became obsessed with pounds, clothing sizes, calories, and grams.

On the outside, Melinda looked very thin. On the inside, she was even thinner. Her spiritual life had dwindled down to nothing. She rarely spoke to anyone, let alone the Lord. She had replaced Him with a new god—her obsession with food. As a result, Melinda was starving herself both inside and out.

■ *Lord, help me remember that recovery is always a spiritual issue. Without sustenance, both my body and my spirit shrivel.*

S.C.

PERFECT IN GOD'S EYES

The LORD will perfect that which concerns me.
—PS. 138:8

Annette's perfectionism was killing her. Her parents were divorced and she lived with her mother, but she spent every other weekend with her father. And Annette's definition of perfection was whatever she thought would make him love her more. Her father did not say much about his feelings directly but told Annette through his attitudes and actions what he valued. For instance, he would put her mother down for the extra weight she had put on since the divorce. Consequently, Annette was determined to keep her weight down—and she did it by binging and purging. It got so bad she kept coffee cans of vomit under her bed to hide it from her mom. She was slowly killing herself.

In order to live, Annette needed to see that she was already perfect. God saw her this way, because she had accepted Christ as her Savior. Remember, God's definition of perfect is not good grades or a slim figure, but faith. The only possible way for Annette to be perfect was to accept Jesus, which she had already done. After that, God wanted her to grow in her faith, which meant learning to give and receive love. In that sense, perfection is within easy reach of all of us—especially since He is the one who will be doing all the work.

■ *As his daughter, I am perfect in God's eyes, so I can relax and let Him perfect that which concerns me.*

J.C.

A HIDDEN DEPENDENCY

And everyone who competes for the prize is
temperate in all things. —1 COR. 9:25

Are you an adrenaline addict? Do you thrive on speed, thrills, risk, deadlines, or emergencies? If so, this hidden dependency may be fighting against your recovery.

Your body manufactures adrenaline to give you extra strength and energy in emergencies. In a crisis, it can save your life. The problem is, high adrenaline also feels good—it reduces pain and makes you feel strong and in control. It's easy to get in the habit of deliberately invoking an adrenaline "rush" through thrill-seeking, pressuring yourself, or getting hooked on hurry. Eventually you forget what it's like to live at a normal level; you need to "psyche yourself up" in order to get anything done. Some doctors even believe you can become physically hooked on your own adrenaline.*

Why is that bad? For one thing, it's rough on your body. High adrenaline has been linked to premature heart disease and other illnesses. But adrenaline dependency also can be a recovery roadblock. It's hard to depend on God and live a sane life when you are really depending on your own adrenaline to keep you operating at high speed!

■ *My recovery may need to include learning to live on*
less adrenaline.

A.C.B.

*See Archibald D. Hart, *Healing Life's Hidden Addictions* (Ann Arbor: Servant Publications, 1990).

DARK SECRETS

*Let us cast off the works of darkness, and let
us put on the armor of light.*

—ROM. 13:12

No one was aware that Chelsea was bulimic. She hid it
well. She knew all the tricks of throwing up quietly and
hiding food in inconspicuous places. She had her stom-
ach muscles trained to purge on cue. On the outside,
everything seemed normal. She ate meals with her
friends and family. She snacked just like everyone else
did. People used to marvel at how much she could eat
and never gain weight. They envied her "high meta-
bolic rate."

But Chelsea's successful secret life was also a lonely
one. Chelsea ate, threw up, abused laxatives, and cried
in isolation. She was too ashamed of her problem to tell
anyone.

Secrecy keeps us locked up inside. It alienates us
from others, makes us feel like we are abnormal or even
crazy, and teaches us to be ashamed. Secrecy is akin to
darkness—and it usually keeps us from facing the truth.

If you find yourself doing a lot of things in secrecy,
examine what you are doing. Dare to hold your life up to
the light. (You will probably need some loving support
in order to do this.) Allow the Lord to remove the hidden things from your life. His light brings liberation,
peace, and hope.

■ *God, I surrender my hidden secrets to you. Remove
the darkness from my life and let light surround my
thoughts and actions for your glory.*

S.C.

DISCOVERING MY GIFTS

There are diversities of gifts, but the same Spirit. There are differences of ministries, but the same Lord. —1 COR. 12:4–5

Do you get the impression that God likes variety? He made short, tall, and in-between people. Auburn, blonde, jet-black, and chestnut-colored hair adorns our heads. Hair texture can be coarse, kinky, fine, or wavy. Personalities can be quiet, flighty, serious, or outgoing.

God likes variety in our spiritual life, too. As part of our spiritual inheritance, He gives each of His children one or more spiritual gifts to help fellow believers grow. These gifts include the ability to give wise advice, teach, offer comfort, and serve others without complaining. (For more gifts, see 1 Cor. 12, Rom. 12, Eph. 4, and 1 Peter 4.)

To find out about your gifts, you may want to go over the lists of gifts and see what seems to fit. Ask those who know you what they think. And listen to the compliments others give you. Comments such as "Your words gave me hope" may tell you that you have the gift of encouragement. A comment such as "When you explain things I understand them better" may indicate a gift of teaching.

Recovery means developing a new identity, becoming that person God intended you to be. And that means becoming aware of the gifts God has given you.

◼ *Knowledge of my spiritual gift is part of knowing who the new me is.*

J.C.

HEAD UNDER THE COVERS

Consider and hear me, O LORD my God;
Enlighten my eyes,
Lest I sleep the sleep of death.

—PS. 13:3

Am I sleeping because I'm tired . . . or because I want to escape? I may not be abusing substances, but I can still find ways to hide from my feelings.

Recovery isn't easy—but I know it works. I had my doubts when I came into the program. I thought I was the only person who ever felt this way—all churned up inside, feeling like no matter what I did it wasn't enough. But God's love for me isn't based on my performance. By the grace of God, I walked away from crazy behavior and destructive addictions. If I can beat that, I can beat anything.

Sometimes sleeping all morning is easier than listening to my parents hassle me. But my parents aren't responsible for what I do with my life. And sleeping it away is a waste.

■ *God, get me up and moving when I'd rather stay in the cocoon of my covers. Let your love for me be louder than my mom's voice.*

D.K.

A HEAVENLY PARENT

If you then, being evil, know how to give good gifts to your children, how much more will your Father who is in heaven give good things to those who ask Him!

—MATT. 7:11

Parents are people who have taken on an incredible task. They are given a tiny person to love and care for, to teach and to mold into a mature, responsible human being. And how they perform that task will make a gigantic difference in their child's life. If they yell, hit, and show disrespect, the child will learn to do the same. If they demonstrate love, fairness, discipline, and support for one another, the child will learn to act in a similar fashion. The patterns they set in motion will affect their child's decisions, beliefs, opinions, and actions. And even if they die or leave home, their very absence will shape their children's lives.

The Bible calls God our heavenly Father. Like earthly parents, He takes on the responsibility of shaping our lives and helping us grow. He promises us His love, as well as His help, His discipline, and His faithfulness. Unlike earthly parents, however, God is an eternal Father. He is not subject to human failings; He gives His children nothing but good. Even when your earthly parents fall short of your expectations, He is still there to help you.

■   *God, please help me always to depend on you as my eternal Father.*

S.C.

UNSELFISH AMENDS

*Love suffers long and . . . does not seek
its own.*   —1 COR. 13:4–5

When I apologized, my little sister didn't say anything. I don't think she believed I meant it." As the oldest in her family, Sharon had often baby-sat her younger siblings and used that opportunity to sneak a drink. Afraid that her sister, Lynn, would tell on her, Sharon had resorted to threats and blackmail. She had also made a big deal about any mistakes Lynn would make—trying to feel better about herself by making Lynn feel bad. Now, however, she was trying to make amends.

"But I think Lynn is still scared of me," Sharon told me. "I want her to tell me how my drinking affected her. I need to hear it from her. I want to make it better."

However, Lynn was still hurting. She was not ready to accept Sharon's apologies. Sharon had already bullied Lynn in order to keep her drinking a secret. Now she was in danger of bullying her again. Sharon wanted Lynn to forgive her right away so she could feel relief. But making amends to Lynn meant Sharon had to prove to her that she had really changed. If there was to be any hope of reconciliation, Sharon would have to go at Lynn's pace. In the meantime, Sharon had to sit on her own guilt feelings and figure how to give them to God.

■   *God, help me not to inflict more injury in making amends. Help me not to further my own selfish agenda.*

J.C.

A PILE OF PROBLEMS

So Jesus said to them, "I say to you, if you have faith as a mustard seed, you will say to this mountain, 'Move from here to there,' and it will move." —MATT. 17:20

In our house, it doesn't take long for laundry to really pile up—just a few days of being out of town, or sick, or just busy. The heap of dirty towels and jeans and T-shirts becomes a mountain—and the job of doing the laundry looks like a hopeless task.

The problems in our lives can pile up that way, too. An argument with someone at school. A bad grade. Too many activities. Tension at home. Before too long, we have a mountain of seemingly unsolvable problems.

If that happens to you, don't give up. Instead, step back from the mountain and take a deep breath. Then begin the task of sorting out your circumstances one by one. Ask, "Is this a problem I have some control over?" If the answer is yes, mentally toss it over in a "Can Change" basket and make plans to work through the items in that basket—again, one at a time. But if your answer is no, toss that problem into the "Can't Change" basket and turn your back on it! When you're through sorting, that's the basket you turn over to God and forget about!

■ *Lord, I ask you for the wisdom to sort through my pile of problems. Thank you that you are there with me in the process.*

S.C./A.C.B.

SAYING NO TO DECEIT

*"Your habitation is in the midst of
    deceit;*
Through deceit they refuse to know Me,"
    says the LORD.
                          —JER. 9:6

Sarah was not the type of person to admit she had a problem. Other people had problems and needed help; she truly believed she could handle things herself. And yet Sarah found herself drinking a little more every day. Before school, she would take a drink from the bottle she had hidden in the closet. She had liquor stashed just about everywhere—in her locker, under her bed, in her car. Between classes, she would find a way to sneak a drink in.

Sarah's friends started noticing that she was becoming more withdrawn and moody. She snapped at them more than she ever had before. But Sarah still would not admit she was an alcoholic. That would be admitting that something had more control than she had.

Lying to ourselves or to others does not make a problem go away. It does not resolve it, change it, or enhance our lives in any way; it just means we stuff the problem down a little further. We can avoid dealing with our problems for a while, but eventually they will be on our doorstep again. And they will stay with us until we stop our deceit.

God calls us to be truthful. This means with ourselves and with others.

■   *Father, when I live in deceit I cut myself off from the
    help I need. Please give me the courage to see my
    problems as they are.*

                                                    S.C.

JESUS IN THE FRONT SEAT*

Take My yoke upon you and learn from Me. . . . For My yoke is easy and My burden is light. —MATT. 11:29–30

Jesus and I decided to take a trip on a bicycle built for two. I sat in the front and He in the back. I knew some of the shortcuts in the neighborhood. I had some places I definitely wanted to go.

My shortcuts led us through some alleys. Broken glass from beer bottles soon punctured one of the tires. "That's OK," He said, "I can fix it." Another shortcut led us to a dead end. After several detours I quit. I sat in the back and He in the front.

Jesus took me out of the familiar neighborhood to places I had never even heard of. At one point I asked Him where we were going. All He did was smile and yell through the wind, "Pedal! Pedal!" After a while, I learned to relax and enjoy the trip more. We had several rest stops, where the host gave us lovely gifts. At certain points during the journey, these became too heavy to carry anymore. Jesus told me to give them away, which I did reluctantly at first. But then I noticed there were always more gifts even better than before.

I still don't know where we'll end up. But I've found I enjoy the trip more when Jesus is in the front seat.

■　*Letting Jesus take the lead lightens the burden and keeps me on track.*

J.C.

*Adapted from a radio sermon by Charles R. Swindoll.

LIVING WITH BUBBLING HORMONES

How fair and how pleasant you are! . . .
O daughters of Jerusalem,
Do not stir up nor awaken love
Until it pleases.
—SONG OF SOL. 6:10; 7:6; 8:4

The first thing you notice about someone is whether they are a girl or a boy—and if you can't tell, it drives you crazy. We are created to be sexual beings. From the word *go*, we are created male and female, and things only get more interesting from there.

For so long I thought no one else thought about sex as much as I did. I wondered what was wrong with me. Did I have overactive hormones, or what? But then in recovery, I found people willing to be honest and real, even earthy at times. I found out I wasn't alone. The AA Big Book says, "We all have sex problems. We'd hardly be human if we didn't. . . . We remembered always that our sex powers were God-given and therefore good, neither to be used lightly or selfishly nor to be despised and loathed."*

Rather than working so hard to control or stifle my sexual feelings and fantasies, maybe I need to give them to God, asking Him what He wants me to do with them. He's faithful with everything else I bring Him; I can trust Him on this one, too.

■ *Sometimes "religiosity" makes it easy to forget that Jesus was wholly human. He must have known what hormones were all about.*

D.K.

Alcoholics Anonymous, 3rd ed. (New York: Alcoholics Anonymous World Services, 1976), 69.

LEARNING TO ASK

Ask, and you will receive, that your joy may be full. —JOHN 16:24

When Caroline was small, she had a difficult time getting the attention she so craved from her parents. They were always busy doing activities of their own. They were involved in their church, the PTA, as well as a few committees at work. So Caroline learned to manipulate her parents. She would often make them feel guilty in order to get something she felt she wanted or needed. And because doing good things seemed to be taken for granted, when Caroline wanted attention, she got in trouble. Then the school would contact her parents and let them know she was not behaving well. Caroline even went so far as to get herself in trouble with the police.

Unfortunately, Caroline's habit of manipulating others brought her problems in other areas of her life as well. For instance, since Caroline felt she had to manipulate her parents to get what she wanted, she also tried to manipulate her friends. It was not intentional, she just did not know how to communicate her needs directly. Out of her desperation, a lifelong harmful pattern had emerged. Changing it was one of her "target tasks" in recovery.

■ *Lord, teach me to ask for what I need instead of manipulating other people. Help me to believe, deep inside, that my need for love and attention isn't a lost cause.*

S.C.

A FRESH START

*Therefore, if anyone is in Christ, [she] is a
new creation; old things have passed away;
behold, all things have become new.*
—2 COR. 5:17

Valerie's eyes welled up with tears. She had lost her
virginity. "He took something from me I could only give
away once, and then he dumped me. You know what
that makes me? A slut! I hate his guts—and I hate myself for being so stupid."

Valerie had a choice. She could choose to see herself
as a slut who did not deserve to be treated well. This
could lead to more promiscuous behavior, sexually
transmitted diseases, substance abuse, and heartbreak.
Or she could choose to see herself as forgiven by God,
precious to Him, and empowered by Him to live a new
life.

Biological virginity can never be restored. However,
there are those who have turned their lives over to God
and let Him restore their spiritual and emotional virginity. Josh McDowell of the "Why Wait?" campaign calls
this secondary virginity. In secondary virginity, God
takes your hurts and lovingly performs His healing on
them. You then can start afresh with the new self He
gives you.

■   *If I let him, God can make me over into a new self
and let me start fresh with a new life.*

J.C.

GETTING REAL

Rejoice always, pray without ceasing.
—1 THESS. 5:16–17

Do you ever want to sneer, "Oh sure! Get real!" when you read something in the Bible? On my more cynical days I want to say that about this verse. Rejoice always? Sounds like someone who just doesn't know what life's like!

But this advice was written by someone (the apostle Paul) who experienced life at its worst—who was laughed at, beaten, and put in prison for his beliefs, and who suffered from a painful "thorn in the flesh" that none of his prayers could remove. What he learned—and what those of us in recovery have discovered—is that to "rejoice always, pray without ceasing" really does work. It doesn't mean brainwashing ourselves that everything is fine. But it does mean choosing to trust that God is involved in our lives and capable of producing good even out of our pain. It means keeping the communication lines open between us and God, not shutting Him off just because we don't understand what He's doing. It's an attitude that keeps us going in recovery. And that's as "real" as it gets.

■ *Lord, help me to "get real" with you—being honest about my problems but still choosing to rejoice, and especially keeping the prayer lines open.*

A.C.B.

MY FEELINGS ARE MINE

Whoever has no rule over [her] own spirit
Is like a city broken down, without walls.
—PROV. 25:28

In Linda's house, saying what you felt or believed was a major "no no." Linda's mother was considered "fragile," and no one was allowed to upset her by disagreeing with her. Several unspoken rules dominated the household: (1) Even if you are unhappy, say you are fine. (2) Don't show how you feel. (3) Assume that other people are correct and that they perceive things accurately, even when your perceptions are different. (4) Above all, protect others from hurting.

By age fifteen, Linda was convinced it was her job to make sure everyone felt OK and everybody's needs were met. She felt responsible for people she didn't even know well. She could never say no to requests, and she could never confront others because she always assumed they were right and she was wrong. She apologized at the drop of a hat. She was also an emotional basket case.

One of the biggest hurdles Linda faced in recovery was accepting that she was not responsible for the feelings of others. She didn't have the right to trample on others, but neither did she have the responsibility of protecting others. The only feelings she was responsible for were her own—and she needed to be honest about them.

■ *Lord, help me remember that I do not have to protect others from their feelings.*

S.C.

PLANS FOR YOU

> *"For I know the plans that I have for you,"*
> *declares the LORD, "plans for welfare and*
> *not for calamity to give you a future and*
> *a hope."*
> —JER. 29:11 NASB

Elizabeth knew the "no makeup" rule before she checked into our hospital inpatient unit, but that didn't stop her from throwing a tantrum about it. And it wasn't just about makeup. Elizabeth went into a tirade every time she encountered a limit she did not like.

Elizabeth's peers confronted her about making such a huge issue over small restrictions. And after a while, Elizabeth started to wonder about her overreactions. Exploring her past, she remembered two incidences of being date-raped while half drunk. She had been physically overpowered, bruised, and even cut. Maybe that was why the thought of letting anyone have any kind of control over her now threw her into a rage.

The problem was, Elizabeth had generalized her terrible experience into the belief that all attempts to establish control over her were harmful. This attitude was causing unmanageability in her relationships with her parents and teachers—and even with her peers. In order to get better, Elizabeth had to give up control—but not to a rapist, staff, or even to her parents. She had to hand the controls over to Someone who could always be trusted: God. Once she did that, she could relax and begin participating in His plans for her life and her healing.

■ *God has exciting plans for your future, but you won't*
know what they are until you give Him the controls
of your life.

J.C.

MAD AT THE WORLD

Be angry, and do not sin.
Meditate within your heart . . .
And put your trust in the LORD.
—PS. 4:4–5

Some things really tick me off. Breaking a nail. Losing my keys. Waiting in lines. Oversleeping. Finding my favorite jeans in the dryer—after I'd specifically asked my mother *not* to dry them. Things used to get to me in a big way. Too often I'd find myself irritable, impatient, short-tempered.

For too long I directed my anger at "safe" things. Confronting the real reasons for my anger was too scary or simply not allowed in my family. But breaking a nail or losing my keys are no longer the determining factors for how my day will go. I no longer lose my cool over simple inconveniences or minor irritations. Now when I'm angry I face it, own it, and figure it out. And when a broken nail does bring a blowup, I know to look deeper. The nail isn't the real issue.

Learning to deal with anger, when I've spent years learning to avoid it, takes time. But part of this program of recovery is learning that there are no failures, only slow successes.

■　　*God, give me time to relearn what I need to and the*
　　　grace to move on from there.

D.K.

WHEN I NEED FORGIVENESS

And whenever you stand praying, if you have anything against anyone, forgive him, that your Father in heaven may also forgive you your trespasses. But if you do not forgive, neither will your Father in heaven forgive your trespasses. —MARK 11:25–26

Learning to forgive is a vital aspect of recovery. But forgiveness has a flip side—asking forgiveness. Because we are human, we inevitably have times when we are insensitive, thoughtless, rude, or offensive. When we act out our anger, our words may be uncalled for or our actions hostile. Asking forgiveness, therefore, is an important part of step nine of the Twelve Steps of AA, which directs, "[We] made direct amends to such people whenever possible, except when to do so would injure them or others."

Pride often raises its ugly head at this point, however. "I'm sorry" may be two of the hardest words in any language to say. And it's true that asking forgiveness is risky. The one who was wronged may not be ready to forgive and may even be angry and vengeful. But *receiving* forgiveness from another person is not really the point of asking for it; the point is reaching out to make amends and thus opening ourselves up to receive God's forgiveness. We can't be responsible for how another person responds to us; all we can do is be faithful to what God directs. After that, the matter is between God and the person we have wronged.

■ *Lord, help me to put aside my pride when I need to ask forgiveness.*

S.C.

THE PURPOSE OF PAIN

*Why is my pain perpetual
And my wound incurable,
Which refuses to be healed?*
—JER. 15:18

The woman had stumps for hands and feet. Dirty strips of cloth covered them, and she covered her face with a veil. She pushed herself in a low cart up the dusty street, begging for money. On the streets of Madras, India, leprosy victims like her were a common sight.

Leprosy is a disease that attacks the nerve cells, so people who suffer from this disease don't feel any pain. And that's no blessing! When a leprosy victim cuts her toe, for instance, she feels no pain and may seek no treatment. The wound becomes infected, and gangrene may set in. Then the toe or foot has to be amputated. This was what had happened to the beggar woman.

God gave us physical pain as a warning sign; its purpose is to point out where we need healing. If we ignore the pain or numb it with painkillers, healing never has a chance to occur. That's true of emotional pain as well. Feeling the pain motivates you to seek healing. But hiding behind substances or behaviors only perpetuates the hurt.

When you experience pain in recovery, try to thank God for it. Use it as an arrow to point out where the emotional wound is. Then work with God and perhaps a therapist toward a real cure, not an anesthetic.

■ *Our pain can point the way toward healing if we don't ignore it or hide from it.*

J.C.

THE LIE OF FAST RELIEF

*Therefore be patient. . . . See how the farmer
waits for the precious fruit of the earth,
waiting patiently for it until it receives the
early and latter rain. You also be patient.*
—JAMES 5:7–8

We're living in the age of instant. Instant food. Instant replay. Instant gratification. We're used to seeing big problems solved in a minute ("Get fast, fast, fast relief") or a half-hour ("Gosh, what a mix-up; glad we got it all straight!") or, at most, a few weeks ("Tune in next Thursday for the exciting conclusion of. . . .".

That "instant" mentality makes recovery hard to take. After all, the whole emphasis in recovery is on slow growth, one day at a time, learning to trust God's timing instead of making things happen. But there's a reason recovery steers clear of the quick fix: it's a lie! And most of us got into trouble in the first place because we fell for the fiction of "fast relief." We swallowed the line that a six-pack or a boyfriend or a chocolate bar could fix our fear or our loneliness or our anxiety. What happened? We still felt fearful and lonely and anxious—and we had a painful addiction to worry about, too.

Sometimes recovery just seems to creep along. But during those "tear your hair out" times, it helps to remember: It's the slow, steady pace of recovery that brings lasting relief.

■ *Lord, I know the quick fix is a lie, but sometimes I just want to hurry things up. Give me patience to value long-term growth over fast relief.*

A.C.B.

BOUNDARY PATROL

So then each of us shall give account of [herself] to God. —ROM. 14:12

Boundaries is a common term in recovery circles. It refers to the instinctive "borders" that define our selves. Boundaries can be physical, emotional, or sexual. Their extent varies from person to person and culture to culture. But having distinct boundaries—and having those boundaries respected—is vital to our emotional health. Boundaries help us identify our values, beliefs, and feelings; they allow us to be individuals and to "give account of ourselves to God."

When a personal boundary has been trespassed, the normal response is anger and a sense of violation. But many people in recovery have had boundaries so violated by abuse or dysfunctional relationships that they have little sense where their personal limits are. They have to relocate their boundaries and then learn to defend them against violation. How? First of all by learning to "feel their feelings" without the anesthetic of a compulsion or addiction. And then by practicing certain specific "boundary patrol" techniques, which include: (1) speaking your mind; (2) refusing to put up with abuse; and (3) learning to say no.

■ *Lord, as I learn to tune in to you, teach me to patrol my boundaries. Teach me where I begin and everybody else ends.*

S.C.

CUTTING THE CLUTTER

I went by the field of the slothful. . . .
And there it was, all overgrown with thorns.
—PROV. 24:30–31

My desktop spontaneously creates clutter on its own. I have nothing to do with it. Put a soda-pop can on the desk, and another appears when my back is turned. Magazines, books, newspaper clippings, three-by-five cards, and paper clips all love to gather on my desktop. If I'm not careful, empty paper cups, cookie crumbs, and opened envelopes follow.

My desk requires regular clearing. Without it, the desk quickly becomes a junk station, not a place to work. It's purpose in life, to be a desk, is lost.

Recovery is like that, too; it requires constant attention. Pulling off the junk of "who cares?" attitudes, "poor me" outlooks, and "I just don't feel like it" laziness takes work. I may not feel like meeting with my sponsor, but I go anyway. I may not feel like working the Twelve Steps, but I do. I may not feel like talking to my mother about my anger, but I work things out with her anyway.

Sometimes the whole process is downright exhausting. And sometimes I may let the clutter build. Then I have more cleaning to do—but I do it. The rewards are worth it. When I keep my life "cleaned up," I find out more about the purpose in life God designed for me.

■ *Laziness and neglect can become habits that crowd out my recovery.*

J.C.

Surprising Myself

*No razor has ever come upon my
head. . . . If I am shaven, then my strength
will leave me, and I shall become weak,
and be like any other.* —JUDG. 16:17

I've always had long hair. Thick, dark, and long. And like Samson, my hair was a significant part of my identity. For Samson, his hair was the source of his strength. For me, it was the source of my femininity. Somehow I felt that without my long hair I wouldn't be attractive. Getting my hair trimmed was always just short of traumatic.

But recovery leads us in strange directions and down unexpected paths. What I never would have dreamed of doing, never have had the guts to do before I came into recovery, I find myself doing now. Confronting an issue at home, saying no, studying for an exam (not just cramming or conning), walking away from a bad situation—even cutting my hair. Short. *Really* short! And I love it.

Now my hair is symbolic of turning a corner. Changing from within. Becoming the person I want to be, not the person I think I should be.

So now my hair is a little funky and a lot of fun, a daily reminder not to take myself too seriously. Samson may have lost his strength when he cut his hair. I gained mine.

■ *When Christ lives within, we are never the same. He
takes our willingness to change and grow and brings
about some interesting surprises.*

D.K.

BLACK AND WHITE

Let me be weighed in a just balance,
That God may know my integrity.
—JOB 31:6

One thing you could say about Terry: She had style. I was impressed when she walked into my office with her hair dramatically slicked back and her sleek figure in a dramatic black-and-white sweater.

As I got to know Terry, however, I came to realize that her thinking was black and white as well—and that was part of her problem. She was great at getting noticed, but she felt abandoned if she wasn't the center of attention. If she couldn't get everything she wanted, she really felt she had nothing. In her mind, she had to be either good or bad, perfect or a failure, beautiful or ugly, right or wrong. And since nobody can be perfectly good, always beautiful, or perennially right, Terry got depressed a lot. Then she would pop a few pills and sleep round the clock.

A lot of Terry's recovery has involved breaking free from her black-and-white thinking. As she came to terms with her tendency to think in extremes, she began to understand why she needed to escape through drugs or oversleeping. She still has style, but she's learning she doesn't have to be perfect.

■ *Be alert for black-and-white thinking; it can be a recovery buster. Moderation and balance are important keys to a healthy life.*

S.C.

NOT FAIR!

For if the word spoken through angels proved
steadfast, and every transgression . . .
received a just reward, how shall we escape?
—HEB. 2:2–3

It's not fair!" That's the standard teenage rallying cry—usually accompanied by a red face and very intense feelings. Such indignation over life's injustices is based on the expectation that life *will be* fair. That kind of thinking just invites disappointment and leads to unmanageable behavior.

But let's say for the moment that life *is* fair. If this is so, then I should never be given a second chance on my driver's test if I fail. That wouldn't be fair to all the people who got it right the first time.

There should never be any makeup exams in school. That wouldn't be fair to the students who made it to the test and passed it the first time.

It's not fair that mothers should pay for prom dresses and shoes—after all, it's not their prom.

If we all got what we deserved all the time, we'd be in big trouble. In fact, we'd be dead. God says we all deserve eternal death. But fortunately for us, God in His love decided not to be fair. So instead of "fair" we get "grace." Grace means we get favors and goodies from God that we don't deserve. That's not fair. But life is not fair, thank God.

■ *Expecting that life will not be fair helps me be grateful for what I have and calm when I don't get what I want.*

J.C.

NOT BY MY STRENGTH

*Come to me, all you who are weary and
burdened, and I will give you rest.*
—MATT. 11:28 NIV

I'm tired, God. Why does recovery have to be so much work? I know I can journal, make calls, take a walk, or talk with my sponsor or friend. But I'm tired of the effort, tired of feeling I always have to police my own behavior. I want to resign from recovery.

But these feelings, too, lead me back to You. In my addiction, I think it's all up to me to "make it better." But I know that's not true. The first step of the Twelve Steps of AA says, "We admitted we were powerless over alcohol—that our lives had become unmanageable." Whether I've abused food, drugs, or alcohol, I'm powerless on my own.

My recovery is not by my strength, resolve, energy, or feelings. My recovery is by Your power within me—a power greater than my feelings of discouragement.

■ *Thanks, God, for carrying me through today no matter how I feel. I still think I can do this recovery bit like an assignment in school—learn the expected responses and get by—but I know that with you only absolute honesty counts. Anything less won't cut it. And I know your strength won't let me down.*

D.K.

A GOOD HARVEST

But the ones that fell on the good ground are those who, having heard the word with a noble and good heart, keep it and bear fruit with patience. —LUKE 8:15

I was raised in the breadbasket of America—Kansas. My home state is known for growing thousands and thousands of acres of wheat. So I have seen firsthand the remarkable amount of labor that goes into raising a crop. Before any seeds can be planted, the farmers have to plow the ground. It may need to be worked and softened before it is usable. The seeds must be planted in the fertilized ground so that birds won't eat them and the sun won't kill them. The farmers have to make sure their crops get enough water and are not overtaken by weeds, nor devoured by insects. And they have to wait patiently for the results; you just can't hurry a harvest!

Positive growth in our lives works much the same way. Our hearts, like the ground, need to be soft and receptive—sometimes God has to "soften us up" so the "seeds" of His grace have a chance for survival. We need to "fertilize" our seeds with prayer. Our tears keep the ground moist, and fun times provide the brightness we need. When our lives begin to change, we usually want to see the end result immediately, but it doesn't happen that way. Plants and people need time to grow. But if your growth is sprinkled with tears, sweat, some good times, and prayer, you have an excellent chance of yielding a good harvest.

■ *What "crop" is growing in your life today?*

S.C.

JUST ANOTHER BOYFRIEND

*Christ also loved the church and gave
Himself for it.* —EPH. 5:25

It's easy to switch addictions. At one time drugs, alcohol, or food was your boyfriend. He comforted you by numbing any hurts you had and was always there when you needed him. However, he was very possessive and demanded all your attention, energy, and time. After a while, you had nothing left for your family, school, friends, and God.

Then you broke up. The pain you had before you met him is still there—along with some new pain.

What do you do with the hurts? Your old "boyfriend" is always ready to take you back. But you don't want to go through that again, so you look around for a new one. Sex looks like an attractive possibility. Being held feels good; you don't feel so alone anymore. The pain is temporarily gone.

But sex is a liar. He promises you immediate intimacy but somehow leaves you feeling still empty—and used. He may give you "gifts" such as venereal disease or even AIDS. He takes away whatever common sense you have, and you find yourself making bad choices just to be with him. Pretty soon, you almost feel as if you're with your old boyfriend.

But there's hope. Jesus made us for Himself. He wants to nourish and cherish us. In fact the marriage relationship was modeled after Christ's love for us. He is the only One who can fill that hole in our hearts.

■ *Do I want "boyfriends" or marriage to Christ?*

J.C.

THAT'S WHY THEY CALL IT FAITH

For we walk by faith, not by sight.
—2 COR. 5:7

It hit me suddenly one day—one of those "aha" experiences. As usual, I was worrying over some decision, afraid to make a move: "What if it doesn't work? What if I screw up again? How do I know it's the right choice?" And that's when it hit me. "Of course you don't *know*. That's why they call it 'faith'!"

Even though I've heard about "acting in faith," I've still clung to the idea that faith is mainly something a person believes. But now I see faith as summoning courage to step out and do something I sense is right—even when I don't know for sure it will work. That's the way I got into recovery in the first place. I had to start living the program even before I had much confidence it would work. (But it does!)

Of course, "acting in faith" doesn't mean just striking out on any course that occurs to me. Having faith doesn't mean being stupid. I need to observe what works in the lives of others, ask for help, spend time in God's Word. And then . . . well, sometimes I have to act before I'm even sure what I believe. But the good news is: When I step out in faith, God moves in to meet me.

■ *Lord, thank you for honoring my little bit of faith. Give me the courage and strength I need to live faithfully, depending on you.*

A.C.B.

GOT WHAT IT TAKES

*In everything give thanks; for this is the will
of God in Christ Jesus for you.*
—1 THESS. 5:18

She was old, really old. Wrinkle-wrapped face, gray hair, clunky shoes. And she was going to a Twelve-Step meeting. We talked for only a few minutes before she headed into her group and I went to mine. "I admire you," she told me. "I wish I'd started when I was your age."

I'd never thought about it like that before. I thought I'd screwed up, really made a mess of my life. Yet she admired me, wished she had done what I was doing. So maybe I need to look at recovery from her perspective: I've got a forty- or fifty-year head start because I'm doing it now. Denial is no longer my masquerade. Avoidance is no longer my automatic response. And numb feelings are no longer my escape. My life is what I make it today.

The Big Book of AA says, "We will not regret the past nor wish to shut the door on it. [We] . . . suddenly realize that God is doing for us what we could not do for ourselves." The redemptive power of Christ has given me my life. I'm grateful that old lady reminded me that I'm just beginning. I've got a head start on life, because I'm living it by God's grace.

■ *I'm forgiven. I've been made new. I've got God's
love and a willing heart. I've got what it takes.*

D.K.

*Alcoholics Anonymous, 3rd ed. (New York: Alcoholics Anonymous World Services, 1976), 83–84.

THE RESULTS ARE WORTH IT

*My brethren, count it all joy when you fall
into various trials, knowing that the testing of
your faith produces patience. But let patience
have its perfect work, that you may be perfect
and complete, lacking nothing.*

—JAMES 1:2–4

Healing is an ironic thing. While it can be one of the
greatest experiences of our lives, it can also cause us so
much pain that we would like to give up. Sometimes we
may wonder whether it is really worth it."

Anne reached a point where she felt that way. "I
didn't think making changes in my life would be this
difficult!" she stated. "It is tough, Anne," I replied.
"Sometimes it takes more energy than you think you
can possibly muster. But I promise that if you can just
hang on, the results will be worth it."

Healing takes time. It takes effort. It takes patience.
Sometimes it takes everything we have. In a society
where we can obtain things quickly (instant coffee, instant credit, instant food), we expect instant healing. It
doesn't work that way though. It took a while to get
where you are and it will take a while to get better.

We don't have to go it alone, though. Counting on
friends, family members, support groups, and—most
importantly—God helps us make it through the rocky
times.

And the healing is really worth whatever it takes. The
changes you make today will make the differences in
your tomorrows. Don't stop trying!

■ *God, please give me the strength to keep trying when
I feel like giving up.*

S.C.

GIVE "IT" TO GOD

Today, if you will hear His voice,
Do not harden your hearts.
—HEB. 3:15

"No. Not that! I can't give that up! I *need* it."

Chris was squirming under God's finger—the finger that was pointing out the need to surrender control over something that was really important to her. She had volunteered to check into the hospital drug rehab program on one condition—that she would be out in exactly four weeks. However, Chris's heavenly Father had different ideas. He wanted her to surrender her right to control the discharge date and to stay as long as she needed to.

Chris began ripping her notebook cover in anguish and anger. Then she stopped. She heaved a sigh and simply said, "OK." She did not look too happy. She had just given "IT" to God. But she had done it as an act of her will, not as something she felt like doing.

That day, Chris began really working at recovery and not just giving lip service to it. Giving up control was painful. It felt unnatural. But the rewards were going to be worth it.

■ *I know I am working at my recovery when I feel the ripping away of my will. I start to grow when I place "IT" into God's waiting hands—whatever "IT" may be.*

J.C.

WHO'S IN CHARGE HERE?

Woe to him who strives with his Maker!
Let the potsherd strive with the potsherds
of the earth.
Shall the clay say to him who forms it,
"What are you making?"

—ISA. 45:9

I really get a kick out of this verse. To me, it paints a hilarious picture of what I must look like to God when I try to manage my life without His help. It's as ridiculous as a lump of clay or a broken sliver of pottery trying to give instructions to the potter!

In my mind, I picture one of those Disney pictures where inanimate objects have human features and personalities. Can you imagine a lumpy gray wad of clay tottering around on its wobbly clay feet and shaking a finger at the busy craftsperson? Or the little chips of china nagging in high, thin voices?

And yet that is exactly what I try to do when I lose track of who's really in charge. I try to take over my own life—and the results are disastrous. Things go much better when I relax and let the Master Potter shape my life. The result may not be what I have in mind, but I can be sure it will be something beautiful.

■ *Lord, help me remember who I am and who you are—and to trust that you know what you're doing in my life.*

A.C.B.

THE WRONG FRIENDS

The things which are impossible with [my own strength] are possible with God.
—LUKE 18:27

She was a good friend, or so I thought. We hung out together, told secrets, had fun. But whenever we spent time together, I found myself overeating, drinking, or doing things I didn't want to do. Making poor choices. Compromising myself.

The further into recovery I went, the more troubled I was by the friendship. Then someone in my support group asked me if she really *was* a friend. Maybe she was undermining my recovery. Maybe I needed to quit spending time with her. But how could I do that? How could I just stop being her friend?

The truth is, some people don't want us to change or get healthy. Some people will drain the life out of us if we let them. And sometimes making the choice to live free of addiction and insanity means walking away from certain relationships.

Knowing how and when to get out of bad or destructive relationships comes with time. My support network in recovery will see me through making tough decisions. The inner strength to do what I need to do comes through prayer and seeking God's will. All I have to do is come to God with a willingness and a desire to do the right thing.

■ *What I can't do on my own, I can do through the power of Jesus Christ.*

D.K.

CHOOSING WISELY

Without counsel, plans go awry,
But in the multitude of counselors they
*   are established.*   —PROV. 15:22

Every day we are surrounded by choices. We make many decisions in the course of a day—some big, some not so big. Over time, the decisions we make determine the course of our lives.

Anna always seemed to end up making poor choices. She didn't set out to make bad decisions; it just always seemed to happen. Anna could not understand why things would not work out the way they were supposed to. But after getting to know Anna, I had some ideas. For one thing, Anna did not like to plan ahead, so she often made decisions in haste. Also, because she did not feel confident in her abilities to make good decisions, she let herself be swayed by the advice of several friends who themselves were prone to poor choices.

When faced with a decision, how do you respond? Do you take the time to think about what to do, or do you just react? Do you receive wise counsel and look to God for guidance? If you need to make a decision, choose wisely. The choice you make may affect your life for a long time to come.

■   *Hasty decisions often result in regrets. Think about*
your options. Talk with people who can help you
make a good choice.

S.C.

A GOOD EXCUSE TO GROW

And do not be drunk with wine, in which is dissipation; but be filled with the Spirit.
—EPH. 5:18

Some people use getting drunk or high as an excuse to have sex, lose their temper, or indulge in other kinds of inappropriate behavior. After the substance wears off, they can look embarrassed when others tell them what they did. But they don't have to feel too guilty—after all, wasn't it the alcohol that made them do it?

In a similar but much more positive way, the Holy Spirit can influence you to do and say things you normally don't. And you can be filled with the Spirit when you transfer the controls of your life to God. The Holy Spirit does not demand. He waits for you to voluntarily give up the controls. He waits for you to ask Him for direction—and then He gives it. But it's up to you to follow His guidance. He doesn't make you do anything you don't want to do.

Being filled with the Holy Spirit is not a once-and-for-all experience, any more than being drunk is. You have to get a refill to get drunk again. With the Holy Spirit, you have to keep asking God what He wants you to do and then go ahead and do it.

Of course, there's a huge difference between getting high and being filled with the Spirit. The Spirit is not a taker, but a giver. When you give Him the controls, He gives you His power for a new life.

■ *God, help me to be willing to defer to you on all my decisions, big and little.*

J.C.

WALK AND NOT FAINT

But those who wait on the LORD
Shall renew their strength;
They shall mount up with wings like eagles,
They shall run and not be weary,
They shall walk and not faint.

—ISA. 40:31

Some days, "one day at a time" feels like too much of a commitment; it's all I can do to stay in recovery one *minute* at a time. The only way I can keep from slipping is to focus my eyes on each little step: "OK, now, just go to the phone instead of the refrigerator. OK, now, dial my sponsor's number . . ."

On days like that, it helps me to remember something John Claypool wrote about today's verse. He says it describes three different ways God gives us strength. In a way, the verse seems backward. Doesn't it make more sense to walk first, then run, then soar with eagles? But as John Claypool puts it, "When there is no occasion to soar and no place to run, then the promise of strength "to walk and not faint," small as it may seem, becomes infinitely significant and appropriate; in fact, it is the best gift of all."*

■ *Lord, thank you that you give me strength when I depend on you. With your help, I'll stay on my feet in recovery.*

A.C.B.

*John Claypool, *The Light within You: Looking at Life through New Eyes* (Waco, Tex.: Word, 1983), 137–38.

A HANDCRAFTED ORIGINAL

You are worthy, O Lord,
To receive glory and honor
and power;
For You created all things,
And by Your will they exist
and were created.
—REV. 4:11

This is an original, handcrafted garment," reads the boutique tag (right above the exorbitant price). "Minor irregularities of color and texture are part of the natural weave of the fabric and serve to enhance the uniquely beautiful design. Please wear and enjoy."

That's the kind of tag that should be attached to you! After all, you are an original, handcrafted design, created personally by the Master Designer. There is not another person just like you anywhere in the world. Even those irregularities that drive you crazy—your crooked nose, your offbeat sense of humor, the mole on your left elbow—are meant to enhance the natural beauty of God's design. God created you with all your special features. He knew what He was doing.

It's easy to fall into the trap of copying others or striving to be what you think others want you to be. But that's like trying to put a designer original on the sale rack at Dollar Mart! Instead of hiding your uniqueness, why not celebrate the fact that you are special? You are a work of art, different from all others and uniquely loved. Please live and enjoy!

■ *You are beautiful just the way you are.*

S.C./A.C.B.

WHY GOD STRETCHES US

> *Enlarge the place of your tent,*
> *And let them stretch out the curtains*
>   *of your habitations; . . .*
> *Lengthen your cords,*
> *And strengthen your stakes.*
>
> —ISA. 54:2

When I was seven, I used to make a tent out of my bed. An open umbrella under the covers made a cozy teepee for two. But one day there were three of us, so we decided to expand from bed to floor. The umbrella was too small, so we draped the blankets over chairs. When a fourth friend came, we had to "enlarge the place of" our tent even further. Blankets were stretched to full capacity. Now there was enough room for all of us and all our fun.

When God stretches us, He does so with a purpose in mind. Meeting difficult problems or challenges head-on can expand our ability to enjoy life later. Meeting the challenge of keeping straight allows us to enjoy relationships instead of depending on drugs, alcohol, or food. After having a time of abstinence, we may become aware of old hurts we used to numb out with substances. God is doing more stretching. Allowing God to heal these hurts brings a new depth to our lives and our relationships. We find we have more energy, more stability. And because God is in control, our tent pegs are deeply anchored into the ground.

■ *God stretches us through the hard times so we can better enjoy the good times.*

J.C.

LETTING GOD BE GOD

Seek first the kingdom of God and His righteousness, and all these things shall be added to you. —MATT. 6:33

Who—or what—is my god right now? Easy to reply almost automatically, "God, of course!" But is that really true? Today? Right now?

What is weighing most heavily on my mind? The thoughts that follow me from place to place, popping into my mind uninvited, are probably a good indicator of what I've placed at the center in place of God. Even after years of recovery, I find it so easy to let God be pushed aside by thoughts of something I've said, something I want, something I'm nervous or worried about. So what is it today that threatens to capture my undivided attention? An exam? A date? Shopping? Family hassles? My period coming late? Whatever fills my thinking to the exclusion of serenity is what I've made my god—at least temporarily.

People, places, and things I find myself obsessing about will never fill me from within. That, only God can do. Letting God be God isn't something decided once and for all. Committing my life to God and putting Christ at the center is a daily act, a decision to be made every day, one day at a time.

■   *God, you know all the things I tend to put in your place. You know my worries, my fears, my wants, and my needs. So today, for this day, I'm putting all of me in your hands.*

D.K.

COMING CLEAN

> *Do not lie to one another, since you laid aside the old self with its evil practices.*
> —COL. 3:9 NASB

There is a phrase I hear a lot these days: "coming clean." It is kind of catchy and, in my opinion, it is powerful. Telling the truth to others can be very difficult. If you've been in the habit of telling "white lies" or even big lies, it's even hard to know what the truth is, much less tell it to others. But admitting past lies, making amends for them, and breaking the habit of deceit are all crucial parts of recovery.

How close are you to coming clean? "Scraping off" dirty spots of lies in your life is not fun. Going back to a person and apologizing for lying to him or her can be humiliating (but it can also be a liberating experience). Telling a parent the whole truth may be tough, and there may be consequences (but it's one more step toward rebuilding trust).

No one ever said honesty was easy or convenient. It is necessary, however, if you are going to recover. Remember, the Lord knows your heart. He knows the truth. And your lies will eventually find you out. Lies are like spider webs: they entrap, entangle, and are difficult to escape.

■ *Father, please help me to come clean before you, myself, and others.*

S.C.

WORKING UP A SWEAT

Now no chastening seems to be joyful for the present, but grievous; nevertheless, afterward it yields the peaceable fruit of righteousness to those who have been trained by it.
—HEB. 12:11

I don't like to sweat when I take an aerobics class. When I sweat I get sticky and smelly. Then I have to take a shower, which takes up more of my time. But I've learned that if I really want to go somewhere with the exercise program, the sweat has to come. Sweat is a sign I'm making an effort. It also means my body is getting disciplined to do things I never thought it could do.

Recovery is a sweaty discipline. God does His job in removing the character defects that keep our addictions alive and well. But we have to cooperate—and that's hard. How nice it would be if God would just dissolve our defects. But recovery doesn't work that way. If I want to get better, I need to work up a little sweat.

What does it mean to "work up a sweat" in recovery? It means being willing to take risks with God—like risking rejection from my partying friends by saying "no" to them. It also means sticking to the disciplines of recovery—like journaling or attending support meetings—even when I don't feel like it. Such effort can be uncomfortable or even painful, but the "sweat" is a sign that the process is working. If I persist, I'll eventually be able to do things I thought were impossible for me.

■ *Lord, give me the courage and endurance to "work up a sweat" in recovery. Keep on reminding me that the results are worth the work.*

J.C.

GOD CAN TAKE MY HONESTY

O daughter of Babylon, . . .
Happy shall he be who repays you as you
*   have served us!*
Happy shall he be who takes and dashes
Your little ones against the rock.
                                —PS. 137:8–9

What a horrible thing to say! Is this really in the Bible?

Anyone who thinks the book of Psalms is just a collection of pretty little poems hasn't read it. Mixed right in with the praise and rejoicing are whiny complaints, vengeful curses, and angry accusations. (Check out Psalm 102, for instance, or Psalm 109.) I'm sure these "negative" Psalms have all sorts of theological and historical explanations. But I believe they are there, at least in part, to show that we can come to God with absolute honesty. The psalmists obviously felt comfortable telling God just exactly how they felt—even when the feelings were less than noble. They knew God is big enough and powerful enough to take our honest attitudes—even the angry, petty, venomous ones—and somehow, eventually, make them positive.

God knows my heart. He is never surprised by my selfishness, my jealousy, my unacceptable thoughts and desires. And He wants me to bring even these sleazy parts of my soul to Him. If I open up my whole self to Him, He will not condemn me. Instead, He will set to work transforming me into somebody I'm not ashamed of.

■   *Lord, thank you that I can talk to you honestly about*
    anything—as long as I am willing to listen to you as
    well.

                                                A.C.B.

A TRAVELING STRATEGY

Commit your works to the LORD,
And your plans will be established.
—PROV. 16:3 NASB

I'm going on a trip next week."

"Really? Where are you going? Are you driving or flying? What are you going to pack? How much money will you need?"

"Well, I don't know . . . I'm just going."

How would you rate that person's chance of getting anywhere? Not great! And yet so many of us seem to think we can move forward in life or recovery without taking the time to consider where we're going or how we're going to get there. Talk about wishful thinking!

If you want to be successful in any endeavor—recovery included—you need to first ask yourself, "Where do I want to go?" If you have no idea what your goal is, how will you know when you have arrived? Second, consider, "What needs to happen for me to reach this goal?" You will probably need to seek the input of trustworthy people, and you will probably need to map out some intermediate steps. Third, get going. Begin working toward your goal a step at a time. Even if you run into problems and must take a step or two backward, you will still be further along than if you had never tried. And if you keep your destination in mind and depend on God as you travel, you will eventually reach your destination.

■ *God, walk with me as I move forward step by step.*
S.C.

MUSIC FOR THE HEART

Keep your heart with all diligence,
For out of it spring the issues of life.
—PROV. 4:23

Patti was furious. "I hate you," she screamed at her mother as she slammed the door of her room. Then she switched on the stereo and sank back on her bed as the words and music flowed all around her.

Music can be powerful. It can move us to tears or bring back a flood of memories. For Patti, it was a way of coping with her anger. She thought that listening resolved her feelings, but usually it only numbed them temporarily. And some of the music actually fed her anger. The songs she liked were those with driving, angry beats and lyrics that talked about how unfair life was and about how people should stand up for their rights. Instead of relaxing her or giving her another way of looking at her problems, they left Patti feeling restless and stirred up.

If the music you listen to feeds your anger, you may be setting yourself up for a possible relapse. God warns us to guard what we allow into our hearts—and "heart" here refers to both our thinking and our emotions. If you constantly feed your "heart" with songs that portray the world as hostile and uncaring, you will probably begin to think and act accordingly. But music that helps you see the world through God's eyes can keep you going in recovery.

■ *I can choose music that supports my recovery instead of feeding my negative feelings.*

J.C.

A WALL OF GRAY

Now Jesus, walking by the Sea of Galilee, saw two brothers, Simon called Peter, and Andrew his brother, casting a net into the sea. . . . And He said to them, "Follow Me. . . ." They immediately left their nets and followed Him. —MATT. 4:18–20

Peter was on the beach when he first met Jesus. I grew up on the coast, and I've spent countless hours walking the beach, listening to the waves' rhythmic surge and the incessant shrieks of the gulls, feeling the wind in my face. Once I stood on the beach, alone, and watched a fog bank roll in. It was eerie—watching a wall of gray move slowly toward me until I was completely enveloped, unable to see the surf beyond five or six feet, the horizon no longer visible. I was alone beneath an incredible blanket of silence.

For those of us in recovery, the tendency to isolate is a common denominator. Isolation creeps in slowly, blanketing our world as quietly as a fog bank rolling in. And isolation is deadly, shutting us off from those who hold us accountable and offer support. Isolation moves us from being a participant in life to being a spectator.

One saying I've heard in my recovery group is, "We may be powerless over our addiction, but we're responsible for our recovery." Part of being responsible is accepting that I can't do it on my own.

■ *Even Jesus had a support group. Now they're called disciples, but when Christ called them, they were every bit as human as we. The only difference was their willingness to walk a daily walk with Christ and each other.*

D.K.

No More Power Struggles

The beginning of strife is like releasing water;
Therefore stop contention before a quarrel starts.
—PROV. 17:14

Julia and her mother were at war. There may not have been any guns used in the battle, but there were battle wounds from the words that were constantly being hurled at each other. They argued over the smallest details. If one said "black," the other said "white." If her mom said "no," Julia screamed "yes." The skirmishes usually had very little to do with the subject being discussed but had everything to do with a gigantic battle of the wills. Mother and daughter were embroiled in a perpetual power struggle.

Julia finally found one way that her mother could not have any say so over her life: She stopped eating. When her mother would try to force her to eat, Julia's desire to starve herself grew even stronger. It was a battle that would have two losers. In Julia's endeavor to win a war, she was destroying both her health and her relationships. And Julia's mother, in her effort to draw Julia closer, was pushing her farther away. A war of the wills typically has no victors, only victims.

■ *Father, the only way I can avoid these insane power struggles is to put the power back where it belongs—in your hands. Teach me to avoid unnecessary strife by depending on you.*

S.C.

MISTAKES ARE MY TEACHERS

Incline your ear to wisdom. . . .
For the LORD gives wisdom.
—PROV. 2:2, 6

Janice's first "step aerobics" class was a disaster. She overestimated her endurance and elevated her platform board too high. This made it hard to concentrate on the instructor and the "lefts" and "rights." By the middle of class, Janice felt she was going to die of muscle cramps and embarrassment. She felt like never going back. However, she really did want to get in shape, so she did go back. This time she kept her platform low. Her endurance was better. She could concentrate. The "rights" and "lefts" made sense this time. She even enjoyed herself.

Janice could have chosen to give up after the first class. That would have been all right, but she would have missed out on something she really wanted. Instead, she tried again. She used her mistakes as a lesson in what not to do the second time.

Proverbs tells us to be attentive to wisdom and understanding. Being attentive means seeing my mistakes as opportunities to learn how to be successful next time . . . or the next.

Of course, some mistakes are bigger than others. Relapse has bigger consequences than a messed-up aerobics class. But even if you have gone through a relapse, don't let it go to waste. Learn about your weaknesses. Maybe like Janice, you overestimated your strength. Like her, you can learn, adjust, and try again.

■ *With God's help, my mistakes can be my teachers.*

J.C.

Build Your Own Family

God sets the solitary in families;
* * *
You, O God, provided from
Your goodness for the poor.
—PS. 68:6, 10

Families are where we learn to live with ourselves and others. But many of us in recovery have been short-changed in the family department. Maybe bitterness and tension reign in your home. Maybe your parents are too caught up in their own problems to help you with yours. Maybe alcoholism or abuse has warped your family experience. If that's true, you can ask God to provide you with a substitute family where you can learn more about love, acceptance, compromise, and support.

Pam unofficially adopted herself out to her best friend's family. By hanging out at their house, she gained a more balanced idea of how togetherness works. Gerry asked an older woman in the church to be her "adopted grandma." In their shared time together, she found a warmth and closeness that were lacking at home. LaKesha thought of her support group as family; from them she learned honesty, acceptance, and love. And Joanie found family at her church, where she saw God's love and unconditional acceptance at work.

■ *Father, I know that I am poor in healthy family experience. Set me in a family so I can learn more about healthy togetherness.*

A.C.B.

THE GOSSIP GAME

Set a guard, O LORD, over my mouth;
Keep watch over the door of my lips.
—PS. 141:3

In elementary school we used to play a game called "gossip." Someone would start at the front and whisper a sentence into the next person's ear. The message would go up and down the rows until the last person received it and announced what she had heard. Giggles would fill the room because the message was always so different from what it had been in the beginning.

Gossip is not just a harmless child's game. Young and old people are willing participants in this destructive activity. Gossip destroys reputations, wounds feelings, smears the truth, and tears people apart—yet most of us engage in it periodically. It is difficult not to repeat a piece of juicy news about someone. After all, the one who holds the scoop generally has a lot of power and gets a lot of attention.

And yet God admonishes us not to gossip about others. The end message will, in all probability, be different from the truth anyway, so why pass it on? Better yet, why participate at all? Isn't it better to love and support others than to pass on information about them?

■ *Father, as the Scripture says, please place a watch on my lips. Help me not to play the gossip game.*

S.C.

A CLUE TO MY HURT

But God has revealed them to us through His Spirit. For the Spirit searches all things, yes, the deep things of God. —1 COR. 2:10

When Veronica's boyfriend was slightly late for a date, she worried that maybe he had gotten into a car accident. When they disagreed, she feared he would break up with her.

When Michelle's parents tried to enforce a curfew on her, she ran away the next day. When they told her she needed to live by their rules at home, she screamed at them for being unfair.

What these two girls have in common is that they both overreacted. After a time of being straight, feelings become more noticeable. They are not being numbed out anymore—and sometimes we overreact to things that trigger them.

Usually, a pattern can be seen in the overreaction. Veronica's overreactions were based on her fears that people she loved would abandon her. Her parents had divorced when she was a baby. On the rare occasions when she saw her biological father, he was drinking. Michelle's reactivity had to do with control issues. She had been overpowered and then sexually abused repeatedly by two neighbor boys. To her, someone's having control over her meant pain.

Overreactions can be our opportunity to ask God's Holy Spirit to reveal what hurts He sees in us that need healing.

■ *The Spirit searches all things in me and points out what he wants me to work on.*

J.C.

NOTHING CAN SEPARATE US

For I am persuaded that neither death nor life, nor angels nor principalities nor powers, nor things present nor things to come, nor height nor depth, nor any other created thing, shall be able to separate us from the love of God which is in Christ Jesus our Lord.
—ROM. 8:38–39

Though my emotions may be fluid, ever-changing, my God is ever faithful. Sometimes past regrets or feelings of failure can seem overwhelming. But without my past, without the decisions I've made and things I've done, I wouldn't be who I am.

When regrets creep into my thoughts, bringing feelings of shame or fear, resentment or anger, I need no longer be captive to those feelings. I can look at my past straight-on, knowing that only in accepting myself for who I am will I be free to become who I'm created to be. Christ doesn't wait until I've got it all together to love me. He loves me in this moment, despite my faults, limitations, and failures. My God is a God of redemption and reconciliation. Nothing I have done, and nothing yet to come, can separate me from the faithfulness of His love.

■ *God, when I feel ashamed, unworthy of your love, open my heart to your healing presence. I've made a decision to turn my will and my life over to you. My decision to trust you isn't based on the way I feel right now.*

D.K.

I CAN'T SEE IT

We grope for the wall like the blind,
And we grope as if we had no eyes. . . .
For our transgressions are multiplied
before You. —ISA. 59:10, 12

Denial is such a tricky thing to cope with. After all, the very definition of denial is that I can't see it in myself. How can I break free of denial if I don't even know I'm in it?

That's one reason recovery doesn't work in isolation. That's why I desperately need God and other people. When I'm in denial, my pain and my guilt and my shame make me absolutely blind to what I'm doing to myself and others—and I can't get over blindness just by deciding to see! Depending on God's insight and on the loving acceptance and gentle confrontation of other people who understand where I'm coming from is the only way I can be healed.

Experience can help, though. Once I've seen how utterly blind I can be about something that is really obvious—like having an elephant right in front of me and not seeing it—I'm a little more willing to listen when others tell me I'm not seeing straight.

■ *Lord, one of your major claims to fame is that you make the blind to see. I need that healing touch for my denial. Help me to accept the gift of sight from you.*

A.C.B.

DEFUSING ANGRY EXPLOSIONS

A soft answer turns away wrath,
But a harsh word stirs up anger.
—PROV. 15:1

If you are an "exploder" when it comes to anger, this verse is for you. It offers hope for better relationships. Emotional blowups or harsh words just make enemies out of friends or family. Even if the other person started it, reacting with a temperamental outburst just creates more hard feelings.

Proverbs tells us that a soft answer will pave the way for possible reconciliation by turning away wrath. But a soft answer is hard to come by for someone who is used to exploding in anger. How do you answer softly when you're already seeing red?

One helpful technique is to consciously slow down your breathing. (Anger will have you breathing fast.) Tell yourself, "Stop! Slow down." Then begin breathing rhythmically: breathe in for three counts, hold for two, and gradually breathe out for three counts. Keep up this rhythm until you begin to feel yourself more under control and less reactive.

Once your body has slowed down, you'll find it easier to think. Opening your mouth and saying something you'll regret later creates unnecessary unmanageability. God has provided you with other options.

■ *Remember: Stop! Slow down. Breathe.*

J.C.

PARENTS ARE PEOPLE, TOO

*A new commandment I give to you, that you
love one another; as I have loved you.*
—JOHN 13:34

Making changes in recovery can suddenly clarify the craziness of others around me. For instance, my addictive/compulsive behavior is often a means of avoiding how painful, difficult, or embarrassing my *parents'* behavior can be.

Parents are people, too—no more, no less. They may be struggling with alcoholism, workaholism, depression, addiction, rage, or abuse. And parents tend to do for their kids what they won't do for themselves. They pay for the finest treatment programs, get their kids into therapy, and genuinely want to be supportive—all the while being blind to their own insanity.

It's quite possible, perhaps probable, that I will become a healthy individual well before my parents acknowledge their own issues. That's tough. The natural temptation is to lash out, judge, or blame. Sometimes I've wanted to scream, "Can't you see what you're doing?!"

But recovery is not about the other person—even if that person is my mom or dad. So for now, I accept that my parents are doing the best they can. And what I have a hard time accepting I give to God, knowing that recovery doesn't happen all at once.

■   *God, my parents' recovery is not up to me. I leave that between you and them, knowing you're in control.*

D.K.

Perfect Peace

You will keep [her] in perfect peace,
Whose mind is stayed on You,
Because [she] trusts in You.
—ISA. 26:3

This is how I imagine it: Howling, screaming winds. Pelting, biting rain. Ear-shattering thunder and eye-assaulting bolts of lightning. And then there's me, right in the middle of it, curled up in a sturdy little shelter under a cozy comforter—aware of the hullabaloo but not particularly concerned because I know I am safe inside.

That is the kind of peace God promises me. And He says I can have it right in the middle of whatever is going on—storms, ridicule, frustration, anger. I can have it right in the middle of chaos at home, as I'm smushed up against my locker in the hallway, or when I'm humiliated in gym class.

If . . .

If I keep my thoughts on the Source of all peace—God himself. If I take the time to get to know Him, praying and meditating on His Word. If I give Him room in my life.

If I do these things, He promises to build me a cozy little shelter right in the center of my being—a comforting nook where I can go whenever the wind picks up and the rain starts hammering down.

■ *Lord, I invite you to come into my life, occupy my thoughts, and teach me the secret of perfect peace.*
A.C.B.

REACHING OUT

> *Be kindly affectionate to one another with*
> *brotherly love, in honor giving preference*
> *to one another.* —ROM. 12:10

In today's "me" society, it is easy to become self-consumed. Thinking only of ourselves becomes a habit. But even though the focus of recovery needs to be on yourself, it is still important to reach out to others. Doing thoughtful things for others blesses givers as well as receivers.

Helping others has a unique way of lifting everyone's spirits. Next time you feel like moping around the house, figure out what you could do to be of service or comfort to another. Cleaning out the garage, baking cookies for someone, mowing the lawn, or even sending a card anonymously would be a better way of spending your time.

If every human being stays wrapped up in herself, very few needs will be met. But each thoughtful deed or kind word adds significantly to the joy that everyone feels. It's like throwing a pebble in a pond. There is a ripple effect.

Look around you. You won't have to look far before you find someone who would be willing to be blessed by you. Reaching out to him or her will do you both good.

■ *Begin today with a small act of kindness*

S.C.

"THE ATTITUDE"

*Therefore by Him let us continually offer the
sacrifice of praise to God, that is, the fruit of
our lips, giving thanks to His name.*
—HEB. 13:15

Some mornings, you may not feel like getting up, but
you do. You may not feel like going to school, attending
a support-group meeting, meeting with your sponsor,
going to your part-time job, going to swim class, speaking politely to a teacher, stopping at a red light, taking
your dog for a walk, or wearing clothes . . . but you do.
If you don't, life goes bananas.

Your spiritual life is the same. Today's verse tells us to
continually offer a sacrifice of praise to God. "Sacrifice" means you may not feel like doing it but you do it
anyway. "Continually" means all the time. No one feels
like doing something all the time. So carrying this direction out can't depend on feelings. What does it depend
on? Your will. It's a decision you make.

Giving thanks and praise must be pretty important to
God if He wants us to do it continually. God wants us to
give up "an attitude" for "the attitude" of thanksgiving.
"An attitude" sees the world as hopeless and hostile.
"The attitude" sees the world through God's eyes. "An
attitude" sees a problem or an addiction as making us
damaged goods. "The attitude" sees it as making us
more dependent on God and thus moving us toward
success in life.

■ *Do I have "an attitude" or "the attitude"?*

J.C.

DON'T SWEAT THE SMALL STUFF

Thus says the LORD, who created you, . . .
"Fear not, for I have redeemed you. . . .
When you walk through the fire, you shall
not be burned. . . .
Fear not, for I am with you."

—ISA. 43:1–5

She was the one who found him. Her father had committed suicide while she and her sister were at school. She got home before her sister, went to the bathroom, and there he was. She had the presence of mind to lock the doors, place a call for help, then go outside to wait for her sister to get home from school.

After all she had been through, one thing amazed me: her attitude. She frequently said, "Don't sweat the small stuff."

That certainly puts things into perspective. *Don't sweat the small stuff.* Those are good words to hang on to. Overreacting to small things, blowing the unimportant out of proportion, placing myself at the center of the universe—that's when I get into trouble. That's when I need to back up, let go, and "let God."

And what if I can't let go? What if something keeps bugging me, causing me to churn inside? That's when I need to seek the outside perspective of another person. Calling a sponsor or friend, voicing my concern at a support meeting, journaling, or praying—all these can help put my life back into perspective.

■ *Don't sweat the small stuff. God listens. God hears.*
Even when something feels bigger than me, it's
never bigger than God.

D.K.

CHECK IT OUT!

You desire truth in the inward parts,
And in the hidden part You will make
me to know wisdom. —PS. 51:6

Do you catastrophize? "I probably flunked the test. I wasn't sure of some of the answers, so I guessed. If I flunk, I'll flunk the course. But I have to pass! If I don't, I'll graduate a year behind everybody else. . . ."

Do you make up motives for others? "I said hi to her, but she just stared right through me when were changing classes. I know she's mad at me. I should have sat with her at lunch yesterday. Now she thinks I'm a snob. . . ."

Do you read too much into a situation? (to continue the above scenario) ". . . but she knew band practice let out late. I couldn't find a seat next to her without moving everyone around. What's wrong with her? Who does she think she is? She expects too much! I thought we were good friends, but I can't take her snobby attitude."

God gave us the measuring stick of truth for our thinking. In the first case, it would have been better if the girl had waited for her test scores before assuming all those catastrophes. In the second case, she falsely assumed her friend was mad, when her friend probably did not see her. In the third case, she assumed her friend expected too much. She needs to check out these expectations to find out the truth. Doing this would avoid a lot of unmanageability and worry.

■ *God, help me to sort out the truth from my assumptions.*

J.C.

DON'T LOOK DOWN

*And when Peter had come down out of the
boat, he walked on the water to go to Jesus.
But when he saw that the wind was
boisterous, he was afraid; and beginning to
sink he cried out, saying, "Lord, save me!"
And immediately Jesus stretched out His
hand and caught him.*

—MATT. 14:29–31

She's amazing. Graceful in spangles and tights, she
steps out onto the wire high above the sawdust floor.
Carefully but confidently, she walks forward, back. She
balances on one leg. She does a handstand. She even
rides a unicycle. And she does it all with steadiness and
poise and a smile on her lips.

What's her secret? She doesn't look down. She
doesn't think about falling. Instead, she keeps her mind
on what she's doing and her eyes focused ahead.

Peter learned that secret, too, when he tried to walk
to Jesus on the water. He looked down at the swirling
sea and immediately began to sink. Only when he
looked back at Jesus and grabbed hold of Jesus' hand
did he stop wallowing in the waves.

When my life feels like a tightrope act or a raging
storm, it helps to remember Peter's secret. I can keep
moving with serenity and confidence—*if* I don't look
down. I can keep my head above water—*if* I keep my
eyes on Jesus and my hand in His comforting grasp.

■   *Father, teach me to keep my eyes on you. Thank you
that you lift me back up even when I forget what I'm
doing, look down, and start to go under.*

A.C.B.

SEEKING EVIL

[She] who diligently seeks good seeks favor,
But [she] who searches after evil, it will
come to [her]. —PROV. 11:27 NASB

Why am I always the one who gets caught?" moaned Staci. Five girls had been involved in spray-painting the building, but she was the one who got in trouble. "It's not fair," she complained. "Just because I have a drug problem, everyone is all over my case."

Staci was missing the point. Her friends may have been guilty, too, but so was she. In getting involved with the prank, Staci had been "searching after evil." She really had no reason to be surprised or indignant when it came "after her."

God tells us we will reap what we sow (Gal. 6:7). If we plant corn, we really shouldn't expect to harvest wheat. And if we sow seeds of trouble, we shouldn't be surprised to get trouble in return. True, sometimes things will happen that we are *not* responsible for (like being abused!). But the general rule still holds: If we search after evil, one way or another it will come after us. Denying our responsibility for what we have done just blocks recovery and hinders our growth.

■ *Lord, help me sort out the things I'm responsible for from the things I am not responsible for—and to take responsibility for the times when I am "seeking evil." Thank you for forgiveness and your gift of a fresh start.*

S.C.

No More Junior Therapist

For each one shall bear [her] own load.
—GAL. 6:5

Amy looked worn out. Her eyelids sagged. Dark circles shaded her eyes. "I was up all night looking for Matt" (her ex-boyfriend). "I heard he had run away from home a couple of days ago. I finally found him with Paul. Paul's been living on the street for three months."

Amy had broken up with Matt over a year ago. She had enough worries of her own: why would she volunteer to take on someone else's? She and her mother were not getting along. In fact, Amy was living with her grandmother, but things were not going well with that relationship, either. Amy also faced the decision of going back to high school or getting a job. So why was Amy expending so much energy on Matt?

The answer to the puzzle was when Amy felt overwhelmed by her own troubles she focused on someone else's. Other people's problems were less painful than her own. In fact, Amy's way of coping—being a "junior therapist"—helped her feel better about herself. Like a drug, it numbed out her own painful feelings of inadequacy. This habit can also be called codependency.

It's not bad to help others. But when one neglects one's own problems as a result, helping can be harmful.

■ *Heavenly Father, help me to see the signs of unmanageability my codependence brings.*

J.C.

THE COURAGE TO CHANGE

Show me Your ways, O LORD. . . .
Lead me in Your truth and teach
me. —PS. 25:4–5

I'm not quite sure how we got to be friends. I didn't start off thinking I was going to hang out with losers. It just sort of happened. And before long, I was right in there making choices and decisions that headed me full-tilt toward self-destruct.

I know I want more from life. I know I'm not a loser. I know they're not the ones I want to hang out with. But we're still in the same school—same classes, same schedules. Sometimes it's like they have an invisible net they throw at me, and I feel snared, trapped, drawn back in. I never knew breaking away would be so tough.

Old patterns don't change easily, and if I hang out with those people, I know what patterns I can easily fall back into. But talking about that in my support group or with a counselor is one thing that helps. Going back and facing the people I used to hang out with is another.

The difference now is knowing I'm not alone. I've got Someone always at my side—believing in me, strengthening me, walking with me, and empowering me to change.

■ *Jesus, teach me your way. Things may be a little rocky at times, but you're leading and I'm learning.*
D.K.

DATELESS, NOT WORTHLESS

I say to the unmarried and to the widows: It is good for them if they remain even as I am.
—1 COR. 7:8

Do you have a date this weekend? If so, you are one of the "chosen ones"; anyone would be lucky to call you her friend. If you don't have a date, you're scum. Nobody wants you; you're basically worthless.

Sound cold? Sure. And it's a lie! But isn't it an unspoken assumption in your school? It's certainly the message that Tammy has gotten. Tammy has only had one date in her life. She hangs around with a group of girls who do not date. And Tammy's dateless state has begun to undermine her self-esteem. At the back of her mind runs the constant question, "What's wrong with me? Why am I such a loser?"

Sadly, the assumption that you have to "be involved with someone" to be worthwhile isn't limited to teens. Our whole society is geared toward couples. People who don't marry or have a "love life" are somehow suspect. (Doesn't anybody want them?) But guess what? The apostle Paul indicates that not only are people without "significant others" valuable in God's eyes; they may be able to contribute more to God's kingdom. That may seem like cold comfort on a Saturday night, but the real meaning is exciting: Your value as a person has absolutely nothing to do with whether you have a date or not.

■ *God, please help me accept myself and others (dating or dateless) the way you do—as your precious children.*

S.C.

NEW POWER

Now to Him who is able to do exceedingly
abundantly above all that we ask or think,
according to the power that works in us.
—EPH. 3:20

As members of God's family, we inherit His power as well as His identity. However, this power is only effective if we are willing to give up our puny power in exchange for His. This process is similar to step three of the Twelve Steps: We make a decision to turn our will and lives over to the care of God. When we do that, then God gives us the ability to make changes and even the willingness to want to do so. He helps us hang in there and persevere when we want to give up.

God also gives us wisdom to make new, wise choices. We used to make choices on the basis of what felt good or would give us immediate gratification. Now we can make choices that are based on God's principles—choices that will give us success.

We have new power over our feelings. Feelings used to toss us back and forth; they made our lives a roller-coaster ride. Anger and guilt are particularly tricky to handle. God's Word gives us specific instructions on how to control these instead of letting them control us.

Finally, we have new power over relapse. This does not mean we will never relapse. But if we do, God promises to help us start over. We don't have to be devastated and forget we ever started to recover.

■ *Our wildest imagination cannot think of what good*
things God will do for us once we let his power work
in us.

J.C.

FREE FROM TYPECASTING

You shall be called by a new name,
Which the mouth of the LORD will name.
　　　　　　　　　　　　　　　　—ISA. 62:2

Most Hollywood actors live in fear of getting typecast. They know it's possible to become so identified with one screen role that they can never break free of it. They will always be "the ditzy blonde" or "the best friend" or "the Jewish mother"—and different kinds of roles will be hard to find.

It's easy to get typecast in life, too—at school or church or even in my family. Whether I'm "the responsible one" or "the troublemaker" or "the class clown," it's frustrating when other people don't seem to recognize I've changed. It's irritating to be seen as a role instead of a person.

But God doesn't see me that way. He gives me the freedom to change roles as I grow—in fact, He expects me to. He even gives me a new name, a whole new identity that has nothing to do with the old, typecast me. That's something to hang on to when I'm chafing at being written off by others. When they call me by my old "name," I don't have to answer. Instead, I can respond as the new person I am becoming in Christ.

■　*Lord, the only name I need to answer to is that of "God's child." Help me break free of my typecast identity and grow into the role you have written for me.*

　　　　　　　　　　　　　　　　　　　　　　　　A.C.B.

BUILDING SELF-CONTROL

*For if you live according to the flesh you will
die; but if by the Spirit you put to death the
deeds of the body, you will live.*
—ROM. 8:13

Serial killer Jeffrey Dahmer testified at his trial that sex had been his consuming interest since adolescence. He was quoted as saying that his "lustful desire overpowered any normal moral choice." Dahmer is an extreme result of the philosophy, "If it feels good, do it." This point of view assumes that the goal of life is self-fulfillment and gratification of our physical desires.

Most of us aren't extremists like Dahmer. We don't believe we have a right to hurt someone else just because it feels good. And yet the primary purpose of our drinking, drugging, "messing around," or unhealthy eating habits was to make us feel good or at least feel better. And after a while our drive to self-fulfillment controlled us. We lost control over our bodies and our lives.

In a sense, recovery is a process of relying on God to help us move from self-fulfillment toward self-control. It starts with maintaining abstinence, then spreads to other self-control measures: not watching too much TV, not gossiping, not sleeping in. Eventually the emphasis shifts to the positive: tithing, exercising, eating a balanced diet. The result is a new, healthy, self-controlled lifestyle.

■ *Every day, to build self-control, I can (1) do something I don't feel like doing; (2) not do something I feel like doing.*

J.C.

THE OTHER SIDE OF PASSION

"Teacher, this woman was caught in adultery, in the very act." . . . "Woman . . . has no one condemned you? . . . Neither do I condemn you; go and sin no more."
—JOHN 8:4, 10–11

There she was. A woman caught in adultery. She'd been fooling around with everyone in town—and everyone knew it. Everyone knew what kind of woman she was, but she didn't care. She knew what felt good, what numbed the pain, and she went after it with a passion. Then along came this Man who turned her world inside out.

Christ knew something we often forget: Passion and compassion are closely related. They both flow from the same inner well. The difference? Compassion is passion turned outward—a giving of self, not a denial of self. Christ didn't shame the woman caught in adultery. He simply said, "Go and sin no more." We're not told what else He said, if anything. But perhaps if we had been standing there, we might have heard Him say, "Go and sin no more. Go and redirect your passion. Go and give yourself in ways that honor me."

■ *Enough said. Amen.*

D.K.

CRYING DAY AND NIGHT

O LORD, God of my salvation,
I have cried out day and night before
  You. . . .
Incline Your ear to my cry.
For my soul is full of troubles,
And my life draws near to the grave.
  —PS. 88:1–3

Depression overtakes most of us at some point of our lives. The overwhelming sadness and hopelessness are hard to endure. Yet depression can be normal and even helpful. When we have suffered a loss, depression slows us down and helps us "process" the loss.

Not all depression is helpful, however. A person who remains depressed for an extended period may be "clinically" depressed—with an actual chemical imbalance in her brain. This usually happens to people who are under intense stress or who have a family history of depression. (You can inherit a tendency to get very depressed.) Whatever the cause, clinical depression needs medical treatment; it rarely goes away on its own. Medication can make a big difference.

If you feel depressed or if a friend seems depressed, ask for help. Talk about the sad feelings and call upon the Lord for healing. But if the depression doesn't lift after a week or so, consider that professional treatment may be part of God's healing. Don't wait; clinical depression usually gets worse over time. But don't give up, either. Depression *feels* hopeless, but it's not.

■   *Father, you know the depths of my pain and you*
    want me to feel better. Guide me to people who can
    help me cope with depression.

S.C.

BACK IN THE SADDLE

> *But may the God of all grace, who called us*
> *to His eternal glory by Christ Jesus, after you*
> *have suffered a while, perfect, establish,*
> *strengthen, and settle you.*
>
> **—1 PETER 5:10**

For several years my family raised horses. We had some ornery individuals as well as some sweet-spirited ones. One quarter horse was absolutely gorgeous to the eye. His bright bay coat would glisten after I washed him. He looked like a jewel to anyone who saw him. In fact, his name was Ruby's Trinket. What a fitting name—or so one would think. But that beautiful animal was far from beautifully-tempered.

Trinket and I had many run-ins. Our wills would clash almost on a daily basis. He was lazy, strong-willed, and difficult. It was my job to "break" him, but I am still not sure who got broke! Many times he would rear up and slide me off. He enjoyed bucking, which also ended up with me on the ground. I was always told, "If you fall off, get right back on. If you don't, it will get harder and harder." So reluctantly, with bumps and bruises, I would climb back in the saddle.

You are liable to have bumps and bruises, so to speak, while you are in the recovery process. You may even fall out of your "saddle." If you do, climb back on. Falling does not mean you failed. It just means you are human.

■ *Success comes with persistent trying. Hang on tight*
and keep working.

S.C.

CLOSE AS A HEARTBEAT

Let not mercy and truth forsake you;
Bind them around your neck,
Write them on the tablet of your heart.
—PROV. 3:3

Denise treasured the little pendant her boyfriend had given her. Once she had put it on, she refused to take it off, even in the shower. To her, it was a constant reminder of their relationship.

God intends for my relationship with Him to be just that constant and just that special. He wants His love and His honesty to be so near to me that I'm always conscious of them—almost as if they were hanging around my neck or engraved on my heart. And I need that to happen if I'm going to stay in recovery. That's why step eleven of the Twelve Steps states: "[We] sought through prayer and meditation to improve our conscious contact with God as we understood Him. . . ."

I can also improve my "conscious contact" with God by hanging out with His friends, reading His Book, singing His songs. The habit of talking to Him all the time, not just during special prayer times, helps keep me conscious of His presence. Even a physical reminder—like a little dove necklace or a scripture written in the front of my notebook—can help remind me of what I already know: that God is with me always, as close as my heartbeat.

■ *God's mercy and truth are always available to me; I need to do everything I can to stay aware of him.*

A.C.B.

THE BOTTOM LINE ABOUT MONEY

For the love of money is a root of all kinds of evil, for which some have strayed from the faith in their greediness, and pierced themselves through with many sorrows.

—1 TIM. 6:10

My mom and dad never have time for me," complained Jo bitterly. "They almost never go to my basketball games or my choir performances—and they're always having to work late. They don't care about me; all they care about is money!" It was an honest, heartfelt complaint with more than a little truth in it. But five minutes later, Jo was complaining again—this time that her parents wouldn't buy her a new car!

A lot of us—teens and adults—are confused about money. We have been programmed to "have it all" in terms of material possessions—the right car, the right clothes, the right stereo. And we have bought the big lie that having the right possessions will help us get the love, attention, and self-esteem we crave. That's why we feel lost when we don't have enough money . . . or bewildered when we do have money but still feel lonely or unloved or worthless.

Facing ourselves in recovery may mean facing the facts about money. Money, like emotions, is neither good nor bad in itself; it's what we do with money that's good or bad. But contrary to popular opinion, money has no power whatsoever to solve our deep problems or brings us real love or healthy self-esteem.

■   *Here's the bottom line: If I trust in money or possessions instead of God, I'll just end up feeling robbed.*

S.C.

SPEAKING IN SANDWICHES

. . . speaking the truth in love. . . .
—EPH. 4:15

Mom, I know you worked hard to buy me nice clothes . . . but I want to be able to pick them out myself now. . . . I promise to return anything you don't think is appropriate." That sentence is an example of what speaker Josh McDowell calls a "sandwich." In this sandwich, the two pieces of "bread" are the first and third statements. They offer something positive to the listener (in this case, the mother). The "meat" is the second statement, which expresses the main concern of the speaker (the daughter). Such a verbal "sandwich" is a great tool for following the biblical guidance that we should speak the truth in love.

The daughter could have said: "Mom, you never take into consideration what I want. I'm tired of dressing like a nerd. I'm going to pick my own clothes from now on." But it would be a lie by exaggeration. (It's very unlikely this mother *never* took her child's needs into consideration.) And because it attacked the mother, it certainly would not be loving.

Besides, which presentation do you think the mother is more likely to listen to?

■ *God's Word tells us how we can get our needs met without stepping all over others.*

J.C.

FOR MY NAME IS MANY

*Then [Jesus] asked him, "What is your
name?" And he answered, saying, "My
name is Legion; for we are many."*
—MARK 5:9

The book of Mark reports a story about a crazy man
who said his name was Legion. The dictionary says *legion* means "many, a large number, a multitude." This
guy is basically telling Christ that what torments him
from within is not a single, readily identifiable problem
or demon—but a multitude.

When I came into recovery, little did I know my
name was Legion. I thought I was there because of my
abuse of food, drugs, or alcohol. I thought I was basically OK, except for this one little nasty problem. Then
I began realizing the issues were numerous. The identities within me—the Dutiful Daughter, the Cool Babe,
the Rebel, the Victim—were all in conflict with each
other. Somedays, the legions living within were waging
all-out war, and I was caught in the crossfire.

Jesus was the master of the unexpected. After healing the man who called himself Legion, He told the
man, "Go home to your friends, and tell them what
great things the Lord has done for you, and how He has
had compassion on you." To maintain my recovery, I
have to do likewise. Christ's directive is simple: Tell my
story. No advice. No problem solving. Simply tell where
I've been, where I am, and what brought me this far.

■ *If I do the telling, Christ will do the rest.*

D.K.

HOUSE RULES

Let your speech always be with grace,
seasoned with salt, that you may know
how you ought to answer each one.

—COL. 4:6

You don't say things like that in this house, young lady!" Tina's dad yelled. He was drunk again, and his words slurred as he attempted to chastise her. She had told him she was sick and tired of being around an alcoholic father and complained that she could never bring a friend home because he was either drinking or passed out on the couch. But Tina's dad didn't want to hear it. All he wanted was for her to shut up and leave him alone.

The dominant house rule for many dysfunctional families is a simple one: "Don't speak. Hold your tongue. Keep the secret. Don't rock the boat. Even if it is the truth, don't say it. Pretend something else is happening instead of reality." And that's one reason kids from dysfunctional homes have a hard time growing up healthy. Talking about problems and facing reality is a primary component of positive living and workable relationships. If you've grown up where the house rule is "Don't speak," it's hard to unlearn the habit of denial and cover-up. But the whole point of the recovery process is unlearning old patterns through God's help. As you continue in recovery, you'll begin operating under a new set of "house rules."

■ *Father, help me unlearn the "Don't speak" rule and communicate with honesty, wisdom, and grace.*

S.C.

PERSISTENT LOVE

But God demonstrates His own love toward us, in that while we were still sinners, Christ died for us.

—ROM. 5:8

Youth pastor Steve was an upright young man. That's why he said no when a hooker came to the church and offered him sex in exchange for money. But Steve was also a kind man, and he helped her get the clothing, food, and shelter she needed. Eventually she became a Christian, and Steve fell in love with her. They were married. But a few years after the wedding, she backslid and went back to her old job. Heartbroken, Steve looked for her day and night until he found her. He begged her to come home; she said she didn't deserve him. But finally his persistent love won her over, and she came home.

Now life was better than ever . . . until the day Steve's wife totaled the family car. Steve came home to find her bags packed; she was sure he could never forgive her. But when she told him why she was leaving, Steve just laughed and hugged her. Gently he told her that there was nothing she could do to change his love. "I loved you at your worst," he said. "This is nothing in comparison."

Satan wants us to think that Christ will cut His help and blessings from us when we sin. But Christ loved us at our worst. Once we belong to Him, nothing we do can make Him stop loving us.

■ *"There is . . . now no condemnation to those who are in Christ" (Rom. 8:1).*

J.C.

THE HONESTY OF EMOTIONS

*And He said to her, "Daughter, be of good
cheer; your faith has made you well. Go
in peace."*
— LUKE 8:48

Good feelings. Bad feelings. So often we put a value judgment on our emotions, rating them good, bad, or indifferent. We too quickly tell ourselves, "I shouldn't be feeling this way," before realizing what the feelings are telling us. But once again, feelings are neither good nor bad. Feelings simply are. All our feelings—joy and sadness, love and resentment, exhilaration and fear— are simply part of being human. To close the lid on painful feelings is to shut myself off from all my feelings. Where good and bad begin are where choices come in.

We may not be able to choose how we will feel, but we can choose what to do with our feelings. And the most important place to begin is with honesty. Emotional masquerade comes all too easily for those of us dealing with compulsive/addictive disorders. We've learned the roles, mastered the games, and paid the consequences. Honesty with ourselves, with God, and with others breaks the destructive cycle. Powerful emotions don't scare God—after all He created them. So why should powerful emotions scare us?

■ *Christ said, "Your faith has made you well." So listen to the honesty of your emotions, go in peace, and trust the Lord.*

D.K.

CUTTING RELAPSE SHORT

*Though [she] fall, [she] shall not be utterly
 cast down;
For the LORD upholds [her] with His hand.*
—PS. 37:24

My relapse started when my mother and I went back to arguing," said Marilee. "So I went to live with my boyfriend and his parents for a while. He and I got drunk one night and had sex. Then I found out he's been sleeping around, and he gave me herpes."

It happens. People in recovery relapse. But people can choose to make their relapse long or short.

Marilee can make her relapse longer by wallowing in self-pity, guilt, and regrets. She can tell herself that her mom will never change, that no other boy will ever go out with her now that she has herpes. She can give up and say that since she's already blown it, she might as well blow it big time.

Marilee could have made her relapse shorter. A slip begins before that first drink. She could have made amends with her mother right after the argument or used her boyfriend's house just to cool off and come home that same day. She could have stopped after that first drink. She can stop now.

Today's verse promises that God is holding out His hand to you if you slip. Go to Him and confess your mistake. Don't shy away from Him; doing that cuts you off from God's power to help. Make your relapse short. Otherwise, there is a danger of being hurled headlong.

■ *In relapse, don't be afraid to grab hold of God's hand. He won't condemn you.*

J.C.

An Alternate Thanksgiving

*As you have therefore received Christ Jesus
the Lord, so walk in Him, ... established
in the faith, as you have been taught,
abounding in it with thanksgiving.*
—COL. 2:6–7

It's about that time again. Once again, Americans troop to the dinner table to stuff themselves senseless. Once again, people slump into darkened rooms to watch television until their eyes bug out. Once again, families gather together to rehearse all the old aggravations until they are thoroughly sick of one another. No, that's not what Thanksgiving is supposed to be about, but that's reality for a lot of families. Somehow we've gotten the idea that the way to be truly thankful is to indulge ourselves in too much of everything. And that, of course, is not a healthy idea for someone in recovery.

So this year, I'm declaring an alternative Thanksgiving. Instead of thanking God for what He has given by taking even more (sort of an insane idea when you think about it), I want to thank Him by reviewing where He has brought me and recommitting myself to His care. I want to thank Him by going out of my way to show appreciation to people who have helped me and by brainstorming specific ways I can help others. After that, maybe I'll have some turkey and some family time and maybe even a little TV. But those will all be side dishes. This year, as my Thanksgiving main course, I'm having growth flavored with gratitude.

■ *Lord, teach me the secret of Thanks-giving, not just Thanks-taking.*

A.C.B.

BASIC RELATIONSHIPS

> *The first of all the commandments is: . . .*
> *"You shall love the LORD your God with all*
> *your heart, with all your soul, with all your*
> *mind, and with all your strength." . . . And*
> *the second, like it, is this: "You shall love*
> *your neighbor as yourself." There is no other*
> *commandment greater than these.*
>   —MARK 12:29–31

Jesus talked a lot about relationships; how we treat each other was obviously very important to Him. During His time on earth, He gave specific instructions for parent-child, husband-wife, master-servant (boss-employee), and neighbor-neighbor relationships, just to name a few. But He summed all of these instructions up in two simple commandments.

Our primary love relationship, Jesus said, has to be with God. But after we put God first, we are to love our neighbors as ourselves. Note the balance here. We are not intended to love only other people and *not* ourselves. (This is the trap of codependency.) And we are not to love *only* ourselves, catering to our own wants and needs. (This is the trap of self-centeredness.) Instead, we are to keep our loves in the proper order: Love God, love our neighbors, love ourselves. If we can stick to this basic relational formula, everything else will fall into place.

■   *Lord, teach me what it really means to love you, others, and myself.*

                                                              S.C.

MEETING GOD'S EXPECTATIONS

Without faith it is impossible to please [God].
—HEB. 11:6

And without good grades, it's impossible to please.
. . . And without church attendance, it's impossible to please. . . . And without being perfect, it's impossible to please. . . . (etc. and ad nauseam).

Trying to meeting other people's expectations can be frustrating. Sometimes I feel it's impossible to live up to what my family and others think I should be. But God expects only one thing from me: faith. This expectation gives me hope. After all, not everyone can excel at school, athletics, looks, or behavior, but anyone can excel at faith.

I was born into God's family by faith, when I believed in Him and accepted Christ as my Savior. And I grow in His family by faith. What does this mean? It means accepting that the Father rewards me when I diligently seek Him—by asking Him questions and looking in the Bible for His answers. It involves realizing that He *will* answer me (even though I don't always get the answer I want). And it means showing my trust in Him by obediently acting on the answer I receive. Such obedience brings me the rewards of growing faith—renewed relationships, greater self-control, and the sense that God is pleased with me.

■ *God's expectations for his children are always attainable.*

J.C.

DOING IT RIGHT ISN'T ENOUGH

Do not be overly righteous,
Nor be overly wise:
Why should you destroy yourself?
Do not be overly wicked,
Nor be foolish:
Why should you die before your time?
—ECCLES. 7:16–17

The Bible holds more than one surprise. We already know about "foolish wickedness"; that's what got us into recovery in the first place. But this other admonition—this bit about "overly righteous"—the Bible's telling us not to be "too religious" is a bit surprising.

But did you know there was only one group of people with whom Jesus really got angry—only one type of person with whom Jesus was impatient, critical, and harsh? In the Gospels they're called Pharisees. They were the overly religious, the outwardly pious, the ones who placed greater emphasis on external religious performance than on inward spiritual wholeness.

So what does that tell us? That we're better off being wild and crazy than religiously rigid? No. Both extremes hold dangers. Both can be deadly. And neither extreme is living true to the call of Christ. We can do all the right things, say all the right words, and go all the right places, but if our heart isn't right with God, we're not doing ourselves or God any favors.

■   *God wants our heart, not our performance.*

D.K.

ONLY GOD CAN READ MINDS

Through presumption comes nothing but strife.
—PROV. 13:10 NASB

Allyson was fuming when she came into the dining room. "What's wrong?" her mother asked as she looked up from the pile of bills she was paying.

"Nothing."

"Now that's a lie. You're so angry, I can see smoke coming out of your ears," her mother joked.

"Very funny, Mother." Allyson was not amused.

Earlier in the day, Allyson's mother had walked by her with a big frown on her face. Allyson had no idea what the problem was, but she had assumed it had to do with her. She then had begun brooding that her mother was thinking the worst of her. Anger at her mother had begun to smolder. Fortunately, Allyson had eventually decided to check out her assumptions with her mother. Her mother, it had turned out, was frowning about the bills, not about something Allyson had done.

Allyson's habit of mind reading had caused many unnecessary fights with her parents. She was learning to correct this erroneous thinking pattern by replacing it with the truth.

■ *Only God can read minds. The rest of us need to check out our assumptions.*

J.C.

MOVING PAST MY MISTAKES

Behold, the former things have come to pass,
And new things I declare;
Before they spring forth I tell you of them.
—ISA. 42:9

Mistakes from the past can be tools for the present. If I learn from them, they are profitable. If I choose to ignore them, I may have to continue to learn the same lesson over and over.

Whether a mistake is disastrous or helpful to me is my call. When I realize I have made a mistake, I need to evaluate it. What caused me to choose as I did? Where was the flaw in my thinking or the emotional need that warped my judgment? What harm has been done? What must be done to reduce the damage or to make sure I don't make the same mistake again? When those questions have been answered, I will be wiser.

No one is perfect. Everyone lacks knowledge in one way or another, and everyone is subject to human emotions and human selfishness. I can't expect to live without mistakes. But I can choose to learn from the past. I can let it be a teacher for my present and my future. I can take action to make sure history does not repeat itself in my life. And I can watch the mistakes others have made or are making as well—obtaining all the information I can so that I have a chance to make my life better.

■ *God, teach me not to let past mistakes hinder my present progress.*

S.C.

SEASON OF EXPECTATION

My soul, wait silently for God alone,
For my expectation is from Him.
He only is my rock and my
salvation. —PS. 62:5–6

This is a forward-looking season, a season of expectation and celebration. Christmas is coming! And this, we are told, is the season of joy and peace, the season of magic. It's a time when families gather in harmony, when people kiss under the mistletoe, when selfish people reach out to others, and children's dreams come true.

Sometimes, miraculously, those things happen. But often, instead, families gather—and squabble. People kiss—and end up using each other. Selfish people—act selfish. And children are left thinking, "Well, maybe next year. . . ."

The sad truth is: Christmas can be a time of disappointment instead of delight. In fact, I wonder if we have inflated our expectations for Christmas to the point that we have set ourselves up for disappointment. If we put our faith in Christmas, we have a good chance of being let down. But maybe that's because we're meant to put our faith not in Christmas . . . but in God.

■   *Christmas can be wonderful. Christmas can be awful. Either way, Christ has still come into the world. And that's cause for celebration.*

A.C.B.

TANGLED WEBS

*Stand fast therefore in the liberty by which
Christ has made us free, and do not be
entangled again.* —GAL. 5:1

Oh, what a tangled web we weave . . ." That old cliché
is about deception, but it paints a vivid picture of what
our dysfunctional behavior does to our lives. Our personalities and relationships get to be like snarled skeins
of yarn, and unknotting them looks like an endless, tedi-
ous, even futile job.

We do have help, however, if we ask for it. Step seven
of the Twelve Steps of AA spells out a strategy for getting our lives unsnarled: "[We] humbly asked [our
Higher Power] to remove our shortcomings."

Untangling the twisted yarns of our lives is slow work.
The Lord points out a loose thread and we gently pull at
it, taking it as far as it will go. Then He points out another thread and we tease it out. If we get impatient and
just yank on the first thread we see, the whole thing
knots up. If we give up in frustration and stop working,
the yarn gets more tangled. But if we continue to work
with God, thread by thread, we have the satisfaction of
seeing the tangled web of our lives begin to straighten
out. If we stick close by Him, we can avoid ever getting
that tangled up again.

■ *Lord, I humbly ask you to help me keep untangling
the tangled web of my life.*

S.C./A.C.B.

NEW HOPE

And now, Lord, what do I wait for?
My hope is in You.   —PS. 39:7

It's no use. I give up. There's no hope." Have you ever said those words to yourself? If you really believed them, you probably wanted to quit trying. Without hope, there is no change.

It's easy to lose hope in recovery. We may have tried to recover and relapsed and relapsed again. It's discouraging; we seem to fall into the same hole again and again.

But Jesus can bring us new hope. Through Him, God has given us everything we need for a successful recovery (2 Peter 1:3). He gives us His power for new relationships—for trust with parents and for making new friends with non-using peers as well as letting go of old, using ones. Jesus gives us a new identity. We are no longer victims. We can have self-respect. We also have new power—once we give up trying to control our lives and give the controls to Him. We have new thinking. We no longer have to believe Satan's lies. And all these "new" things translate into what we need most: new hope.

■   *Jesus is the hope of your recovery.*

J.C.

So MUCH

For God so loved the world that He gave His only begotten Son, that whoever believes in Him should not perish but have everlasting life.
—JOHN 3:16

God loved the world—that means me—so much that He sent His only Son—that's Jesus. Why? So that if I hook up with Him, I can have everlasting life instead of the death I deserve.

But there's more. The kind of life God intends for me to have is not only "everlasting," but available now. In fact, it's the kind of life I've begun to experience in recovery. Life that is real and honest, not based on lies and self-deception. Life lived in dependence on God and in community with others instead of isolation and loneliness. Life that offers a way out of the cycle of pain that has crippled humans ever since the first man and woman chose death instead of life—the same pain that was ruining my life.

Granted, I only get a taste of it in this world. But that taste is enough to keep me hungry for the life only Christ can provide.

■ *Thank you, Lord, for loving me so much. Help me to trust your love enough to keep on the path to your kind of life.*

A.C.B.

FAILING SUCCESSFULLY

*And let us not grow weary while doing good,
for in due season we shall reap if we do not
lose heart.*
                                        —GAL. 6:9

In order to be successful, we have to learn how to fail successfully. Inventor Thomas Edison made over 5,000 dud light bulbs before he made the one that worked. What if, after the 4,999th failure, he had said, "I'm no good. I'm stupid. Nothing ever works for me"? We'd all still be reading by candlelight!

Prime Minister Winston Churchill gave speeches that rallied a discouraged England during World War II. Many people today still quote him. Would you believe he earned low grades in English as a child and that he had a speech impediment?

Teacher Anne Sullivan repeatedly tried to teach just one word to a blind, deaf, and mute girl. She got bit, scratched, and hit for her efforts. But finally she succeeded. Helen Keller not only went on to college, but became a renowned speaker.

These are world-famous people. But what about you? How did you learn to ride a bike? By failing successfully. Our failures tell us what needs adjusting. If we keep fine-tuning our efforts, we'll eventually succeed.

Addict thinking says everything has to be done right the first or second time—and you turn to substance abuse to numb the pain when you can't. But healthy thinking expects failure. In fact, it sees failure as a stepping-stone to success.

■ *A baby falls down many times as it learns to walk,
but it gets up again.*

                                        J.C.

GUILT TRUE AND FALSE

I said, "LORD, be merciful to me;
Heal my soul, for I have sinned
against You." —PS. 41:4

Some people never feel guilty. Other people feel guilty over everything. And neither extreme is healthy!

We experience *true guilt* when we have disobeyed the Lord or been responsible for hurting someone. This kind of guilt is healthy. It motivates us to right whatever wrong we have done, and it also helps keep our hearts softened and open to others. (That's why the Bible says that God loves a broken and contrite heart.) Most important, true guilt has a remedy: We ask forgiveness and make amends to those we have hurt.

False guilt, on the other hand, comes from accepting responsibility that does not belong to us. We have not disobeyed God or done anything wrong, but we feel guilty anyway. False guilt grows out of human tradition, superstitions, or family myths, not the Word of God. This counterfeit guilt cannot be forgiven or remedied— it just weighs down our lives. Healthy recovery depends on recognizing our false guilt and then letting it go.

■ *Father, I depend on you to show me where I'm truly guilty so I can seek forgiveness. Grant me the insight and the strength to jettison the false guilt from my life.*

S.C.

BLAME OR RESPONSIBILITY

The heart is deceitful above all
*   things,*
And desperately wicked;
Who can know it?
I, the LORD, search the heart, . . .
Even to give every man according
*   to his ways.*   —JER. 17:9–10

My mother messed me up by throwing me in this psycho hospital. This is messing up my school year. I probably won't graduate on time. What's the use? I might as well sell drugs and at least make money." Cindy's escalating drug use had brought her to our adolescent unit. Now she was blaming everyone else for her problems.

Blaming is a form of denial. Cindy recognized the unmanageability of her life, but she took no responsibility for it. Yes, her mother had remarried three times, and none of the men had really liked Cindy—but she had alienated them all with her sarcasm. Yes, the hospital stay would require her to catch up with her classes at home—but cutting classes had already put her behind.

Jeremiah tells us that our hearts are deceitful. We tend to blame everyone but ourselves for the unmanageability of our lives. But God says different. He lets us reap the consequences of our own conduct, and He expects us to take responsibility for our lives. The good news is that, with God's help, we can give up blaming and self-deception and continue on the road to wholeness.

■   *God, teach me to give up blame and take up responsibility.*

J.C.

MAKING AMENDS TO ME

For I have given you an example, that you should do as I have done to you.
—JOHN 13:15

If I treated anyone else like I've treated myself at times, I'd for sure have to make amends to that person. I've abused my body, set my expectations ridiculously high, demanded perfection, lied to myself—the list goes on and on. Perhaps one person to whom I need to make amends *is* myself.

The first time I heard someone in my recovery group say she needed to make amends to herself, I thought, "I could never do that." Upon examination, I realized I didn't think I deserved it. Yet that kind of thinking is what landed me in a downward spiral of crazy behavior in the first place. I do deserve to be treated with the same respect I give others. And I do at times need to make amends with myself.

After all, if I can't forgive myself, if I can't make amends with myself, how can I truly forgive others? Excluding myself from the same tolerance, compassion, and respect I have for others makes the Golden Rule null and void. I can't "do unto others as I would have them do unto me" if I'm doing a number on myself.

■ *God, when I'm harder on myself than I would be on others, quiet the harsh voices within and let me hear your word of grace.*

D.K.

THOSE WHO REFUSE TO LOVE ME

> *You have heard that it was said, "You shall love your neighbor and hate your enemy." But I say to you, love your enemies, bless those who curse you, do good to those who hate you, and pray for those who spitefully use you and persecute you.*
>
> —MATT. 5:43–44

Years ago, I read a quote that went something like this: "Our lives are shaped by those who love us and by those who refuse to love us."

That saying has echoed many times in my mind, especially when I've banged my nose up against rejection . . . or someone I trusted has let me down . . . or someone, for some reason, has just seemed out to get me.

The people who refuse to love me do shape my life—but *I can choose the way they shape it*. I can allow their indifference or spite to mangle my self-esteem. I can let myself get all twisted up with anger or revenge. Or I can use their rejection as an opportunity to get in better shape. I can examine myself and my expectations. (Am I in denial about some character flaw? Am I expecting more than another person can deliver?) I can turn in gratitude to those people who really do care. Most important, I can ask God to help me love those who refuse to love me. When I voluntarily give up my right to get back at my enemies, I let my life be shaped by the only One who will ever love me with pure, unselfish love.

■ *Lord, thank you that you do love me—even when others refuse to. I choose to let your love shape my life in a positive way.*

A.C.B.

ACCEPTING CORRECTION

*[She] who keeps instruction is in the
way of life,
But [she] who refuses reproof goes
astray.* —PROV. 10:17

Sue Ann hated to be corrected by anyone. No matter how gentle the reproof was, she became angry and defensive. People avoided being around her or working with her because she was so sensitive. She would blame others for not explaining things to her when, in reality, she was too upset to listen. Because Sue Ann was unable to separate who she was from what she did, she felt that someone who corrected her actions was attacking her.

Life is a learning process. And some of the most valuable teaching comes in the form of instruction or correction. Listening to correction helps us gain skills and knowledge and avoid serious mistakes. A wise person is one who has learned to accept criticism and learn from it.

If it is difficult for you to accept reproof, consider the alternatives. You probably will be tense most of the time for fear of making a mistake (because then you might be corrected). You will have to learn about life from "the school of hard knocks" (because minor mistakes will lead to big ones). And people will find it difficult to be around you (an angry, defensive person is no fun!). Receive instruction . . . do not refuse correction.

■ *God, teach me to separate who I am from what I
do—and to be grateful for those who do me the favor
of correcting what I do.*

S.C.

Focus on Praise

If there is any excellence and if anything worthy of praise, let your mind dwell on these things. —PHIL. 4:8 NASB

Try this experiment. Describe your strong points to a friend. Then describe the weak points. Which list comes easier and faster? Your answer tells you what you habitually focus on.

Most of us find it easier to list what we consider as our weaknesses. This may be because of perfectionism. Perfectionism takes even our good qualities and knocks them down a notch or two. Say that someone compliments you on an outfit. You say, "Thanks, but it's not new." (So what? It still looks good.) Your friend says she likes the birthday poster you made for her. You say, "Well, yeah, but the colors didn't come out exactly right." (So what? She liked it, and you really did spend a lot of time and some money on her.)

Today's verse knocks out perfectionism. It says that if there's *any* excellence, we should zoom in on that. It doesn't say something has to be perfect before we can praise it. Instead of obsessing about how we could have done something better, we need to dwell on what was good about it. God goes on to tell us (in v. 9) to practice this way of thinking. He wants us to make it a habit. Habits take time and effort to form. But the payoff is His peace: "The God of peace shall be with you" (Phil. 4:9 NASB).

■ *Focusing on* any *praiseworthy parts of a situation helps me break the habit of perfectionism.*

J.C.

OPEN-ARMED LOVE

*But when he was still a great way off, his
father saw him and had compassion, and
ran and fell on his neck and kissed him.*
—LUKE 15:20

Filthy, smelly, sick, and thoroughly disgusted with himself, the young man trudges homeward. He's been away so long, and he's thoroughly messed up his life. He's really ashamed to go home, but the sad truth is, he doesn't have any other options. So on he trudges, head hanging.

The weary father leans on his front gate, looking out into the distance. He's waited like this every day for so long, and nothing has happened. But today is different. Today, in the distance, he spies a scruffy but familiar figure. And at that moment the old man loses every trace of his dignity. Arms outstretched, robe sleeves flapping, he goes running down the road. He loses a sandal and leaves it in the dust. He trips and scrambles back to his feet, not even feeling his scraped knees and elbows. All he can think about is throwing his arms around his son.

That, says Jesus, is the kind of welcome I receive whenever I finally come to the end of myself and come home to God. All that huge joy, that open-armed excitement—and it's all for me. Me!

■ *Getting a clear picture of my heavenly Father's
open-armed love can keep me going when the shame
of where I've been and what I've done has me discouraged.*

A.C.B.

I AM WHAT I THINK

For as [she] thinks in [her] heart, so is [she].
—PROV. 23:7

When you first saw Joy, she looked rather plain. She was large boned and slightly overweight, and she rarely wore makeup. But when you started to talk to Joy, a transformation quickly took place. Her sparkling eyes needed no mascara. Her enthusiasm energized her bulky form into a dancing expression of her words. You realized you were in the presence of someone fascinating and attractive. Joy believed what she had to say was important and interesting, so it was easy to feel the same way about her.

God tells us that in Christ we are new creatures and that the old has passed away (2 Cor. 5:17). When I choose to believe that, I'm transformed from the inside. The old me had no choices about my addiction and about where my life was going. Now I know I do have choices, and that confidence helps me decide more wisely.

The old me felt alone and had no support. But the new me has the support of my church and my recovery group and others who help me in recovery—and the new me can reach out to others. The old me believed I was unloved and so acted unlovable, pushing people away. The new me revels in God's promises that He will never leave me or forsake me. I can choose to believe I'm precious to Him, and so I feel loved. I am loved!

■ *The choice is mine: I am what I think.*

J.C.

FORGIVE FOR YOUR OWN GOOD

Then Peter came to Him and said, "Lord, how often shall my brother sin against me, and I forgive him? Up to seven times?" Jesus said to him, "I do not say to you, up to seven times, but up to seventy times seven."

—MATT. 18:21–22

Forgiveness is a tough commandment to obey. Holding a grudge seems easier—sometimes even pleasurable. But there is a reason Jesus tells us to forgive: Forgiveness benefits the forgiver as well as the "forgivee."

It's easy to see this benefit for one who has been forgiven; she is released from the burden of guilt. But the benefits reaped by the forgiver are just as real and just as important. Forgiving allows us to feel all our emotions, not just anger. It also lets us off the hook physically—holding a grudge is stressful and can cause headaches, stomachaches, or disturbed sleep and appetite. And forgiveness frees us from the bondage of bitterness. People who don't take care of their grudges eventually grow resentful and hateful—far from happy.

One word of caution about forgiveness, though. We need to feel our anger and acknowledge our hurt before we can forgive sincerely and completely. Premature "forgiveness" can be a form of denial, a way of stuffing down emotions we don't want to face. There truly is a time for everything—even forgiveness.

■ *Dear Lord, teach me to forgive—for my own good.*

S.C.

HE WON'T LET YOU DOWN

Do not trust in a friend;
Do not put your confidence in a
*   companion. . . .*
Therefore I will look to the LORD.
        —MIC. 7:5, 7

When someone doesn't meet all your expectations, be glad. You've been given an opportunity to learn dependence on God. If everyone always came through for us, we'd feel less of a need to go to Him. Times of deep disappointment in people can be sweet times of closeness with God. They are also necessary reminders that people are . . . well . . . human. If we expect people to come through 100 percent of the time, we are setting ourselves up for bitterness. Bitterness is fermented anger. It leads to unmanageable behavior.

Today's verse doesn't mean we can never trust people. Instead, it reminds us that it's better to put our hope in God. People will come through sometimes, but God comes through all the time.

The same truth also applies to your own failures, of course. If you have felt a lot of guilt about disappointing others, try to give it up. This does not mean you should go failing others on purpose. Shortcomings should be confessed and dealt with. But obsessing about your failure just brings relapse closer. It also puts you in God's place. God is the only One who never makes mistakes. And who knows, maybe God can use your failure to bring someone else closer to Him.

■   *I can choose to think of my disappointments with*
    people as opportunities to depend on God.

                                                J.C.

A JUDGMENTAL SPIRIT

Judge not, that you be not judged. For with what judgment you judge, you will be judged; and with the same measure you use, it will be measured back to you.

—MATT. 7:1–2

Have you ever noticed how easy it is to be critical of other people? Have you ever laughed at the way someone dressed or the way her hair was done? Have you ever disagreed with someone and walked away thinking he was a jerk?

Judging others seems to be a favorite pastime for some people, but we are all vulnerable to developing a judgmental or critical spirit, especially if our own self-esteem is low. We tear down others because we feel insecure ourselves; we try to build ourselves up by belittling others. But it doesn't work! No number of put-downs can make us feel lifted up.

The Lord cautions us about being judgmental, partly because He knows a judgmental spirit hurts us as much as it hurts the people we criticize. How can we face and recover from our own problems when our attention is focused on others? How can we get the support we need from others when we have cut ourselves off from them by passing judgment? And how can we accept God's kindness when we have no experience in being kind to anyone else?

■ *Lord, help me to treat others the way you treat me— with compassion and tenderness and understanding, not with judgment and criticism.*

S.C.

NEW AND IMPROVED

For all the Athenians and the foreigners who
were there spent their time in nothing else
but either to tell or to hear some new thing.
—ACTS 17:21

Those "Athenians and foreigners" Paul gave a speech to in the Bible were just like me. I always want the scoop—I want to be the first to hear and catch on to something new. Why? I wonder if it's because I'm afraid that my life is going to be nothing but the same old thing (or even worse, a repetition of my parents' lives). Cynics say nothing ever really changes—and that's a scary thought.

But to this crowd of people who were hungry for a scoop, Paul introduced some truly new news—the story of a man who was dead and then alive again (Acts 17:30–31). It must have sounded like *National Enquirer* stuff to those jaded listeners. And with it came the message that God was not only calling people to change their lives, but making that change possible through His risen Son.

I need that message when my recovery falters, and I wonder if change is really possible when I get discouraged and hungry for something new in my life. God's message (supported by the experience of others in recovery) is not only "You must change," not only "You can change," but also "I'll help you change."

■   *Father, help me keep in touch with how fresh and*
exciting your story really is. Teach me to be hopeful
instead of cynical—give me a glimpse of the new
thing you are doing in my life.

A.C.B.

LIVING WITH A DICTATOR

"They will fight against you,
But they shall not prevail against you.
For I am with you," says the LORD,
"to deliver you."
—JER. 1:19

Katherine lived in a home run by a dictator. Her father was opinionated and controlling, and he could not tolerate any questions or disagreements. Even when Katherine was referred to our program for treatment of her drug addiction, her father tried to tell the staff how to run the program.

This totalitarian atmosphere at home made recovery difficult for Katherine. In her experience, the only freedom she could find was in outward revolt or covert manipulation, so she tended to approach life as a sneak or a rebel. Learning to relate responsibly to others was a challenge to her. In addition, Katherine needed to learn how to live with her father without "setting him off" unnecessarily or being completely dominated. She learned to "choose her battles" carefully, deciding ahead of time what issues were truly important (and enlisting the support of others in these) and which issues she should just give in about. She leaned heavily on God and her group for moral support as she worked at building a new, sane life in the shadow of the dictator.

■   *Father, I pray you will help me find healthy ways to deal with controlling people—something more positive than rebellion or manipulation.*

S.C.

RED FLAG WARNING

Who can understand [her] errors?
Cleanse me from secret faults. . . .
Let them not have dominion over me.
—PS. 19:12–13

Red-orange warning flags—we see them at road construction sites. A worker waves the flag, warning of difficult travel ahead. We slow down. We are more observant. Depending on what we see, we alter our driving.

We need to do that with our recovery too. What are some red warning flags of relapse? For Jacque it was when she felt tired from focusing on other's problems while her own were begging to be solved. For Melody, it was when she began to have an increase of negative thoughts. For Marilu, it was an increased urge to have control. The red flags are different for each person. One way we will learn to recognize our own personal red flags is to attend a support group. Counseling from a pastor, a sponsor, or a therapist can also help.

Once the red flags are identified, daily time with God can help us stay alert for them. Psalm 139 tells us that He lovingly made us, so He knows us inside out. He knows of our tendency to get off the road, our blindness to the potholes that may be obvious to others.

Today's scripture admits that it's hard for us to see our own mistakes. They seem hidden even from us. It is only God who can open our eyes to them. He can keep these bad habits from controlling us.

■ *Heavenly Father, show me where the red flags of relapse are waving.*

J.C.

EMERGING FROM THE SHADOWS

*"I will put My Spirit in you, and you shall
live, and I will place you in your own land.
Then you shall know that I, the LORD, have
spoken it and performed it," says the LORD.*
—EZEK. 37:14

For so long I lived in my older brother's shadow. He was the responsible one; I was impulsive. He was the methodical one; I was spontaneous. He was the serious one; I was the bubbly airhead. Then one day he read something I'd written and said, "I wish I could put words together like you." That statement nearly knocked me over. I'd been so busy comparing myself to him, seeing what he was and I wasn't, that I'd completely missed seeing what *I was*.

We are each uniquely gifted with talents, skills, and abilities we have yet to embrace. Perhaps your friends comment on the flair with which you put together unexpected combinations of clothes, yet you minimize your sense of style, design, and color. Perhaps you've journaled, kept diaries, or loved telling stories since you were a kid, yet you have never thought of yourself as a writer. Perhaps you're the one all your friends want to talk to when something is really on their minds—and you've never recognized your gifts as a listener.

Accepting ourselves means more than accepting our failures, character defects, and shortcomings. Accepting ourselves also means embracing our strengths, delighting in our gifts, and opening ourselves to the talents with which we were created.

■ *God, open my eyes so I can see myself as you see me.*

D.K.

TRUST HIM FOR TOMORROW

Do not worry about tomorrow, for tomorrow will worry about its own things.
—MATT. 6:34

Do you ever get tired of people nagging you about "your future"?

"It's about time you started thinking about your future," they say. Or "think about what you're doing to your future." How can they expect you to be mapping out your education and career when sometimes it's all you can do to keep going in the present?

What a relief to realize that God doesn't expect us to have the future all sewn up. Jesus said specifically, "Do not worry about tomorrow." He didn't mean we shouldn't prepare. He didn't mean we shouldn't set goals or make plans. He just meant that deciding to trust God today is the only dependable way to prepare for tomorrow.

After all, you can't prepare for every possibility. You can't be sure your goals will never change or your plans will never go awry. You can't promise never to make a mistake. But putting God first and developing the habit of relying on Him will help you handle unforeseen developments, redirect your goals, revise your plans, acknowledge your mistakes, and keep moving forward. Sure, you need to prepare responsibly. But then, instead of worrying about "your future," you can trust God to take you there.

■ *Father, keep reminding me that I can trust you instead of worrying about tomorrow.*

A.C.B.

"NORMAL"—BUT NOT HEALTHY

Thus says the LORD:
"Do not learn the way of the Gentiles. . . .
For the customs of the peoples are futile.
—JER. 10:2–3

When I get mad at my mother, I go to my room, close the door, put on my headphones, and jack the stereo up. I can't hear her and the music pushes everything out." Beckie was describing a way she numbed out her anger, at least temporarily. (The same issue with her mother would resurrect itself a few weeks or days later, only worse.)

Beckie was not doing anything abnormal. Most of her friends did the same thing when they had problems with their parents. But Beckie was not doing anything abnormal when she was drinking, either. Most of her friends did that, too.

In our nation, it is increasingly becoming common even for elementary-school children to use. But being "normal" doesn't necessarily mean harmless! Today's verse warns against following the futile ways of dominant culture.

Listening to music may be an easy way to deal with anger and one that everyone is doing. But it may be a futile way of coping in that it doesn't resolve the issues you were initially angry about. In fact, it can create another dependency problem. You might ask yourself (and answer honestly) if you can go a month without your music. If not, ask God to help you learn healthier ways of using music.

■   *Is my music hindering me from facing problems?*

J.C.

AN UNQUALIFIED YES

> *Then the angel said to her, "Do not be afraid, Mary, for you have found favor with God. . . . You will conceive in your womb and bring forth a Son, and shall call His name JESUS." . . . Then Mary said, "Behold the maidservant of the Lord! Let it be to me according to your word."*
>
> —LUKE 1:30–31, 38

Some things I'm asked to do seem so hard. Like owning up to the tests I've cheated on, or making things right in the places where I've shoplifted, or even going to my mom or dad and making amends for some of my not-so-cool behavior. The thought of making amends is pretty tough, pretty scary. But God was asking Mary to do the unbelievable—subjecting herself to ridicule or rejection (like who would believe she was really a pregnant virgin!?). No matter how scared she was, no matter how tough she thought it was going to be, she said yes. She had the confidence and faith to know that somehow God was going to make it OK.

Abbie Jane Wells says, "For all I know—for all anybody knows—God may have 'proposed' (or propositioned?) . . . through the ages, but *as far as we know,* Mary was the first one to say an unqualified 'yes.'"*

■ *When I say an unqualified yes to doing the right thing, no matter how hard or scary, God will see me through.*

D.K.

*Quoted in Reuben P. Job and Normal Shawchuck, *A Guide to Prayer for All God's People* (Nashville: Upper Room, 1990).

TROUBLED BEGINNINGS

And she brought forth her firstborn Son, and wrapped Him in swaddling cloths, and laid Him in a manger, because there was no room for them in the inn. —LUKE 2:7

An exhausted and worried young man tries to find food and lodging for his family in a strange town. His pregnant wife, well into labor, doubles over with pain. She is forced to give birth in a stable full of donkeys and cows. And almost before she has a chance to clean up, she has to cope with visitors—a bunch of smelly, low-life shepherds.

Despite the signs, despite the angels, it must have seemed a troubled beginning. I wonder if Mary and Joseph had difficulty seeing the hope, at least at first.

I think that real, positive change often feels that way. The first time in a support group, you feel awkward and out of place. The first few weeks of therapy seem to bring pain out of the woodwork. The first days in a re-hab center can be hell.

But the baby born in that smelly cow stall redeemed the world. And the painful first steps of recovery lead to new life. Uncomfortable beginnings really can be worth the price.

■ *Father, surely by now I must be getting the message that life with you is always worth the price. On this Christmas Eve, keep me looking through the stable door to see the star, through the pain to see your hope.*

A.C.B.

SHOW AND TELL

And the Word became flesh and dwelt among us, and we beheld His glory, the glory as of the only begotten of the Father, full of grace and truth.
—JOHN 1:14

Talk about a comedown! This huge, powerful God chose to squeeze Himself into a puny little package, a human body. He made himself vulnerable to human pain and temptation and weakness—even death! And all because it was the only way to get through to us.

For centuries, God had been trying to show us human beings how we could live healthy and whole lives in relationship to Him. And somehow we just couldn't get it. We kept thinking it was up to us—or that it was so totally beyond us there was no point in trying. We were like two-year-olds listening to a college professor; we just couldn't grasp the message. No wonder we were frustrated and rebellious!

So what did God do? He got down on our level. Like a nursery-school teacher who sits right on the floor with the kids, this great God chose to come down to us, to actually become a human being. It was the ultimate "show and tell." Jesus came to show us by example and tell us in our own terms that it really is possible, in Him, to be a healthy, growing, un-screwed-up human being. Isn't that the whole point of recovery?

■ *Lord, sometimes I still just don't get it. So thank you for coming down to my level and surprising me again with the Christmas gift of yourself—the Word made flesh.*

A.C.B.

NEVER ABANDONED

For He Himself has said, "I will never leave you nor forsake you."
—HEB. 13:5

Four-year-old Jennie woke up one morning to find herself alone in the house. Her mother had briefly stepped outside to do a chore, but Jennie didn't know that; all she knew was that the house was empty. Even though she had never been left alone and had no reason to believe she would be left now, she just knew she had been abandoned. Her terrified wails brought her mother running.

There is a deep-seated, instinctive fear of abandonment in all of us; we fear we will be left alone. If we have experienced significant loss in our lives—divorce, death, cross-country moves, or other separation—we find it hard to believe that it won't happen again. And it might! People are weak. People are imperfect. People let us down—and it hurts.

That's why God's promise never to leave us can bring us both health and comfort in recovery. No human being can make that promise with honesty. But God is God: His promise to be with us always is a promise that He keeps.

■ *Lord, I praise you for your consistent presence and love in my life. Thank you that you will never abandon me.*

S.C.

FAMILY CONNECTIONS

*In love, having predestined us to adoption as
[daughters] by Jesus Christ to Himself.*
                                        —EPH. 1:4–5

When you accepted Christ, God the Father adopted you into His family. As His daughter, you now have certain privileges and resources you did not have before.

Part of this inheritance is unconditional acceptance. You are the daughter of a King. Because you have a perfect Father, you don't have to be the perfect daughter. You are already loved and accepted by Him the way you are. Another advantage of being the King's daughter is the fact that you have many brothers and sisters— your fellow Christians. You can enjoy their love and power—you have a natural support system out there. Being part of this important family means you have certain leadership responsibilities. As you find out what these are, you find that you can influence people in a good way. And having the King as your Father also means you deserve respect—from others and, most importantly, from yourself. When you respect yourself, recovery comes more naturally.

The perfect Dad, a royal family; unconditional love, leadership responsibilities and self-respect—all these are part of your new identity. Taking advantage of "family connections" will help you in the recovery process.

■   *Knowing what family I belong to promotes my recovery.*

                                                      J.C.

BEYOND DOG-EAT-DOG

But if you bite and devour one another,
beware lest you be consumed by one
another!
— GAL. 5:15

Remember the gingham dog and the calico cat—and other ravenous creatures from nursery-rhyme land? They got so angry and spiteful that they ate each other up!

Sometimes I think we try to do that to each other, too—not physically, but emotionally and spiritually. Isn't that what the expression, "It's a dog-eat-dog world," means? Somewhere deep inside, we believe that the only way we can win is to make sure everybody else loses, the only way we can be safe is to destroy everybody else, the only way we can get what we need is to make sure nobody else gets anything.

But the natural results of this kind of thinking should be clear to anyone who has ever read a nursery rhyme: When dog eats dog, everyone gets eaten! That's why Jesus' instructions to "love your enemy" and "turn the other cheek" really do make sense. They're hard—in fact, without God's help, they're impossible—but they are the only way out of the old, destroying cycle of dog-eat-dog.

■ *Father, when I'm tempted to lash out at others, re-*
mind me that I will be hurting myself as well. Teach
me to trust in your love instead of getting caught up
in "dog-eat-dog" thinking."

A.C.B.

A PROBLEM IS AN OPPORTUNITY

*And we know that all things work together
for good to those who love God, to those who
are the called according to His purpose.*
—ROM. 8:28

Crisis in the Chinese language is composed of two
other Chinese words: *danger* and *opportunity*. In any
problem we face, we have two choices. We can see it as
a tragedy or as an opportunity.

David Ring was born with cerebral palsy, which
causes spastic muscle control and speech problems. He
was labeled a cripple and told he'd never work. He was
told no woman would ever want to marry him, that he'd
never have kids. David had every right, by the world's
thinking, to see his life as a tragedy.

David tells of lying in bed, minding his own business,
when God called him to preach. As David recalls, he
told God, "Lord, me preach? I have CP!" And God
replied, "Really? Tell me something I don't know."
David protested some more, but fortunately God won.
Today David is the Reverend David Ring. He is married, with four children. He has spoken on TV and radio. Yes, it is hard to understand his speech at first and
painful to watch his struggle to control his body. But
after a while all that disappears. What one hears and
sees is God using David Ring in a mighty way because
he saw his CP as an opportunity instead of a tragedy.

■ *"Difficulties are our opportunities for advancement,
for increased self awareness, for self-fulfillment"
(from a saying on a calendar).*

J.C.

PASSING IT ON

Encourage one another daily, as long as it is called Today, so that none of you may be hardened by sin's deceitfulness.
—HEB. 3:13 NIV

A new girl in our support group just called. She wants me to be her sponsor. This is so weird. Me. As if I had it together enough to help someone else.

But when I think about it, I *have* learned a lot in recovery. I know from experience that it really is possible to get better. I know what it feels like to depend on God instead of my own efforts and to live one day at a time instead of tackling all my problems at once. I'm learning to be really honest with myself, even when it hurts. I'm starting to be alert to signs of slippery abstinence and weakening sobriety—and I'm learning to ask for help.

Most of all, I know how much I need the encouragement of my group, my sponsor, and my therapist. When I am feeding myself a line of B.S., they call me on it. When I am depressed or discouraged, they listen and urge me on. Sometimes they're the only thing that keeps me going. Sure, I'm depending on God, but they become God's face for me. Wouldn't it be cool if I could be that for someone else?

■   *God, it feels a little strange, but I want to give to someone else the encouragement I've been given. Help me to be what others have been to me—as I depend on you.*

A.C.B.

I'VE COME A LONG WAY

Finally, [sisters], farewell. Become complete.
Be of good comfort, be of one mind, live in
peace; and the God of love and peace will
be with you. . . . The grace of the Lord
Jesus Christ, and the love of God, and
the communion of the Holy Spirit be with you
all. Amen. —2 COR. 13:11, 14

Addiction starts out seductively. At first it feels good—an easy source of pleasure. Then a subtle change takes place. Somewhere along the way, it turns on you and begins to destroy you from the inside out. Soon the addiction becomes your whole focus; you can't think of anything else but getting it, doing it, or sneaking it. Then you face the self-hatred, the vows of future reform, the self-punishment of patterns repeated despite your strongest resolve.

Sometimes the intensity of that vicious cycle grows dim and I become lax in my recovery efforts. All I have to do, though, is remember. When a newcomer comes into our group and tells what brought her here, the memories flood in—the pain so raw, almost afraid to hope that things could be different.

It's helpful to realize that even though I may not be where I want to be, at least I'm not where I was. I have come a long way. And for my recovery, I'm so grateful. Grateful to a God of healing, grateful for those who've walked with me through the process. I don't ever have to go back to the old patterns.

■ *Lord, by your grace, I'll never go back. Thank you*
for leading me into recovery and moving me into a
life of faith, hope, and love.

D.K.

About the Authors

Jane Cairo is a family and individual therapist for the Minirth-Meier inpatient adolescent unit in Wheaton, Illinois. She received a master's in clinical social work from the University of Illinois and a bachelor's in family relations from Northern Illinois University. She also received a bachelor's in communication and writing from Moody Bible Institute.

Sheri Curry is an outpatient therapist for the Minirth-Meier Clinic in Richardson, Texas, and an inpatient therapist for the North Texas Medical Center, Westpark Campus in McKinney, Texas. Sheri specializes in working with children and adolescents dealing with physical, emotional and sexual abuse, depression, school problems and self-esteem. She graduated with a master's degree in clinical psychology from Wheaton College in Wheaton, Illinois. She received her undergraduate degree from Kansas State University in Manhattan, Kansas.

Anne Christian Buchanan is a free-lance writer and editor (and former teenage girl) who has been active in Christian publishing for more than fifteen years. A graduate of Baylor University in Waco, Texas, she served as an editor at Word, Inc. for twelve years before establishing her freelance business. She currently lives in Knoxville, Tennessee.

Debra Klingsporn is a free-lance writer and publicist who has worked with adolescents and has been involved in recovery groups for several years.

For general information about Minirth-Meier Clinic branch offices, counseling services, educational resources, and hospital programs, call toll-free 1-800-545-1819.

Library of Congress Cataloging-in-Publication Data

I can't, God can, I think I'll let Him : daily devotions for
   teenaged girls' recovery / Jane Cairo . . . [et al.].
      p.   cm.
      "A Janet Thoma book."
      ISBN 0-8407-3458-1 : $7.99
      1. Young women—Prayer-books and devotions—
   English.   2. Alcoholics—Prayer-books and
   devotions—English.   3. Narcotic addicts—Prayer-
   books and devotions—English.   4. Compulsive
   eaters—Prayer-books and devotions—English.
   5. Devotional calendars.   I. Cairo, Jane.
   BV4860.I22   1992
   242'.66—dc20   92–19115
                                          CIP